Advance praise for *Legacy of the Heart* by Wayne Muller

"I found Wayne Muller's book full of surprises. In a very direct and lucid way, richly illustrated with stories of human brokenness, he gently moved me beyond the questions of Why? and Why me?, helped me step over the barriers of my guilt and shame and encouraged me to look through my wounds as through a window that opens to a new view of who I am and where I am called to go.

"This is a truly hopeful book, psychologically sound and spiritually challenging. It offers many invigorating thoughts for those who are thinking about their painful past, and many practical suggestions for those who want to know what to do.

"This is a brilliant, warm, inspiring book that will bring consolation, comfort and a desire to live a full life to many people."

Henri Nouwen
Pastor of L'Arche Daybreak Community in Toronto

"Muller's keen awareness of how spiritual and bodily suffering interact makes the comparison with Augustine especially vivid. Of course, Augustine focused on his own past, and Muller examines that of many people. Also, Muller calls on the resources of several faith traditions. Still, this is a fine book, interesting not just to therapists and theologians but to many nonspecialists."

Harvey Cox
Professor of Divinity, Harvard University School of Divinity

Legacy of the Heart

The Spiritual Advantages of
a Painful Childhood

WAYNE MULLER

SIMON & SCHUSTER

New York   London   Toronto   Sydney   Tokyo   Singapore

While the case histories in this book are as accurate as memory and transcription allow—though condensed and edited—clients' names have been changed to honor their privacy.

Simon & Schuster
Simon & Schuster Building
Rockefeller Center
1230 Avenue of the Americas
New York, New York 10020

Designed by Rhea Braunstein
Manufactured in the United States of America

1   3   5   7   9   10   8   6   4   2

Library of Congress Cataloging-in-Publication Data is available

ISBN 0-671-76119-6

Material from *Seeking the Heart of Wisdom: The Path of Insight Meditation*, by Joseph Goldstein and Jack Kornfield, copyright © 1987 by Joseph Goldstein and Jack Kornfield. Reprinted by arrangement with Shambhala Publications, Inc., 300 Massachusetts Ave., Boston MA 02115.

This book was given life through the loving support of Christine Tiernan, my wife, best friend, playmate, and spiritual companion. Every word has Christine's voice in it, and without her wisdom and guidance this project would never have come to be. At every step she has shown me where to look, how to listen, and what to remember, always with great love and tremendous patience. She opened my mind, my heart, and my spirit. With deep love and gratefulness I dedicate it to Christine.

I offer this book with a prayer that it will, in some small way, serve to alleviate the suffering of all beings.

ACKNOWLEDGMENTS

I have had so many wonderful teachers, friends, and guides throughout my life that it would be impossible to acknowledge them all. Perhaps the most potent voices belong to the women and men who have placed their trust in me over the years as we struggled to heal their deepest wounds. I am indebted to them all for what we learned together about healing, courage, and love.

There are also many people who, when they came into my life, brought with them exactly what I needed to learn. Denton Roberts, with his humble wisdom, first showed me how the inner workings of the child's mind took shape in our adult lives; the entire staff of the Family Education and Counseling Center, especially Dr. Lynn Cantlay, all opened their hearts and took me in, and taught me that therapy could be playful, exciting, and healing for everyone concerned; Dr. Steve Aizenstat and Dr. Gary Linker generously allowed me to use the Human Relations Institute in Santa Barbara for my endless investigations into the nature of psychology, community, and spirit, and unconditionally supported me each step of the way; Judy Hay, Valerie Russell, David King, Bill Webber, and Harvey Cox each in their own way taught me that spiritual healing comes to full flower only in the healing of the larger human community; Father Henri Nouwen lovingly reminded me always to balance the practice of psychology with the practice of spirit; Erik and Joan Erikson helped me realize that all psychology is ultimately rooted in the body, heart, and spirit; and Jack Kornfield, a loving teacher who speaks from the heart of the Buddha, taught me to sit still and listen with humility, humor, and compassion.

Many kind people have accompanied me on the journey of this book. Stephen and Ondrea Levine have been exceedingly generous with their friendship, their loving company, and their kind assistance on this project. Their work in the field of healing helped prepare the soil from which this book has grown. Ram Dass, who has shown so many of us how to be playfully curious about matters of the heart, generously offered his comments and support when I was just beginning and dearly in need of confidence; Daniel Goleman lent his valuable help, advice, and guidance from the start; Dr. Richard Heckler, who has accompanied me at various points along this journey for the past twenty years, provided love, humor, and compassionate collaboration; Peter Guardino first told me to write this book in 1974; Dianna Whitley made sure I sent it to the right person; Sister Mary Lou Kownacki at Pax Cristi helped me with some of the quotes; and Jai Lakshman, whose friendship, loving care, and enthusiastic support as a dharma brother and golf partner continues to endure beyond measure.

I would also like to especially thank Liz Perle, my editor and publisher, for the creative way in which she showed me how to listen to my own work, and for having the insight to recognize the jewel in the mud; and, finally, I thank Loretta Barrett, my agent and friend, for believing in me when no one could have been expected to. Her gentleness, wisdom, and care have been a comfort and a blessing.

CONTENTS

We must learn to reawaken and keep ourselves awake,
    not by mechanical aids,
but by an infinite expectation of the dawn,

which does not forsake us
    even in our soundest sleep . . .

—HENRY DAVID THOREAU

PRELUDE

Reawakening

When we are hurt as children, we can quickly learn to see ourselves as broken, handicapped, or defective in some essential way. As we remember with excruciating precision the violations and injustices that devastated our tender hearts, we come to view our childhood as a terrible, painful mistake. At times, the enormity of our childhood sorrow can fill us with a sense of hopelessness, disappointment, and despair.

For the past eighteen years, in family therapy agencies, hospitals, schools, prisons, churches, and private practice, I have worked exclusively with adults who grew up in troubled families. As a therapist and minister, I have been privileged to witness the tremendous courage of women and men—rich and poor, black and white, Hispanic and native American, gay and straight—who sought to heal the painful residue of their childhood suffering. Even as they struggled to be free, the reverberations of family sorrow continued to infect their adult lives, their loves, even their dreams.

Yet, at the same time I have also noted that adults who were hurt as children inevitably exhibit a peculiar strength, a profound inner wisdom, and a remarkable creativity and insight. Deep within them—just beneath the wound—lies a profound spiritual vitality, a quiet knowing, a way of perceiving what is beautiful, right, and true. Since their early experiences were so dark and painful, they have spent much of their lives in search of the gentleness, love, and peace they have only imagined in the privacy of their own hearts.

A painful childhood invariably focuses our attention on the inner life. In response to childhood hurt, we learn to cultivate a heightened awareness, and sharpen our capacity to discern how things move and change in our environment. Childhood pain encourages us to watch things more closely, to listen more carefully, to attend to the subtle imbalances that arise within and around us. We develop an exquisite ability to feel the feelings of others, and we become exceptionally mindful of every conflict, every flicker of hope or despair, every piece of information that may hold some teaching for us. Thus, family pain broke us open and set our hearts on a pilgrimage in search of the love and belonging, safety and abundance, joy and peace that were missing from our childhood story. Seen through this lens, family sorrow is not only a painful wound to be endured, analyzed, and treated. It may in fact become a seed that gives birth to our spiritual healing and awakening.

Beginning the Practice

I realize that it requires a tremendous leap of faith to imagine that your own childhood—punctuated with pain, loss, and hurt—may, in fact, be a gift. Certainly the unhappiness you felt was not, in itself, a blessing; but in response to that pain, you learned to cultivate a powerful intuition, a heightened sensitivity, and a passionate devotion to healing and love that burns deep within you. These are gifts that may be recognized, honored, and cultivated.

You are not broken; childhood suffering is not a mortal wound, and it did not irrevocably shape your destiny. You need not remove, destroy, or tear anything out of yourself in order to build something new. Your challenge is not to keep trying to repair what was damaged; your practice instead is to reawaken what is already wise, strong, and whole within you, to cultivate those qualities of heart and spirit that are available to you in this very moment.

Your life is not a problem to be solved but a gift to be opened. Just as the pain, hurt, and suffering that came to you as a child were powerfully real, so is the tangible resilience of your spirit equally vital and alive. This book will help you reawaken that inner strength and discover a reliable sense of safety, belonging, and peace.

In this book I outline twelve distinct manifestations of childhood sorrow: lingering wounds that express themselves as points of tension between our emotional history and our spiritual unfolding. Each chapter begins by examining the shape of a particular childhood wound, and reveals how the scar from that wound affects our emotional and spiritual life. We then gently observe, explore, and massage those places where we feel caught, where we are ready to grow, and where we ache to be free. And finally we listen as the spiritual teachers of the world describe these same points of tension as doorways of the spirit, doorways that may lead us into deep healing and liberation.

The spiritual search you inherited as a child of family pain is at once a profoundly confusing, exciting, and intimate dialogue with your heart and spirit. Indeed, the persistent questions that occupy the heart of the wounded child are invariably the same questions pondered by the saints, seekers, and spiritual teachers of the world: Why must we have pain? Where do we belong? What is most important in our lives? How can we recognize what is beautiful and true? How may we be joyful? How do we learn to love?

As children, these questions were difficult for us to ask and impossible for us to answer. Isolated and alone within ourselves, we were wary and confused about trusting anyone to help us wrestle with the infinite complexities of being human. Now, as we grow older, we feel a surging readiness to be healed. Perhaps we may now allow these same questions to become the seeds of our reawakening.

You may use these spiritual teachings to cultivate the healing that is *already present within you*. You can explore those practices that directly correspond to your childhood wounds, and use them to uncover and reawaken the resources you have within you to heal and to grow. Finally, you will be able to investigate your childhood pain in the context of the larger human family, allowing your past to place you in compassionate kinship with others who suffer loss, injury, grief, or injustice.

As you move through this book, you may begin to reawaken your natural energy, curiosity, and wonder, rediscovering a place within yourself where you are strong, clear, and whole. Some name this place soul, or spirit. Some call it our inner light, which softens the darkness in our hearts. Others call it the Divine, or the Beloved; still others describe it as our true nature, or our Buddha nature. Many of us simply name it God.

Throughout the book I have included teachings from Christian, Buddhist, Hebrew, Sufi, Hindu, and native American traditions. I have also included writers and thinkers from our contemporary culture who speak of the heart and spirit with some precision. These saints and guides are not the answer to our quest—they simply indicate the path, like a finger pointing to the moon. They help our eyes to see and show us where to look.

Take your time; be patient with yourself as you read this book. The scars of childhood cast long shadows deep in the heart, and are not readily let go of. All healing requires gentleness, attention, and care. But keep in mind that you need not repair, reconstruct, or remake yourself into someone else. Your practice is simply to reawaken what is already wise and strong, to claim what is deep and true within you, to rediscover your own intuition, to find your inner balance, and to reaffirm your intrinsic wholeness in the eyes of God.

Everything you will ever need may be found within your own body, heart, and spirit. Your most difficult task is to believe in yourself. Using the practices, exercises, and meditations at the end of each chapter, perhaps you will learn to reawaken that trust in your own wisdom, courage, and creativity.

We do this work in the name of love—love for ourselves, love for our family and friends, love for all the children of the earth who have suffered. As the capacity to love expands within you, your love, kindness, and generosity become more available for others—and the family of the earth is in desperate need of your love, your care, and your participation in the growth and healing of us all. This book is an invitation to heal, to reawaken the spirit of life within you, to fulfill the dreams of your deepest heart, and to claim your place of belonging in the human family as a courageous and loving member.

CHAPTER ONE

Pain and Forgiveness

Every one of us felt some pain as a child. Whether the hurt came intentionally or unintentionally, we undoubtedly experienced some measure of suffering in our family. For some, it was the physical pain of illness, accident, or family violence. For others, it was the emotional pain that came with the death of a parent, divorce, abuse, or neglect. Still others may have simply felt the pain of growing up, partaking of the inevitable losses and broken dreams that litter the stage of every childhood.

When we experience suffering or pain, questions inevitably arise in the mind: Why? Why me? Why did this happen? What did I do to deserve it? In the grip of suffering, we reflexively seek the reason why we hurt. We are convinced that if we find the cause, perhaps we may somehow prevent pain from ever coming again.

But what if pain is beyond our control? What, after all, is pain, and what is its function in our lives? Is pain always a mistake, some imbalance that must be corrected? Or is pain simply an injustice, something inflicted from outside that must be fought and guarded against at all costs? Is it punishment for bad behavior, or is it more like a reward, something that is "good for us," something given to bring us strength and character? Conversely, is it even useful to assume that pain has any function at all beyond the fact that it plainly tells us we've been hurt?

How do we understand pain? Psychological and emotional distress come in many forms, and we react to different kinds of pain in a variety of ways. More important, our beliefs about the nature of pain can actually change our response to our own suffering. If we feel that the pain we are given is a violation or mistreatment—if we feel pain as an injustice—then we harden

1

ourselves, fight against it, and fill with anger and rage at the person or situation that caused us hurt. On the other hand, if we believe that this particular pain is the one that will push the baby out of the womb and into our arms, we somehow try to make a place for that pain in our heart. Pain is still there: excruciating, terrible pain. But at the moment of birth, we rarely feel betrayal or rage; we somehow feel that this is simply pain that has come with life.

As Daniel Goleman, the psychologist and author, has observed, "The brain has discretion in how pain is perceived . . . As with other senses, the psychological experience of pain depends on far more than the simple strength of nerve signals: fear of the dentist's drill and the joy of childbirth each alter pain, in entirely opposite directions."

Why Pain?

At the end of his life, Jesus was arrested by the occupying forces in Jerusalem and condemned to die. He was impaled with a crown of thorns, forced to carry his cross to the hill where he was to be crucified, and was stabbed and ridiculed as he slowly died. Before his death, Jesus cried out: "My God, my God, why have you forsaken me?"

We have all come upon moments in our lives when, in deep pain and suffering, we felt that same cry rise in our own throats. We have all felt deeply hurt, wounded, or betrayed by some person, event, or tragedy. And we have undoubtedly sought to know why it happened to us.

Pain and suffering are not exceptions to the human condition; they are inevitable players in the drama of our lives. Pain arises in a thousand ways, through a symphony of unanticipated events that bring injury, loss, disappointment, and defeat. Like anger, fear, or joy, pain is simply one ingredient in our emotional stew—but it is one of the ingredients we feel a desperate need to explain.

Why do we hurt? As children, we were forever trying to explain the pain that came our way. We tried to understand why our hearts ached when someone yelled at us or when we lost something precious. Why did Mom yell at me? Why did Dad hit me? Why couldn't they listen? Why didn't they hold me? Why were they so angry? Why didn't they leave me alone?

With each painful event, we renewed our efforts to explain the causes of our suffering. Perhaps Dad was angry with me because I didn't do well enough in school. Or was it because he had a bad day, or too many drinks? Mom must have yelled at me because I didn't help her enough in the kitchen—or maybe she was mad at Dad, or feeling sick. Maybe my brother beat me up because I wasn't nice enough to his friends. Or was it because he got in trouble at school, or had trouble with his girlfriend?

The mind frantically seeks relief in some certainty, some cause for the pain that fractured our hearts, ruptured our bodies, and quietly tore at our spirits. We take comfort in the discovery of a reasonable explanation for our suffering, since the pain itself is so uncomfortable.

We used these childhood explanations of the causes of our suffering to shape the trajectory of our lives. If I think pain came to me because I was not good enough, then I will spend my life working to improve myself. On the other hand, if people hurt me because I was not caring enough, then I may dedicate myself to helping everyone around me. If I got hurt because the world was unsafe, or people were bad and could not be trusted, then I will protect myself and not get close to anyone.

Our psychological culture sometimes falls prey to the idea that it was our childhood suffering that brought pain into our lives. We hurt now because we were hurt as children; if we were not hurt as children, we would not be hurting now. So, the thinking goes, if we can heal what happened in our childhood, we can heal ourselves of any pain from now on.

Because I hurt, something must be broken; if I fix it, maybe I will never get hurt again. Thus, every childhood explanation of pain becomes a secret theology designed to prevent any further suffering.

Childhood Suffering

Any child who is hurt will seek the comfort of loving parents. Yet some families, through denial or inattention, will not feel how much the child is hurting, or will pretend that the child's hurt is not real, not justified. The experience of pain is so strong that when others ignore it, we seem to feel it all the more. This can make the child feel crazy, who then redoubles the efforts to name the suffering and try to find the truth about it. Thus, in addition to the initial suffering, we add anger at being ignored, or we add confusion, or shame.

In this way we increase our attachment to our suffering as the one thing that is most true in our lives: I was hurt. The memory of that hurt is so strong, it has colored who I have been, and has shaped who I have become. This is one of the most powerful attachments to our families—the memory of being hurt. There are few greater obstacles to emotional freedom than the obsessive fascination we bring to the injustices, assaults, and sufferings that came to us as children of our biological parents. While it is critical to name and heal those tender places, as we analyze and dissect our child-hoods we may trap ourselves in an endless search for whatever we lost when we were small. This preoccupation with discovering the reasons behind the childhood injustices can sometimes blind our hearts to the tremendous opportunities for healing and liberation available to us in this very moment. But it is so difficult for us to let go of the search for the answers to our questions: Why did we hurt? Why me? We pick at the scabs and scars in our heart, waiting for an answer that may never come.

Why Me?

One day Maria came to my office. When Maria was young, her father had frequent episodes of anger that seemed to arise out of nowhere, episodes that usually ended with her father severely beating her. She told me with some pride that she would never cry when he was yelling and hitting her. Only later, when it was over, would she go away to her room and there, in private, she would cry and hold herself, and repeat over and over the same question: Why? Why are they doing this to me?

Maria and I explored many painful moments together, moments that included other forms of violence and more intimate forms of abuse. Each time, she would ask, "Why did this happen? How could this have happened to me? I tried being good, being quiet, not causing trouble, staying out of his way—and it still happened, over and over. It was horrible," she said, "but it was most horrible because I couldn't understand why he was doing it to me."

One day I asked her to talk to me about her father and to tell me about his pain. She was quiet for a moment, and then explained that her father had been adopted, did not know his real parents, and was beaten often as a boy by his adopted father. I then asked her to tell me about her father's father's pain, and she said that he was an alcoholic, frequently unemployed, and depressed. So, I asked her, why did you get hit? Was it your fault, because you did not get out of the way fast enough? Was it your father's fault, because he could not control his temper around his own fragile offspring? Was it *his* father's fault because he was alcoholic? And whose fault was his alcoholism?

As long as Maria kept asking her childhood question—why did this happen to me?—she was subtly avoiding the very painful fact that it *did* happen to her. "Maria," I said one day, "it happened. You were hurt very deeply, violated horribly. Why did it happen? I don't know. I am sorry it happened, but it did happen. For just a moment, imagine letting go of the 'Why' and just allow yourself to say, 'I hurt.' Nothing more, just repeat that phrase a few times slowly, 'I hurt.' "

She resisted at first; she insisted she needed to know the reason why, as a small child, she should even have to hurt. No child should have to hurt that badly, she said. But very slowly she began to say the words, letting them quietly sink into her. "I hurt . . . I hurt." And slowly she began to cry, deep and full, grieving the terrible pain in her heart. Now she could feel it, the sadness, the ache, the wound. She was hurt.

We would rather explain our hurt than feel it. For many of us it is easier to say "I hurt because my father never understood me" than it is to say "I hurt." When we were small we attached stories to our pain, stories about how it came and why it was there. And so now, whenever we hurt, we do not feel simply the sensation of pain—we feel the story of our suffering. "I hurt because I was never held, I hurt because I was beaten, I hurt because my parents were clumsy in this or that way." When we feel the old childhood story so strongly, it is hard to feel the truth of our pain in the present moment.

For Maria, our work in therapy could help her understand the causes of certain historical events that were very painful for her. We could learn to accept the anger, fear, and tightness in her heart that were born of those painful moments. But, more important, her early suffering had become the deepest truth on the altar of her life. And to set her free from her father, from her family, from the confines of life at home, we had to leave behind the old story about injustice and bad parents—even though it was true— and invite her to enter into the pain itself. She had to begin simply to grieve. Only then could she allow her heart to open, to feel the deep healing that came from gently surrendering to her deepest feelings—not listening for the explanation or the blame or the injustice, but simply feeling the unspeakable pain of a child.

When Pain Is Given

We live in a time when many of us identify ourselves in relation to the particular forms of misfortune we were given. We say that we are alcoholics, or adult children of alcoholics, or adult children of dysfunctional or chemically dependent or codependent families. We name ourselves through the events that happened to us, and, when possible, through the people who brought us pain.

But there is a subtle principle that underlies this naming process, that *pain is a mistake*. We tell ourselves, "The pain that happened to me could have been prevented; it should never have happened to me."

This is a very human response to pain. A hospice worker once told me that when he visited the home of a ninety-six-year-old woman who was terminally ill, he expected to find someone who had lived a full life and was preparing to die. But rather than wanting to reflect and reminisce about the joys and sorrows of her life, the woman seemed dismayed by her misfortune and was ready for a fight. "Why me?" she asked.

Even at ninety-six, we still want to know why we have to die. But what if suffering and death are simply given to us, just as joy and wonder and hunger and ecstasy are given? What if pain is not an injustice, not something to be figured out, not someone's fault?

The Buddha said that in this life we would experience ten thousand joys and ten thousand sorrows. He understood that suffering is a thread that runs through the entire fabric of our lives. Whatever we desire, whatever we own, whatever we covet, will pass away. All that we have, including our very lives, we will someday lose. Even when we get what we want, we worry about the day it will disappear. And so we all experience suffering. This, said the Buddha, is the First Noble Truth.

Jesus said it in another way: "In the world you shall have tribulation." Jesus knew that pain and suffering would come to the children of creation. He said that the poor and wounded would "always be among us," and that even he himself could not escape from the pain the world was to give him.

But rather than accept the pain we are given as simply one moment among others, we habitually seek to blame the ones that "caused" us this or that particular pain—as if it weren't for *them,* we wouldn't have had any pain.

One day I watched my five-year-old daughter spill her milk as she was trying to pour it on her cereal. When she saw the spill, she quickly looked around, saw my wife standing on the other side of the room, and said, "Christine, you made me spill my milk."

Our desire to find the person who caused our suffering can appear humorous in the life of a child. But for people who have been given much unhappiness in their lives, the quest for someone to blame can often serve to increase their misery. I have seen this tragically played out in the lives of some people who come to me with AIDS. Often they are filled with shame and anger about the disease: "I feel like this is some punishment, some curse because I am gay. I know I got AIDS because of the life I have led." They have convinced themselves that they are ill because of who they are, because of their character, because of their sexuality. The world, too, seems all too quick to agree with their judgment. If we can argue about the morality or the politics of the illness, perhaps we can distract ourselves and avoid the devastating pain of watching thousands of our brothers and sisters suffer and die.

I often ask, "What if AIDS just came to you because it is what you were given? What if the virus is blind to your strengths and weaknesses, what if AIDS is simply a meditation, a very painful meditation, in this moment of your life? Is there enough mercy, can you find enough love in your heart to imagine that this pain might not be your fault?"

Accepting the pain we are given requires us to soften our hearts and allow the pain to break us open, to acknowledge and to grieve the terrible sadness that comes with abandonment, loss, illness, and disappointment. In this moment we can feel most human, in kinship with all who have felt the deep despair of a broken heart. This is not angry resignation, born of defeat; this is a deep, loving acceptance that what we are given has become our companion and our teacher, regardless of how painful, unwelcome, or unjust.

One day I was called to the bedside of an old Hispanic man, a carpenter. He had spent so much of his life helping his neighbors build their homes over the years that he never had time to finish building his own. So I walked into a house cluttered with boxes stacked against half-finished walls and old plywood floors. This man had AIDS, and would probably die in a few days.

I had been told by a social worker that the man was in denial about his illness and needed a therapist to help him confront his feelings about death. But when I arrived, he didn't want to talk about his "issues" at all. "You're a minister, aren't you?" he asked me. I replied that I was. "Why don't you just pray with me?" So I sat and prayed with him, both of us on the small bed in his uncompleted room.

When we finished praying, I finally questioned him about his illness. Why, I asked, did he think he had AIDS, why did he feel he was given this illness? He thought about my question, turned slowly to me, and said, "So I could have more time to think about Jesus."

Who knew why he had AIDS, whose fault it was, or who had given it to him? All he could do, in the depth of weariness and fear, was listen for the merciful voice of God. He was dying in great pain. But in that excruciating moment he was listening for a deeper healing, for the love and faith that would fill his heart with grace as he made his way home.

Some people once brought a blind man to Jesus and asked him, "Rabbi, who sinned, this man or his parents, that he was born blind?" They all wanted to know why this terrible curse had fallen on this man. And Jesus answered, "It was not that this man sinned, or his parents, but that the works of God might be made manifest in him." He told them not to look for why the suffering came but to listen for what the suffering could teach them. Jesus taught that our pain is not punishment, it is no one's fault. When we seek to blame, we distract ourselves from an exquisite opportunity to pay attention, to see even in this pain a place of grace, a moment of spiritual promise and healing.

Freud once explained that when one looks at a crystal, the place where that crystal is broken is the place that most clearly reveals its structure. We can discover its essence by examining where it is cracked. In the same way, our own wounds can be vehicles for exploring our essential nature, revealing the deepest textures of our heart and soul, if only we will sit with them, open ourselves to the pain, and allow ourselves to be taught, without holding back, without blame.

Many years ago I was asked to convene a commission in California to evaluate and make recommendations on the problems of teenage delinquency and juvenile justice. Before I accepted the appointment, I asked several people involved what they thought needed to be done. Most people said the task was impossible and expressed a great deal of hopelessness about the whole system. I found that merchants blamed the schools for not keeping kids off the streets and away from their stores; teachers blamed the parents for not supervising the kids more closely; parents blamed the kids for not listening to them; kids blamed the police for hassling them; and police blamed the kids, the teachers, and the parents. It was clear we were in big trouble.

I went back to the commission and told them I would take the appointment on the condition that we immediately adopt as our guiding principle the following statement: *Pain is nobody's fault.* Second, I said, we must immediately hold a meeting with representatives from every group in each community. I believe they secretly thought I was crazy, but they agreed to adopt these principles, and appointed me nonetheless.

What happened on that commission was beautiful. Once everyone was released from blaming or being blamed for the problem of delinquency, they were free to open their minds and hearts and playfully collaborate on some very exciting, innovative programs. We held meetings where teachers, police, juvenile offenders, parents, probation officers, gang members, and students were all working together to develop strategies that are still in place more than ten years later—because the people who designed them never had to decide "whose fault" it was. Once we could see that we all had felt tremendous pain, sorrow and disappointment, we were free to work as allies, giving birth to fresh approaches that would alleviate the turbulence in our community.

Grief and Our Parents

If pain is no one's fault, then pain is not the fault of our alcoholic father or our inattentive mother. Our pain was simply a wind that blew through our lives, a powerful meditation that opened us to great depths of emotion and sensation. Once we remove the question "why," we may see our pain face to face, accepting it for what it is. Then we can begin to truly grieve, which softens the pain. The deep hurt and anger and sadness can then lead us to letting go, to forgiveness, and to healing. Stephen Levine, who with his wife Ondrea, has done such beautiful work with those in pain and suffering, wrote in *Healing into Life and Death:*

> Examining what we feel, not analyzing why, we discover the labyrinthine patterns of our grief and unfinished business . . . That which has seemed so untouchable in the past is cradled in the arms of forgiveness and compassion, and the armoring begins to melt. The path to the heart becomes straight and clear, recognizing how this exploration of our grief, of the ways of our old suffering, opens the path to joy.

As we make the journey out of childhood, we are invited to grieve what we have lost. However, many of us who explore our childhoods are not ready to let go of the old stories. For some, the anger we feel toward our parents has become a source of personal power; we were treated badly, and now we deserve to be heard. Like Maria, we have a deep remembrance of the way it should have been for us, and we want to convince our parents to apologize, to love us, and to make right what was done so horribly wrong. We are still trying to work out the same old story, trying to make it turn out right, trying to wrestle a happy ending from the protagonists in our unsatisfactory childhood.

Perhaps we were never given the father we wanted, never had the gentle touch of a man who cradled us in the strength of his arm, never sat and listened as we spoke of how hard it was to be small and afraid. Or maybe we never had a mother who truly loved us, someone who would dry our tears or give us a party or make us laugh just because she loved to see us happy. How can we allow that loss to simply be true, to feel the truth of our emotional orphanage and know that it has never changed, and probably never will?

We begin by acknowledging that the old story is over. How long will we keep looking for someone who can make it all turn out differently? Our challenge is simply to let what was true be true: We were hurt. We never had the parents we hoped for, never had Ward and June Cleaver, never had Ozzie and Harriet. We were denied the perfect father we dreamed of, never had exactly the mother we wanted. When we feel the deep sadness of that loss, the pain and the loneliness, we simply grieve the loss of our childhood, the childhood that never was and never shall be. That story is over.

Some of us have a hard time believing that we are actually able to face our own pain. We have convinced ourselves that our pain is too deep, too frightening, something to avoid at all costs. Yet if we finally allow ourselves to feel the depth of that sadness and gently let it break our hearts, we may come to feel a great freedom, a genuine sense of release and peace, because we have finally stopped running from ourselves and from the pain that lives within us.

When we finally accept our pain, we may begin to feel we are not being singled out for special punishment. We are simply feeling, as Pierre Teilhard de Chardin described, "the tears that are in things." Feeling that pain, we claim kinship in a new family—a broad and rich family of everyone who has ever rejoiced and who has ever suffered, who have sung and grieved just as we have done. Sitting still with our sorrow, we may even start to feel ourselves opening to the suffering of other people who were hurt as children.

The Sufi teacher Pir Vilayat Khan urges us to consider pain in this way:

Overcome any bitterness that may have come because you were not up to the magnitude of pain that was entrusted to you. Like the mother of the world who carries the pain of the world in her heart, each one of us is part of her heart, and therefore endowed with a certain measure of cosmic pain. You are sharing in the totality of that pain. You are called upon to meet it in joy instead of self-pity.

Forgiveness

We take a tremendous step toward freedom and awakening when we imagine we might forgive our parents, the ones who brought us pain. This is often a most difficult practice, and requires strength, courage, and a great deal of time. For to let go of the ones who hurt us is to let go of our identity as the one who was hurt, the one who was violated, the one who was broken. It often feels like the bad guys are getting off scot-free while we are left holding the bag of pain.

But forgiveness is not just for them. The point is not only to let them off the hook. Forgiveness, especially for us, allows us to be set free from the endless cycle of pain, anger, and recrimination that keeps us imprisoned in our own suffering.

What are we required to forgive? Those of us who have been deeply hurt often want to know how much we have to forgive, and how soon? Must I really forgive this or that hurt, this or that injustice or horrible violation? I am not ready, it is too soon, I still hurt too much to say that what happened to me was okay and now everything is fine.

What we are forgiving is not the act—not the violence or the neglect, the incest, the divorce, or the abuse. We are forgiving the actors, the people who could not manage to honor and cherish their own children, their own spouse, or their own lives in a loving and gentle way. We are forgiving their suffering, their confusion, their unskillfulness, their desperation, and their humanity.

As long as we hold onto how this or that person hurt or dishonored us, we are trapped in a dance of suffering with that person forever. We feel their abuse every time that person enters our thoughts. Again and again we must relive the suffering, calling it up over and over, as if by sheer repetition we could erase the tape. But each repetition only strengthens the habitual rut of anguish that sears our psyche.

We are set free from this cycle of suffering when we forgive our parents and we allow them to be who they were, nothing more, nothing less. Less than the ideal mother or father, perhaps, but children of God still, with all their suffering and distress, who need all the grace and mercy available to them. Through forgiveness we are all set free to go our own ways and follow our own destiny.

Once St. Peter asked Jesus, "How many times shall I forgive someone who hurts me? As many as seven times?" Peter knew that the old law stated that you had to forgive any offense at least three times. More than that and you were off the hook. So when Peter said "seven times?" he was being charitable, and he figured Jesus would marvel at his generosity. But then Jesus said to Peter, "No, not seven times, but seventy times seven."

Forgiveness is required of us in rich measure, not because the hurts that come are not painful but because it is forgiveness that sets us free, that heals the unspeakable wounds, that allows us to grow in heart and spirit. The deeper the hurt and the more powerful the injustice, the more we are invited to grieve, to sink into our pain, and to let go into forgiveness. Those who pray the Lord's Prayer ask God to "forgive us our trespasses, as we forgive those who trespass against us." When we forgive one another our clumsiness, we are set free of the past, we are free to be born fresh into this moment, unencumbered by our endless struggles with the old stories.

This is not an easy thing to ask. Should blacks in South Africa or the United States forgive the whites who oppressed and enslaved them? Should native Americans forgive the conquering Spanish? Should Jews ever forgive the Nazis who put their parents and their children in the ovens?

Jack Kornfield, a gentle, loving teacher of Buddhism, tells a story of going with Maha Gosananda, a respected Cambodian monk, into the refugee camps where thousands of Cambodians had fled the terrible holocaust conducted by Pol Pot. Every family had lost children, spouses, and parents to the ravages of genocide, and their homes and temples had been destroyed. Maha Gosananda announced to the refugees that there would be a Buddhist ceremony the next day, and all who wished to come would be welcome.

Since Buddhism had been desecrated by Pol Pot, people were curious if anyone would go. The next day, over ten thousand refugees converged at the meeting place to share in the ceremony. It was an enormous gathering. Maha Gosananda sat for some time in silence on a platform in front of the crowd. Then he began chanting the invocations that begin the Buddhist ceremony, and people started weeping. They had been through so much sorrow, so much difficulty, that just to hear the sound of those familiar words again was precious.

Some wondered what Maha Gosananda would say. What could one possibly say to this group of people? What he did next, in the company of thousands of refugees, was begin to repeat this verse from the *Dhammapada,* a sacred Buddhist scripture:

Hatred never ceases by hatred;
But by love alone is healed.
This is an ancient and eternal law.

Over and over Maha Gosananda chanted this verse. These were people who had as much cause to hate as anyone on earth. Yet as he sat there, repeating this verse over and over, one by one, thousands of voices joined together in unison: "Hatred never ceases by hatred: but by love alone is healed. This is an ancient and eternal law." Out of the mouths of people who had been wounded, oppressed, made homeless, aggrieved, and crushed by the pain of war, came a prayer proclaiming the ancient truth about love, a truth that was greater than all the sorrows they had seen and felt.

"If you want to see the brave, look at those who can forgive. If you want to see the heroic, look at those who can love in return for hatred." This quote from the Bhagavad-Gita reminds us how terribly difficult it is to forgive those who have hurt us. It requires a tremendous amount of courage and is not easily done. I do not expect forgiveness to bubble up in you simply because you finish reading this chapter. Forgiveness can be very hard, and for some, the journey to forgiveness may be long and difficult.

At the retreats I conduct with my wife Christine, when we speak of forgiveness, some who have experienced violation or abuse are reluctant to forgive, and even become angry at the suggestion that their victimizer should be forgiven. It is true that child abuse is a horrible act, and we should do all we can to prevent such gross mistreatment of children. Forgiveness, while it may bring healing, has its own timing. It should be nurtured and invited, but never pushed. Any fear and rage must be honored and allowed to be true for as long as it is present. The heart knows when it is ready to forgive.

The ancient Greek language has two words for time. The first, *chronos*, describes chronological time, the measure of minutes and hours and years. The second is *kairos*, which in the Bible is translated as "the fullness of time." This sense of time describes the deeper readiness of things to be born, to blossom in their own time. So it is with forgiveness.

Ette Hillesum, a victim of the Nazi concentration camps, writes of the healing surrender into grief and forgiveness:

And you must be able to bear your sorrow; even if it seems to crush you, you will be able to stand up again, for human beings are so strong, and your sorrow must become an integral part of yourself; you mustn't run away from it.

Do not relieve your feelings through hatred, do not seek to be avenged on all Germans, for they, too, sorrow at this moment. Give your sorrow all the space and shelter in yourself that is its due, for if everyone bears grief honestly and courageously, the sorrow that now fills the world will abate. But if you do instead reserve most of the space inside you for hatred and thoughts of revenge—for which new sorrows will be born for others—then sorrow will never cease in this world. And if you have given sorrow the space it demands, then you may truly say: life is beautiful and so rich. So beautiful and so rich that it makes you want to believe in God.

EXERCISE
A Place of Refuge

As you begin this series of exercises and meditations, you may find it helpful to create a place of refuge in your home, a place where you feel safe and welcome.

Find a small corner in a bedroom or some other quiet place in your home. This will become your place of refuge, your personal spiritual sanctuary. Many spiritual practices make use of some kind of shrine, puja, or altar that helps focus the attention on matters of the heart and spirit. Find a low table, bench, or even a cardboard box, and drape it with some pleasing material, using this as a focal point for your own journey.

Sit down in front of the table for a few moments in silence. Allow yourself to visualize what is most beautiful, inspiring, or sacred in your life, those things that represent the healing, inward journey of your heart. They need not be religious symbols, only those that hold some deep meaning for you and the life you wish to lead.

Opening your eyes but remaining silent, begin to collect a few of those meaningful objects and place them on the table. You may want to include photographs of people you love, a special quote, flowers, a candle, or something from nature. Arrange them in a way that feels right to you.

Now, for several minutes, sit still in front of the table and have a silent conversation with those things that mirror the voices of your heart. Feel their presence and allow them to nourish you. This is your place of refuge, of belonging. Welcome.

You may feel like reciting a special poem, prayer, or song. Feel free to follow the impulses that arise within you. This is a time to gently allow yourself to feel at home in your body, your spirit, your own life.

Make time each day to sit in your place of refuge. You may find yourself gradually wanting to spend more time here, other days perhaps less time. Nevertheless, try to allow this to become a daily practice.

In this place, there is nothing for you to do. No need to figure anything out, fix what is broken, or become enlightened. You only need sit, feel, and listen. Allow this to be a place without judgment or expectation, a new home, a place of rest.

Meditation
LETTING GO OF FAMILY SORROW

Throughout this book, we use mindfulness meditations to deepen and expand our awareness of the strength and wisdom of our spirit. Meditation is a practice that allows us to focus our attention and sharpen our concentration, to open what is closed, to explore what is hidden, and to restore our center of gravity when we are scattered or distracted. Through meditation we may become more fully present to receive the multitude of sensations that accompany simply being human. Cultivating mindful awareness, we explore the depth and breadth of our true nature and begin to enter into compassionate relationship with the spirit within.

Many forms of meditation use breathing as a means of focusing our attention. Letting the mind rest in the breath can generate an experience of that place of belonging that resides within us. We will use these meditation techniques throughout the book.

Make a list of the most painful memories from your childhood. The list may include people who hurt you, poignant losses or disappointments, or particular situations that brought you sadness or harm.

Collect photographs, mementos, or symbolic items that remind you of these particular people or events. If there is a person, event, or situation for which you have no photograph or object, take some crayons and a piece of paper and make a drawing of the situation as you remember it.

Now sit in front of your table in your place of refuge, gathering these photographs and objects beside you. Begin by choosing one that feels especially painful, the one that seems to bring up the most grief, the most anger, the most sadness within you. You may find it helpful to begin with someone who hurt you deeply as a child, perhaps your father or mother. Place their photograph or object on the table in front of you, and, sitting still and quietly, allow your gaze to rest on them.

Feel the memories as they flood your heart. Feel the sensations that arise in your body as you look at them —feel the tightness, the shallowness or quickness of the breath, the anger, the disappointment, and the sadness. Let your awareness be gentle and heartfelt, exploring and acknowledging with compassion all of the suffering and grief that has lived inside you. Feel the resistance to the pain, the armoring, the reluctance to feel the depth of your sadness. Allow the pain into your heart, allow your heart to feel the deep sorrow of these memories. Feel the grief that you have held back for so long and draw the pain in, make room for it, breathe it into your heart. Continue to breathe in the pain until you fully experience the reservoir of hurt within you.

Now, looking at your mother (or father), slowly begin to say goodbye. "Mom (or Dad), you hurt me badly. Whether you meant to or not, you hurt me. But I will not hurt forever because of what happened between us. I will not hurt just because of your pain. It is time for me to go. It is time for me to say goodbye to you, to your pain, to what you did to me. Goodbye, Mom. Goodbye. I set you free as my mother. I may never be your child again. I let you go as my mother. Goodbye, Mom. I am no longer your wounded child. I set you free. I wish it could have been different, but it has been so painful, I have to let you go. Goodbye, Mom. Goodbye. Goodbye, Mom. Goodbye.

I set you free. I set myself free. I am free of you, I am free of the pain we shared."

As you say goodbye, allow the pain to go with them, each breath, each exhalation releasing the pain of a lifetime. Say goodbye to them as your parents and allow them to go their own way. Set them free. Set yourself free. You are no longer their child. "I am a child of the earth, a child of creation, a child of God. I take my place with them. And I set you free to take your own place, to make your own way." Continue this exercise until you begin to feel a genuine sense of release.

Next, we begin to invite a healing forgiveness into our relationship. Forgiveness is the enzyme that makes possible our freedom and liberation from family pain and sorrow. For some, this may be the most difficult part of letting go. Be patient and gentle with yourself. Allow the words to come slowly, honoring the resistance, yet taking the risk to imagine true forgiveness taking birth in your heart.

"For all that you may have done that caused me pain, intentionally or unintentionally, through your actions, your words, or your thoughts, however the pain came to me through what you did or didn't do, I forgive you. I forgive you. I set you free." Let them be touched for a moment by your forgiveness. Let them be forgiven. Let go of the walls of resentment, so that your heart may be free and your life may be lighter.

Feel the resistance to forgive. Feel the heart try to harden and hold the anger, fear, and hatred. When fear or resistance arises, allow your awareness to gently settle on your breathing, taking a moment to feel at home in the gentle rising and falling of your breath. Even in the midst of understandable, natural resistance, we may invite an emotional softening. Then begin again: "I forgive you. I forgive you." Let the heart soften. Let them go. Allow the war between you to be over. Set them free. Set yourself free. "Forgiving you, I set you free. Forgiving you, I set myself free. I take my place as a child of God, and I let you go. We are no longer at war. I no longer struggle with the pain of you in my heart. I set you free. I am free. God bless you. Go in peace."

Take as much time as you need to allow the feelings of sadness and release to arise within you. Stay with this person or situation until you feel a sensation of relief flood your heart and body. You may want to repeat this exercise, focusing on one person, every day for a week. It may take many sessions in front of the table to feel a deep sense of closure and relief. Repeat the meditation until you feel complete with this person or event.

You may repeat the meditation with as many people or events as you need. Each person may require several repetitions of the exercise in your place of refuge. This is fine. Forgiveness has its own timing and may not be rushed. Allow yourself to take as long as you need. Letting go takes time, courage, and compassion. There is no hurry and no place to get to. This is simply a gentle invitation to practice letting go of childhood sorrow and to make a new home in your own body, heart, and spirit.

CHAPTER TWO

Fear and Faith

A writer once asked me to help her explore some unpleasant emotions that were recurring in her life. I started by asking her to write a short story about her childhood. When she presented it to me the following week, I was struck by the first line: "This is the story of how I learned to be fearful and what I learned to be fearful of."

The story of her childhood was a story about fear. As a child of an alcoholic who later became an alcoholic herself, fear was a constant theme in her life. "I am afraid to let anyone know me, or see me, or be close to me," she wrote.

Just as with pain, fear is something we all experience. As human beings, we naturally fear hunger, want, illness, and injury. On an emotional level we are frightened of abandonment, criticism, intimacy, and pain. We also fear economic hardship, social disrepute, and we are all afraid of the time when sickness or death will come to us or to our loved ones.

When fear arises, we often harden our bodies and hearts, closing inward to protect ourselves. Sometimes we feel tense, paralyzed, unable to move; at other times we may race around faster, trying to make ourselves into a moving target, something harder to hit. We build up walls and barriers, call up armies, and pay insurance companies, doctors, and governments to protect us from danger as we try to minimize the risks of being human.

When we live in fear of everything that may bring us harm, we effectively insulate ourselves from life itself—because pain, sorrow, illness, and death are unavoidable ingredients in life. Despite our fearful preparations, many things that frighten us will inevitably touch us at some moment in some way.

In addition to the generic fears that accompany being human, we also experience other fears, terrifying fears that we inherit from our childhood, those painful memories that refuse to fade away. The writer's story continued: "The thing I was most fearful of was what my mother's moods might be on any given day. I was afraid of being punished for things . . . I was afraid to be caught . . . at almost anything, depending on the day or time of day."

The betrayal, the lies, the abuse, the fighting, the desertion—we remember each moment in vivid detail. The tender heart of the small child is like a page on which each transgression is indelibly stamped. For the child who has been hurt, fear is not simply a vague concern about the possibility of harm; it becomes a reflexive response to the certainty of danger.

When Zenia was young, her father would come home late after the bars were closed, bellowing and cursing through the house in the dark of the night, until he eventually made it to bed sometime later. From the moment her father walked in the door, she would lie awake, gripping the sides of her bed, staring at the door, paralyzed with fear that he would burst into her room. Only after he finally collapsed would she relax enough to be able to sleep. As an adult, when Zenia goes to bed she still feels the familiar anxiety she felt as a child. This woman, now in her forties, carries this old fear born in childhood smallness, relentless and unceasing, that continues to disturb both her sleep and her waking.

Children raised in family confusion or uncertainty come to experience deep and lasting fears that lodge in the body and heart. There is a perpetual sense of imminent danger that saturates every moment. No single instant is truly fearless—even the most loving or playful setting seems to hold some unseen promise of danger.

Fear can have many faces. Nancy, sexually abused by an uncle who eventually committed suicide, remembered driving in a car with him when she was small. Terrified he would make a move toward her, she kept her hand on the handle of the passenger door, ready to jump out. She said she still feels as if she has her hand on the escape lever for most of her life.

Richard, who was molested by his mother, told me that when women try to get close to him, he feels paralyzed with terror. This fear, he said, had ruined his marriage.

Carla's mother, a manic-depressive, would have terrible personality shifts. One minute she was a kind and loving mother, and in the next instant she would be yelling, screaming, and pulling out her daughter's hair. With no warning, what was safe and warm became frightening and dangerous. As an adult, Carla carried enormous tension in her body, constantly protecting herself from the inevitable onslaughts that would come from an unpredictable world.

As we grow older, why do we still hold so tightly to what terrified us as children? Because the wounds were deep and powerful, and came when we were tender and vulnerable. When we were small, we had to rely on powers greater than ourselves for our every need—for our food, clothing, shelter, warmth, and safety. Our very lives were absolutely dependent upon these larger beings for all of our care. So when Mom ran out of the house, or Dad passed out, or someone was beat up, or someone got divorced, or died, or went away and never came back, it felt as if our very lives were in danger. We were literally frightened for our survival.

Our childhood fears were compounded because the people who claimed to be the guardians of our safety were inevitably the same people who caused us hurt. The father who said he would always be there for us was the same father who went away and left us. The mother who said she would never let anyone or anything hurt us was the same mom who yelled and screamed at us. So just as we learned to be afraid, we also came to believe that no one could be trusted to give us shelter.

Some of us attempted to minimize the danger by trying to take total control of our environment. Perhaps if we could stop our parents from fighting or drinking, or help them get along better, or make sure the dinner was ready on time, the napkins were folded, and the toast didn't burn, then things would be all right, then we could ward off any potential flare-ups. Once we got all the ducks in a row, once we were firmly in control of all the things that could possibly go wrong in our family, then we would be safe. Exhausted, but safe.

Unfortunately, the existence of pain and sorrow in our family was totally beyond our control. Our parents' suffering, confusion, anger, or grief was deeply woven into our common family story, and there was little or nothing we could have done to prevent its taking shape in our lives. Their pain could erupt in clumsiness, anger, or desertion at any time. And regardless of how many ducks we managed to coax into a neat, protective row, there would always be that one we missed, and the drama would begin again. There was nothing that any child could do to stop it.

Christy, troubled by a pervasive insecurity for most of her life, asked me to help her discover some sense of safety, some experience of sanctuary. We began by exploring a few of the childhood fears that arose in her very troubled family, and then I suggested we do a guided meditation. After helping her relax into a meditative state, I invited her to allow an image of safety to emerge, an image of a place where she felt absolutely, completely safe, and then to rest for a few moments in the comfort of that image. When the meditation was finished, I asked Christy to describe her image of safety. "It was wonderful," she said. "I was dead, and in outer space." We both laughed at how far she had to go to feel any sense of security. This powerful sense of danger had permeated the cells of her body so deeply that she could only imagine herself safe when she was dead in outer space! Clearly, fear had become one of the strongest voices in the chorus of her psyche.

The Costs of Fear

Our fears made us feel powerless and vulnerable, and so we desperately constructed any strategies we could to protect ourselves: If we thought that our true feelings would be disruptive, we learned to conceal them; if someone seemed angry or displeased with us, we would instantly disown ourselves and pretend to be whatever they wanted us to be; we could even pretend to love, when loving was required. Out of fear and desperation, we learned to cultivate an emotional and spiritual dishonesty to protect ourselves from harm. Fear became a primary motivator for much of our behavior. For some of us, it became our most familiar and reliable feeling.

But this kind of fear gradually and unquestionably corrodes our lives. Dr. Herbert Benson, professor of medicine at Harvard Medical School and author of *The Relaxation Response,* explored the "fight or flight" response that exists in humans as well as in animals. When we experience fear, our body produces specific changes in pulse, respiration, and secretion of certain hormones. Our body prepares to defend itself or to flee. This can prove to be a useful biological response to real danger—as when we are physically attacked or must act quickly to save a drowning child.

But Benson notes that many of us regularly maintain inordinately high levels of fear and stress in our lives, even when we are in no real danger at all. Our chronic psychological fears that linger from childhood produce tremendous levels of stress that invite all manner of illness and disease into our bodies. When we live our lives in fear, regardless of whether those fears are real or imagined, we lower our resistance to disease and actually help bring about those illnesses we fear the most.

In addition, our culture effectively replicates our childhood worries about fear and safety. We live in a dangerous society that places a tremendous premium on protecting ourselves from harm. In one year, Americans spend more than $50 billion on security equipment to protect their homes and property. As a nation, we spend more than $300 billion a year on nuclear weapons, tanks, guns, and soldiers to protect ourselves from everyone else on the planet. We spend countless billions on health and life insurance to shield us from the costs of illness and death. And with all of these expenditures, thousands of dollars for every man, woman, and child in the United States, hardly anyone feels truly safe. We still listen for the things that go bump in the night.

"Where there is fear," said Mohandas Gandhi, "we lose the way of our spirit." When we are in fear, we focus all our attention on the point of danger and lose our capacity to find any courage, security, or peace within ourselves. We become so obsessed with what threatens us that the inner strengths of the heart become inaudible. Perhaps this is why, in the Christian New Testament, the phrase "be not afraid" is found more than three hundred times. When we are afraid, we lose our ability to feel our own inner strength, and things precious and vital within us are smothered by our anxieties. When we spend all our days worried about how things will turn out, planning for whether we will have enough food, clothing, money, or love, then what kind of life have we protected? In spite of our plans and strategies, we never feel at peace.

The Perpetuation of Danger

In the 1950s, some Japanese soldiers were found on remote islands in the Pacific, still fighting the Second World War, which had actually ended years before. It was very hard to convince these poor hangers-on that the war was really over and it was safe to go home.

How do we know when the war is over? How do we know when to protect ourselves from danger, and when to allow ourselves to feel safe? Children raised in troubled families are uncertain which fears are justified—like the fear of rape, or of nuclear war—and which are simply habitual ghosts from our childhood, phantom fears without any real substance. The fears of childhood cast such long shadows across the psyche that after a time, almost anything can generate a fearful response. We even learn to wait for trouble to arrive—the fight, the angry word, the slamming door; it is almost a relief when it comes, so certain is its coming. All of our intuitive wisdom and emotional sensitivity is designed to predict when the ax will fall, so that we may do what we do best: try to protect ourselves from hurt.

The problem is this: Skills learned in danger require the presence of danger to be effective. If our greatest skill is getting ourselves out of trouble, then we are at our best when we have discovered some trouble to get out of. In a strange way we feel safer in fear and danger than we do in tranquility, because we know how to survive danger. We have no idea how to manage peace.

For many of the young men who fought in Vietnam, the truest thing that ever happened to them was war, booby traps, and death in the night. Those that made it back had learned to survive situations of tremendous danger and great terror. When they returned home, many of these young men found it difficult to adjust themselves to "normal" American life; their skills were applicable only in the murderous jungles of Southeast Asia. Many gradually came to recreate for themselves lives of reckless danger, seeking familiar ground on which to battle the enemies they knew best. Others carried deep within them many debilitating fears that terrorized their inner lives.

How can we be sure that our fears and terrors are not telling us the truth, that we should not be on our guard at every turn? And how can we know when it is safe enough to allow some of our fears to fall away and risk the vulnerability of being human?

Fear Without Danger

When we are raised in family distress, we learn to fear many things: We fear that things will change, or go wrong; we worry about what others will think of us; and we fear the hurt that comes from verbal or physical abuse. We fear abandonment and rejection. We even worry about ourselves, afraid that what we have inside may not be enough, may not measure up to the task of living. We fear that our gifts, our intuition, even our spirits are tragically deficient.

Consequently, as we grow older, whenever we feel afraid, we naturally presume that we are afraid of *something*. We assume that there is some person, circumstance, defect, or event that genuinely threatens our well-being. As soon as we feel frightened, we usually try to identify a particular danger to justify our fear. If no threat is immediately apparent, we may even manufacture one to give our fears credibility. Those of us who experienced fear as children habitually tie our fears to some memory of the past; when fear arises, we instantly seek a childhood explanation: "I am afraid because my father used to beat me up," or, "I am frightened because my mother never protected me." In our rush to calm our fear, we frequently look first to our childhood to explain and justify our anxiety.

But now we are no longer small and vulnerable, and when we feel afraid it does not necessarily indicate that we are, in fact, in real danger. It may simply be a response to a *misperception* of danger. There may be no danger at all; our anxiety may simply be a signal that something in this moment is in need of attention. Something in our body, our emotions, or our environment may be somehow disrupted or off balance, and needs our care.

Perhaps, in these moments, our fear is merely asking us to pay attention, indicating a need to watch for something happening that we are not watching closely enough.

Fear may arise for any number of reasons: Perhaps we are simply tired or feeling fragile that day, or maybe we are preoccupied, or require loving care, or need to attend to some feeling we have been pushing away. There may be no real, external danger at all, just a sensation of anxiety arising within us. Jack Kornfield says the presence of fear may even be a sign of growth, a moment in which we are "about to open to something bigger than the world we usually experience."

As children, we fear what can harm us, but as adults, fear may often arise when we unexpectedly encounter those things that would heal us. The story is told that when Jesus was born in a small country town, there were shepherds nearby keeping watch over their flocks. In the dark of the night, "an angel of the Lord appeared to them, and the glory of the Lord shone around them, and they were filled with fear. And the angel said to them, 'Be not afraid.' " When the shepherds met with something they had never seen before—even though it was a miraculous moment filled with light, announcing the birth of the Christ-child—still they were afraid. But just because they were afraid, it did not mean they were in danger. They were terrified merely because they encountered something outside their experience: They had inadvertently bumped into God.

If fear, then, is not always an indicator of danger, what can we do when fear arises? How, in the face of our anxiety, fear, and terror, do we cultivate a sense of safety, a sense of faith that all will be well, a place of sanctuary in which we may rest?

Fear and Faith

Since we are rarely in mortal danger, we may discover that most of our fears are generated by the mind. Most of us are fortunate to have enough to eat, enough clothes to keep us warm, and a place to sleep at night. Even though we are reasonably safe and cared for, we still go about our lives with fear and trembling. Why? Not because we fear the present but because we fear the future. We almost always seem to handle what we are given in this moment; but we expect that some day we will be given more than we can handle, and we are terrified that it will be more than we can bear.

We have seen how the pain of our past can give birth to bitterness, anger, and grief. Just as grief arises in response to pain in the past, fear is our response to pain in the future. Thus, if we are to understand our fears and learn to heal what frightens us, we must first explore how we react to the anticipation of pain.

Fear arises when we believe we will not be strong enough to handle the pain we will be given. As children in troubled families, we were given so much hurt, and we felt so small and fragile; we learned powerful lessons about the kinds of deep pain that could tear at the heart and body. We felt how much it could hurt when we were rejected by our own parents, when we were yelled at, or hit, or simply forgotten. There were times we weren't sure we could take any more pain, and that if it ever got worse, we might just give up. We didn't know if we could trust ourselves to survive the emotional and physical batterings that came from being a child, from being a member of our family.

As adults, we still carry much of that uncertainty within ourselves. We are not yet convinced we can withstand all the discomforts, losses, and torments in store for us in this lifetime. At times we don't feel strong enough to be human, to be big, to be a grown-up. Even now, we still feel little, we don't trust ourselves or have faith in our ability to hold our own against the sufferings and sorrows the world can bring.

When we are uncertain and tentative about our ability to handle the pain of being human, we become worried and afraid. When we feel fragile or weak, when we are convinced that the next loss, rejection, or failure will be the one that will somehow do us in or break us apart, then we will approach each day of our lives with tremendous anxiety.

In the Christian scriptures there is a story about Jesus and his disciples as they were crossing the Sea of Galilee in a small boat. Suddenly, without warning, a great storm rose up, the winds tossed the boat to and fro, and the boat began to fill with water. The disciples were overcome with fear; yet Jesus, in the stern of the boat, remained asleep. The disciples, terrified for their lives, woke Jesus and screamed, "Master, don't you care if we perish?" Jesus turned to the ones who were with him and said, "Why are you afraid? Have you no faith?"

In the middle of great danger, Jesus was at peace. The disciples could not rest until the danger had been extinguished, while Jesus' sense of safety rested in a deep faith that all would be well—even in the midst of a life-threatening storm.

What do we mean when we use the word *faith*? For many of us the word can be awkward. It may be uncomfortable to hear or understand, even more difficult to use, because for centuries it has been interpreted by certain religious traditions as a litmus test for spiritual worthiness. A specific quantity of "faith," in these traditions, has been used as an entrance requirement for the kingdom of God. If you have "enough" faith, then you get into heaven, you become a child of God, and you will be granted whatever you desire. If you pray hard enough, if you have faith in God and the doctrines of the church, if you affirm your "faith" in those teachings, then you will be worthy, you will be cared for, and God will look favorably on your life.

This antiquated definition of faith taught that if we "had" enough of it, we could change the world around us to make it more to our liking. With enough faith, we could conquer our fears simply by making those things that frightened us miraculously disappear. If we were poor, faith could bring us more money; if we were sick, faith would make us well; if we were alone, faith would give us company; and if we were feeling inadequate, our faith could bring us a successful career. An adequate supply of faith would assure us that all would turn out the way we hoped.

All too often, however, the zealous application of this religious maxim has been used to drive a wedge between the "faithful" and the "unfaithful," as a way to tell the "good" people from the "bad" ones. Many people have been deeply hurt by those who felt a moral obligation to judge the spiritual worthiness of others by taking a measure of their "faith." This has been especially abusive when applied to people who are poor, hungry, culturally or sexually "different," or terminally ill with cancer or AIDS. Too often the religious assertion is made that if these "unfortunate" people only had enough "faith," then God would feed them, clothe them, and heal them of their deviance, their cancer, or their AIDS. If the AIDS or cancer didn't go away, then the fault must be with the victim; they must surely be lacking in faith. Thus, many of us have felt "faith" used as a weapon against us, as we have been judged relentlessly and without mercy—an experience not unlike the pain we felt in our childhood families.

How can we reclaim the word *faith* so that we may use it for our own healing? We may begin by noting that in most ancient scriptural texts, the word *faith* is not a *noun,* it is a *verb.* Faith is not something that one person "has" and another "doesn't"; faith is not a thing, and so cannot be measured or possessed. Faith is a *way of being.* It is a spiritual practice, a way of discovering what is reliable and true, a way of expanding trust in our inner wisdom. It is a place inside where we are in a compassionate relationship with what is strong and whole within ourselves, where we listen to the still, small voices of our heart and soul. When we are practicing a path of faith, we are in intimate conversation with what is deepest in our mind, heart, and spirit.

For the Hebrews, faith involved a deep trust in the watchful love of God for all God's children. According to the prophet Isaiah, even in the midst of the most terrible circumstances, those whose hearts are centered in the faithful care of God "shall renew their strength, they shall mount up on wings like eagles, they shall run and not be weary, they shall walk and not faint."

The Buddhist word for faith, *sraddha,* also suggests much more than a belief in theological doctrine. *Sraddha* implies a sense of trust, clarity, and confidence—it literally means "to put one's heart on." It is etymologically akin to the Latin *cor,* from which we derive the words *heart* and *courage.* Thus, the practice of faith is clearly the practice of a strong and courageous heart. "If you set your heart aright," says the Book of Job, "you will lie down, and none will make you afraid."

Another Buddhist teaching about faith is found in the concept of equanimity. Equanimity is the ability to experience the changes in our lives, circumstances, and feelings and still remain calm, centered, and unmoved. The image most often used to illustrate the quality of equanimity is that of a mountain. The mountain sits there as the sun shines on it, the rain drenches it, it is covered with snow, and struck by lightning. Through it all, through all the changing conditions, the mountain remains unwavering. As we cultivate equanimity within ourselves, we learn to be more like the mountain, finding that place of strength and courage within ourselves that enables us to withstand the slings and arrows of being human without feeling overwhelmed by fear.

As we explore the practices of faith, *sraddha,* and equanimity, one thing becomes clear: Genuine faith is born of the ability to trust in what is most fundamentally true within ourselves. Circumstances will change, and all manner of things pleasant and unpleasant will arise and fall away; sometimes our lives will be touched with joy, and at other times we will be given tremendous pain and sorrow. Many times we will be afraid. But the object of faith is not to eliminate difficult circumstances, nor is faith about trusting in a God who will rescue us from hurt, or who—if only we believe strongly enough—will make everything better. The real question of faith is when pain and loss inevitably come our way, do we withdraw in fear that we will be destroyed, or do we deepen our trust in our innate capacity to endure them? Can we find a strong and courageous heart, a place of clarity and wholeness within ourselves in which we can place our ultimate trust, gently allowing both the fear and the pain to simply move through us?

Faith is a centering response. The search for faith is a search for our true nature, for the spirit within, the divine strength that lives in our deepest heart. When we were small, we sought safety in trying to control the dangers that populated our daily lives. We kept waiting until everything was okay, until everyone was finally asleep, until the fighting was over. But as we grow older we discover that the hazards and discomforts that threaten us never totally disappear from our lives. We begin to see that true safety is not the *absence* of danger but rather the *presence* of something else—the presence of a sense of faith, born in the heart and sustained by a spirit of serenity, trust, and courage. If we seek our safety within ourselves and not in the manipulation of environment and circumstance, then our practice becomes a pilgrimage to uncover a deep and abiding faith in our own gifts, our own strengths, and our own spirit.

Approaching Our Fears

If faith reflects a confidence in our own inner strength, then as we cultivate faith we become more able to accept whatever we are given. Regardless of whether we are given pleasure or pain, sorrow or delight, we gradually come to feel confident that we are strong, resilient, and creative enough to survive and endure the perils of being human. Our first challenge, then, is to learn to approach our fears directly. Often our first response to fear is to feel our own fragility, and so we move away and hide, we make ourselves invisible and inaccessible to whatever might bring us harm, thereby exaggerating the experience of fear. When we run from circumstances that feel dangerous, we generate additional fear and anxiety. Have we run far enough? Can they still see us? Have we thought of everything? Are we secure yet? We still seek to find safety by eliminating external danger rather than relying on our own inner resources for sanctuary and protection. We may discover that we actually feel safer when we move *toward* those things that frighten us, not when we move *away*.

Daniel was a man who, as a young boy, was molested by his mother. As an adult, he had always found it difficult to sustain lasting relationships with women. There would inevitably come a moment when it felt to him that they were getting too close, and he would feel afraid. At that point he would feel a need to run away and would often end the relationship.

During a therapy group, Dan announced that he had begun a relationship with a woman he cared for, so he wanted to work on his problem with fear. He said the woman was extremely kind and understanding, and he felt very much loved. At the same time, he was already beginning to feel an impulse to run, to hide, to get out. How could he protect himself and be safe, yet still remain close and open to her?

I asked him to pick a woman from the group to role-play the woman he cared for. Then I placed them several feet apart and asked Dan how he felt. "I feel okay, a little frightened, but basically fine." I asked him to move closer, about three feet away. How did he feel? "Still okay, but I feel more tightness in my stomach. It's a little scarier." I asked him to move two feet from her. "This is much scarier," he said. "I feel very uncomfortable. I start to go numb, I want to disappear, run away."

I kept asking him to move closer, until they were face to face, maybe eighteen inches apart. "I feel really bad. I want to just run away, just go away somewhere else. I feel numb, my stomach feels nauseous, I'm frightened." At this point his body was visibly shaken, and I could see he wished this exercise to be over so he could return to his chair and forget the whole thing. "Move a bit closer," I asked, and also requested the woman to place her hand on his. At this point their bodies were almost touching, and Dan was ready to bolt. Yet after a moment in this position, something shifted. Slowly, everyone in the group saw him relax, and he seemed much more comfortable, even allowing a half-smile to emerge. "This feels better," he admitted. "This close, where I can see her eyes, and with her hand on mine, I feel okay. I'm not thinking about her, I'm just being with her. Somehow, this feels safer."

Daniel had spent his whole life running from what frightened him. Because of his early sexual abuse, the unpredictability of intimacy had caused so much fear to arise in his body that he would always run away. But every time he ran away, he would generate so many worries and anxious fantasies that he would inevitably create even more fear in himself for the next time. It had never occurred to him that moving closer, moving *toward* her rather than *away* from her, could bring a sense of safety. As he moved closer, he could see in her eyes something that brought comfort and serenity; he could see her own fear, her deep caring for him, her own uncertainty, and her own willingness to be human and vulnerable. By changing his relationship to what frightened him, he discovered a deeper sense of faith in himself, a sense that he could handle whatever was to come.

When we grow up small and afraid, we come to believe that true sanctuary and serenity can only come when we develop foolproof mechanisms for shutting out danger, for hiding, for running away, for not being open to what could hurt us. Yet as we move closer to our fears, as we accept them, explore them, and examine our response to the anticipation of danger, we may begin to discover that *we have within ourselves all that is required to feel protected and safe.* When we directly face what frightens us, we often discover our own capacity to survive whatever we have been given. The more we are present with ourselves in fear, without withdrawing, hiding out, or armoring ourselves, the more trust we develop in our own resources, our own creativity, resilience, and wisdom. Slowly we begin to cultivate a much deeper faith that, despite the hurts and disappointments we are given, somehow, within ourselves, all will be well.

Faith In Ourselves

Unfortunately, many of us as children even learned to mistrust ourselves. If our families rarely talked about their feelings, we learned to mistrust the reliability of our own emotions. If our parents were uncomfortable and unable or unwilling to speak the truth, we began to mistrust our own perceptions of what was true. And if we constantly felt we were in danger of being hurt, we learned to mistrust our ability to protect ourselves. Even as we grew older, whenever we felt afraid, we would immediately focus our attention on our weakness and vulnerability, acutely aware of the disparity between the powerful threat of the danger without and the fragile, vulnerable, untrustworthy person within.

However, the truth is that often we are much stronger than we imagine. Curiously, few of us realize how much strength it took simply to grow up in our families. As children, we drew upon tremendous determination, spirit, and courage as we strove to maintain our daily lives, to survive the repeated injuries, and to protect ourselves from danger. We developed a remarkable intuition that could warn us of any imbalances or irregularities within ourselves or others; we became attentive and aware of subtle shifts in loyalty, strategy, or intent in those around us; and we became adept at redefining our survival strategies at a moment's notice. In addition, in response to the emotional uncertainties of our families, many of us managed to uncover a place of refuge deep within ourselves where we inevitably found some source of strength and comfort, even in the midst of an environment without sufficient nourishment, support, or care.

For many of us, this exceedingly private place of inner fortitude has actually been our closest and most trustworthy ally for much of our lives, yet it is a place to which we go with remarkable infrequency. It is a place that others are rarely privileged to see. Only when we are terribly hurt, frightened, or unsure about our lives do we go deeply inward to that place. It is a place to which we go when all feels lost, when our strategies and manipulations have finally failed, and the world has become unmanageable. Then, in despair, we turn inside, in search of our deepest strength.

Unfortunately, many of us must be devastated by some tragic moment before we will reluctantly place our trust in what is deepest within ourselves. Many of us never imagine the depth of our inner strength until we find ourselves confronting a terminal illness, experiencing a divorce, or suffering the loss of a spouse, a friend, or a child. Face to face with tragedy, illness, or death, many of us actually become less fearful—not because life holds any less danger but because in those moments we are propelled deep into ourselves, reaching to uncover what is strong, reliable, and whole within our own hearts and spirits. Even in the midst of a personal hell, we rediscover within ourselves a heart of courage.

Not long ago, Bob, a recovering alcoholic and a dear friend, telephoned me. He had spent a good deal of his life accomplishing great things, accumulating wealth, and cultivating positions of power. Yet in the midst of it all, he was always afraid he wasn't quite good enough, and he somehow had to prove his worthiness through his accomplishments. He was always working to calm his inner fears and anxieties and rarely felt strong or peaceful inside.

Bob's son had died of AIDS just two years before, so both he and his wife had been working with death for some time. Their courageous ability to use their suffering as a teaching for others had helped them become less fearful about their own lives, and they were quite beloved in the community as people to whom everyone could come with their pain and always feel welcome.

One morning Bob called to tell me he had been diagnosed as having terminal cancer, and the doctors said he had only months to live. "All my life," he told me, "I have prayed for inner strength and serenity. I have gone to workshops, read books, and asked God every day to give me a sense of centeredness and peace. But now I know I might die very soon, I don't feel afraid at all. It's strange, but I feel so calm. After living with our son's death and being so close to my own, something in me finally feels peaceful. I certainly don't want to die, but I'm ready to go if this is my time. This close to death, I have a strong feeling of faith, that somehow, whatever happens, it will be all right—just what I've wanted my whole life."

Perhaps the greatest fear is the fear of our own death. Yet many of us have witnessed those who, as they suffered the consequences of cancer, heart disease, AIDS, or other life-threatening illnesses, actually became more peaceful and serene as the moment of their death drew closer. The nearer they came to the actual moment of death, the less frightened they became. Somehow, in proximity to their greatest fear, a corresponding awareness of tremendous courage emerged within them.

This seems to be a potent, reliable equation—that as we wholeheartedly approach what frightens us, a parallel reservoir of strength arises to meet it, and we are no longer eclipsed by our fear. It is not fear alone that makes us seek this place so much as a willingness to confront our fears directly, thereby opening up within us the full potential of a courageous heart. Here we go deep within ourselves to rediscover that place of faith, of *sraddha,* to feel the comfort and power of our own spirit, our true nature that, even in the face of death, emerges as a trustworthy and reliable ally.

How many of us have lost this place of faith? How many of us have misplaced this trust in ourselves, this conviction and confidence in our own inner strength? In reality, we never lose that inner place of strength, but in fear of danger, we desperately place our trust instead in our external strategies to defuse and neutralize the perils of the world. Relying on our complex psychological manipulations, trying to reconstruct a world without pain or peril, we tend to ignore the persistent fact of our own inner strength.

Our childhoods taught us many things about ourselves and compelled us to cultivate a variety of skills in perception, resilience, creativity, endurance, and determination, all of which remain at our disposal if we will only use them. Growing up in our families, many of us learned to understand things that no one else ever spoke about, to notice what no one else claimed to see, to consult with ourselves in solitude, and to nourish and nurture ourselves when we were hurt, forgotten, or ignored. This quiet, intimate place of hidden strength is the place where God lives within us, where what is eternal and trustworthy has been our private ally and companion. When we live our lives by acting out of this deep place of knowing, when we listen to the voices that speak to us from this inner place of sanctuary, then we may truly begin the practice of faith.

The Buddha taught his followers to "be lamps unto yourselves; be your own confidence; hold to the truth within yourselves." Are we willing to trust this place within us? Are we willing to place our confidence in the wisdom of our own heart and spirit? What if, every time we felt frightened or confused, we trusted our intuition? Most of us, because we mistrust ourselves, habitually second-guess our feelings and perceptions. But what if we trusted ourselves, our gifts, our inner voice? What if we assumed our feelings were accurate and were telling us something important about ourselves and the world? What if we trusted our hearts, relying on our ability to receive sensitive information from those around us, and acted as if what we felt were true? How much more courageous we would be if we felt that all of the perceptions of our mind, heart, and spirit were intact, fully functional, and working perfectly on our behalf.

The following is an exercise that many people have used with much success. I ask them to try this behavior for a single day: Resolve to go through an entire day assuming that you are trustworthy, that all your feelings are accurate, that all your perceptions and intuitions are reliable. As you approach each person or situation, ask yourself the questions, If I knew that I was absolutely trustworthy, how would I handle this moment? What would I do? What could I say that would be true? What would be the right action to settle this situation with safety and clarity? Once we begin to imagine that we have all we need to answer the questions of life within ourselves, it is amazing how quickly our habitual fears begin to melt away.

Faith, Acceptance, and Serenity

Throughout our lives, our jobs will change, our bodies will grow old, people will come and go, and we will have success and failure, health and disease. Nothing will belong to us, nothing will stay, nothing will remain the same. And yet, in the midst of it all, still we breathe, our hearts beat, our days go from morning until night, and we remain present and alive. With the equanimity of the mountain, the courageous heart feels it all, yet remains faithful and assured that within ourselves, all will be well.

There is a Zen story about a certain general who, during a civil war, led his troops through the countryside, overrunning everything and everyone in his path. The people of one town, having heard the tales of his cruelty, were terrified when they heard he was coming in the direction of their village, and they all fled into the mountains. The general marched into the empty town and sent his troops to search for any who remained. Some of the soldiers came back and reported that only one person remained, a Zen priest. The general strode over to the temple, walked in, pulled his sword, and said, "Don't you know who I am? I am the one who can run through you without batting an eye."

The Zen master looked back and calmly responded, "And I, sir, am one who can be run through without batting an eye." Hearing this, the general bowed and left.

Faith is not a fortress against danger; faith unfolds like a lotus flower, resting deep within us, a quiet place of deep trust. It is not a magic formula that prevents suffering; it is a place of strength where we feel most vitally present in heart and spirit. As children of family pain, we learned to withstand the changing events and circumstances that punctuated our lives. As adults, we may rediscover this same inner strength and use it to cultivate faith in our spirit, our true nature, and our deep, inner wisdom.

As we become more centered in what is deepest in ourselves, we slowly uncover a place of serenity where even the memory of a drunken father or an angry mother cannot disturb the waters of our soul. This is a very difficult place for many of us to find, and even more difficult to sustain. We may cultivate our sense of faith through a daily practice of prayer or meditation, where we consistently revisit that place within us that is strong enough even to hold what frightens us and to endure the sorrows of being human. Thomas Merton, the monk, poet, and spiritual scholar, said that through prayer and meditation we may find sanctuary in those fearful moments when sanctuary seems impossible. In dialogue with these voices of our heart and spirit, we take refuge in the Buddha, in the heart of Jesus, in what we call "the God within us." And through practice, we learn to place our faith and trust in those inner voices of clarity, strength, and wholeness.

Finally, we may even discover that our sense of humor, our ability to laugh at ourselves and our fears, can help us invoke a playful sense of faith that, despite the slings and arrows of life, somehow all will be well.

Sally came to see me because she had been terribly frightened of many things in her life and wanted to learn how to feel more secure and self-assured. We spent many hours exploring the wounds of her childhood. We explored the afflictions she suffered at the hands of her parents. We did several guided meditations, collages, and journals—in short, everything we could think of to help her feel protected. Yet despite our best efforts, she still felt very much afraid.

Then one day Sally came bouncing into my office with a big grin on her face and bright, raspberry-colored, high-top sneakers on her feet. "I bought these yesterday and put them on, because I thought wearing raspberry sneakers would definitely protect me. From now on, I am going to wear raspberry sneakers every day for safety." We laughed together, enjoying the freedom that came when she allowed her playfulness and courage to melt away some of the fears that had locked up her heart.

Rumi, the Sufi poet, speaks of the moment when we meet our fears with deep faith, playfulness, and love:

Today, like every other day, we wake up empty
and frightened.

Don't open the door to the study and begin reading.
Take down the dulcimer.

Let the beauty we love be what we do.
There are hundreds of ways to kneel and kiss the
ground.

Meditation
CULTIVATING A PLACE OF SAFETY

Find a comfortable sitting position in your place of refuge. Allow yourself a moment to relax, then gently close your eyes. Let your awareness come to your breath, noting the sensations of rising and falling as the air moves in and out of your body. Allow the rhythm of your breathing to bring a sense of calm and quiet to your body and mind.

Take a few moments to scan your body from within. Beginning at the top of your head and very slowly moving downward, note the variety of sensa-tions that are occurring in your body. Feel the top of your skull, your forehead, eyes, mouth, tongue, and teeth. Feel the bones and muscles of the jaw, neck, and shoulders. Take as much time as you need with each section of the body, noticing any tension or relaxation that arises as you focus your awareness on each area.

Allow your awareness to drift downward through the chest, back, arms, wrists, hands, and fingers. Let your attention move through the internal organs of the stomach, the kidneys, the intestines. Feel the lower back, the pelvis, the pressure of your buttocks on the ground. Be aware of the thighs, knees, ankles, feet, and toes. Keep noting any sensations you discover as you make your way through your body.

When you are finished, allow your attention to rest gently back on your breathing for a moment or two. After you have centered yourself fully in the breath, you may try the following meditation.

Ask your mind to allow an image of safety to emerge from deep within you. Allow an image to arise in which you feel absolutely, completely safe. It may be a place, a person, or a time in your life. Simply allow a picture to emerge in your awareness in which you feel totally protected, nurtured, and safe from all harm.

As the image arises, what does it look like? What do you notice about the color, the temperature, and the texture? Are you alone or with some-one? What do you feel when you are in that picture? Let the experience surround you like a soft garment, allowing yourself to linger for several moments, letting yourself feel the full comfort of being absolutely safe and protected.

After some time, choose a place in your body where you may anchor the image. Imagine that you are actually placing that image somewhere in your body, somewhere it will remain and stay with you always. It may be in your chest, your heart, your arms, legs, or hands—in short, anywhere you feel it will be most helpful, where you will have access to that image whenever you need it. Anchor it deep and strong in your body, so that it may be a constant companion.

When you feel you have the image planted within you, slowly allow your awareness to return to your breathing, letting the image become a part of you. No longer separate, it lives inside you. With each breath, allow the image to find a permanent home in your body.

After a while, continuing to let your awareness rest on the breath, you may gently open your eyes.

When you are finished, you may want to try drawing the image of safety that arose. With an easy and playful attitude, take a few minutes to visually record your experience of safety with some simple drawing materials like crayons or pastels. Don't be afraid of not being an accomplished artist— just choose the most potent images and colors, and draw what you saw and felt.

If you like the drawing, you may place it somewhere you can see it often, perhaps in your bedroom. Use it as an additional reminder of the place of safety you hold continuously within yourself.

EXERCISE
Exploring Fear in the Body

The next time you feel afraid, instead of watching for the danger outside yourself, focus instead on your breath for a moment. Using your breath as the center of your attention, first let yourself become aware of the physical sensation of breathing as your abdomen rises and falls, as your lungs expand and contract. As you begin to relax, let the object of fear arise in your heart. Without allowing the fear of it to overcome you, let whatever is causing fear to simply exist as an image in your mind, without judgment and without trying to change or eliminate it. There is no need to protect yourself from this moment. At the same time, keeping your attention centered on the breath, let your breath become the mountain of equanimity, the place within you that remains unmoved.

As the fear arises, we may simply note its coming: "Ah, fear, fear. There it is again." Then we may explore the feelings that arise: Where is the sensation strongest? In the chest, the muscles, the belly? What additional images arise along with the fear? Watch where the fear stays longest, watch as it begins to recede. Simply investigate this fear, making peace with the sensations that arise. If we resist the urge to protect ourselves and move gently into the experience of fear, what other sensations or impulses arise?

As each impression or sensation arises, silently acknowledge it to yourself: "Fear, fear" or "tightness, tightness." You may also make a note of your thoughts: "Despair, despair" or "ruin, ruin." With each breath, begin to make peace with whatever you have been given, opening your heart to the possibility that this may not be a disaster but simply an unexpected variation in the color or texture of your day. Perhaps there is no danger at all, merely a shift in sensations. Practice this for several minutes, observ-

ing how your body and heart respond as you bring mindful awareness to the sensations of fear.

You may end this exercise with a meditation on equanimity. You may want to recite this serenity prayer: "God grant me the serenity to accept those things I cannot change; the courage to change the things I can; and the wisdom to know the difference."

You may also repeat, silently within yourself, the following phrases: "May I be balanced and at peace. May I be undisturbed by the changing events of my life and the world around me. May I have faith in myself. May I have faith in the strength of the spirit within me."

Acknowledge to yourself that all created things arise and pass away— joys and sorrows, pleasant events, unpleasant events, friends, loved ones— even whole nations will come and go. "May I learn to see the arising and passing away of all things with equanimity and balance. May I have faith in the spirit within me. May I be open, courageous, and peaceful."

CHAPTER THREE

Performance and Belonging

When we are born, all creation shifts to make space for each child given birth. Rich or poor, black or white, gifted or foolish, as children of God we inherit a rightful place where we may live and grow, free and without condition. But many children raised in painful families rarely experience this sense of belonging. Regardless of how loving or attentive our family may have appeared, we still may have felt unwelcome even in our own home.

One of our greatest fears was that there would never be a place of safety, care, and belonging for us. Certainly those of us whose families were troubled, unstable, abusive, or alcoholic rarely felt we belonged anywhere. While we may have been granted a place of belonging when we were born, we soon discovered there was little safety or sanctuary to be found in our own family. This was no place like home.

Our childhood experience of belonging seemed conditional on our performance. We learned to anticipate and satisfy ridiculous demands, figure out what our parents wanted before they asked, and always try to do everything right, just so they would let us stay. But every success was temporary; there would always be some new threat to our tenuous sense of belonging, and there was rarely any sanctuary, never any rest.

We were grateful for being allowed to stay anywhere at all, and our fears and our gratitude mingled in a confused, secret litany we recited in our hearts:

They let me stay because I always try to make Mama feel better. They keep me around because I take care of the other kids when they argue, and I sit up with Mom when she cries. They have to like me because when Dad yells at me I don't cry or fight back. They like me because I never ask for anything. I know they love me, because they let me stay.

We felt as if we were valued for not making trouble. By amputating our hearts and feelings, we minimized our undesirability and made ourselves harmless. Only then could we take up space. It was hard to experience belonging when our parents were so addicted, unconscious, and wounded that they could not, in the midst of their own unhappiness, find a place for us in their lives. They, too, must have experienced great pain and disappointment, living their lives without the playful, loving company of their own children.

Thus, while we may have been promised a rightful place of belonging, it was not always easy to know where that place was. We learned to guess, tried to figure that place out, tried to earn it somehow. But we never really felt we had captured our niche, and it felt as though we could be exiled at any moment. So we learned to grab whatever position was offered, thankful for being allowed to stay somewhere, anywhere. This is how we defined belonging: the temporary postponement of certain exile.

Some tried to earn their place by being the clown, or the savior, or the invisible one in the family, and they carried these strategies into their adult lives. Alex, a salesman, learned to transform himself—complete with accent, posture, and manner of speech—into whomever he was talking to. Then everyone seemed to like him, and he felt he belonged with them. Sheila studied long and hard to be an actress because only a theater filled with applause could convince her that she was truly loved.

Claudia told me that as a child she convinced herself she was adopted; as far as she was concerned she did not really belong with these people who were raising her. Every morning she would gaze out her parents' front window, looking out onto the street "to pick out a nicer family. Each day I'd pick out a new one." She would spend the rest of the day pretending she belonged with her new family. "I was dying to be kidnapped," she said.

We have cluttered our lives with these strategies for belonging, trying through some combination of performance and cleverness to make ourselves look attractive and valuable so that those who really belong will let us stay around. But trying to earn our belonging by pleasing others is like shoveling mercury with a pitchfork. As hard as we try, sooner or later it all slips away, leaving us feeling homeless and bereft of a place we can call our own.

Sharecropping

The promise of a place of belonging is difficult to resist, no matter what the price. Often we will do almost anything in exchange for a place to belong. *But finding a place where they let us stay is not the same as belonging.*

The terrible conditions of sharecroppers in the nineteenth century demonstrated how fear could induce people to make painful bargains just for a place to stay. Sharecroppers were poor, often black, and worked land belonging to another in return for a small portion of whatever harvest they could produce. Nothing belonged to them, and anything kept from the owner had to be kept in secret. They had few rights, and the owner had unlimited access to the home and possessions of the sharecropper. Sharecroppers were granted a place of belonging absolutely conditional on their accommodation of the demands of the landowner.

Nate Shaw, a black sharecropper working the land of a white owner in 1907, spoke of the sharecropper's contract:

> Now it's right for me to pay for usin' what's yours—your land, stock, plow tools, fertilize. But how much should I pay? The answer ought to be closely seeked. How much is a man due to pay out? Half his crop? A third part of his crop? And how much is he due to keep for hisself? You got a right to your part—rent; and I got a right to mine. But who's the man ought to decide how much? The one that owns the property or the one that works it?

In this short paragraph Nate Shaw clearly describes a fearful bargain in which he is allowed to stay only if he remains a caretaker of someone else's belongings. He has no home, no sanctuary, no rightful place of his own. This is the sharecropper's contract. And, like the sharecropper, many children raised in family pain feel they have no place of their own. They, too, feel in their heart that they owe someone else for their right to belong, a right that may be taken from them at any time and in any place. If they don't keep everyone happy, they may be kicked off the planet. Like the sharecropper, they live in fear that they will never be allowed to belong anywhere.

The Hiding Place

In the troubled family, this kind of conditional belonging required hard work to stay in a place that brought very little harvest. Consequently, some of us sought other ways to survive. If we could not please our parents enough to earn a safe place, then we would take what seemed to be the only other choice: self-imposed exile. With a good hiding place, we could simply disappear in secret, avoiding the problem of belonging altogether.

Some of us hid out in our rooms, others in books; some hid out in the woods, or in the attic; some created a world with their pets; still others retreated into the television. Most of us found a secret place where we felt less likely to get hurt, where only we and no one else belonged. Brad told me that every night, after a few drinks, his parents would start to fight. And so this little boy, beginning at about five years old, would sneak out of the house, climb into the family car, and sit there waiting for them to stop fighting and go to bed. Even in winter, this was his place of refuge.

Maria drew a picture of her most familiar childhood memory. It was a drawing of a little girl sitting all alone on the front steps of a house, the door closed behind her. There she sat, her head in her hands. She explained that her parents were fighting inside the house, and she was waiting for it to be over. Sometimes she waited for them to stop beating her brother. Sometimes she just waited.

When we are hiding out, waiting sometimes takes the place of belonging: waiting to be discovered, waiting to be asked in, waiting for it to be safe. Waiting and hiding are strategies of powerlessness where our belonging depends on not being found, depends on the fighting to stop, depends on when this terrible night will end.

Some children chose to hide out deep in their own bodies. They were physically present and accounted for, but they withdrew so far inside that it seemed there was nobody home. Children who were painfully abused cultivated an ability to pretend to be paying attention even when deep inside they were far, far away.

Elizabeth

A few years ago, when Elizabeth came to see me, she sat down and said, "I don't even want to be here." When Elizabeth used the word *here,* she wasn't speaking of my office; she was speaking of the company of the human race. She did not belong to it, she insisted, nor did she wish to. She could not justify the need to belong to a species that was so hurtful and dangerous.

In some ways I could agree with her argument. I had always found the world to be painfully in need of healing, and had worked for years in my own small ways trying to help people and institutions to treat one another more compassionately. But the problem for Elizabeth was not the level of danger or safety that existed in the world. Her problem was that she had long ago stopped feeling safe even in her own body.

Elizabeth had a strong meditation practice, and she was respected by many as a teacher, healer, and friend. But there was an ache, a deep pain in her heart that had been there forever. She wanted me, she said, "to help her get rid of it."

We both suspected something traumatic in her childhood, and we soon discovered repressed memories of sexual abuse by her alcoholic father when she was quite small. Unprotected by her mother—or by anybody else—Elizabeth had apparently decided early on that it was much too terrifying and dangerous to fully occupy her body. If this world was a place where three-year-old girls could be so painfully violated, she would rather not be here, thank you. She would rather not show up for her life.

Like so many victims of family violence, young Elizabeth had disappeared. The terror of her childhood taught her to hide out, to refuse the invitation to belong in such a world. "I remember not wanting to accept my incarnation into this body. I prayed that I could go back, to start over, back before this violation. I felt so broken," she said.

Elizabeth and I worked long and hard, and we uncovered much pain. During one tearful session she found herself screaming, "Get off of me! I will not have you on me!" as she struggled with the images of her father's incest. Elizabeth was very brave and quite strong. Together, we patiently and gently worked the soil of her heart's memory, feeling the terror, the rage, and the fears about being here and about ever again being a target for that kind of violence.

As we touched the core of her pain, Elizabeth, like all children of abuse, had a decision to make. She could learn to be more comfortable hiding out—which was certainly a merciful and justifiable choice—or she could decide to belong in her own body, to bravely claim her inheritance as a child of creation, and take her place on the earth. Elizabeth and I deliberated at great length on the danger she felt when she was present in her body. We worked together on strategies she might use to feel safe. We used meditations that allowed her to experience different ways of being present, exploring the physical sensations of fear and safety that arose with each new level of being fully alive. Slowly she began to feel slightly more at home with herself. Still, it was a long time before Elizabeth could imagine that taking her place in the world could ever be preferable to escaping from it altogether.

Years later, after we finished our work together, Elizabeth was diagnosed with breast cancer. This was a particularly difficult cancer, and she struggled for a long time with the toxic effects of radiation and chemotherapy. I went to visit her in the hospital, and asked her how she felt about her body now that she was in such pain.

"I feel like I am finally here. Not only that, I *want* to be here," she told me. "It seems strange, especially now that I have this cancer—but I am glad to be here, glad to be alive and in this body. I think that finally accepting my place here will be the thing that helps me heal." Elizabeth closed her eyes, and we were both silent for several moments. Then, with a quiet strength in her voice, she said, "I feel safer now. Learning to accept my life gives me a kind of sanctuary. I have a place for my spirit, even in this body."

How should we feel about belonging? If we either must work hard to be allowed to stay—or simply hide out and disappear—then we rarely feel we can belong anywhere in peace and safety. These kinds of choices justifiably produce a great deal of ambivalence about whether we want to belong at all. Some who come to see me are so tired of trying to belong somewhere that they are on the verge of leaving the whole thing behind and finding a cabin in the woods to hide out for the rest of their lives. Others have playfully suggested that the only place for them must be in a convent or a monastery, a temple or ashram where they wouldn't have to talk or interact with anyone in the world, some isolated place where they could belong in safety.

When we feel ambivalent about belonging, we are probably feeling trapped by the expectation that we must earn our place in a world where it feels as if there is no room for us. Healing this ambivalence can happen in several ways. First, we can *accept* our ambivalence about belonging and bless our reluctance to open ourselves to the pain of exile and rejection. That we are afraid is understandable; we were hurt, and hurt deeply. By forcing ourselves to belong where we are not yet comfortable, we are ignoring our pain. For the moment, we might allow the ambivalence to stay. There is no rush, no place to go.

The second step, however, is one that asks us to see our belonging in a larger perspective. For this we must reenvision our sense of belonging, reimagine our lineage: No longer simply as children in exile in a painful family, we now begin to share our belonging with all creation as children of the human family. This step is awkward at first, and requires practice, but it is a step that allows us to discover a much deeper, richer place of belonging. Without denying the real pain of our particular childhood, we slowly begin to imagine that we can claim our rightful kinship within the human family.

The Larger Family

If we slowly pan back the camera to get a broader view of our lives, we see that our childhood family is not the only stage on which the struggle for belonging is fought. Our legacy is not only about Mom and Dad and how they treated us and how we felt about them. Belonging is about the place we claim among our larger human family, with whom we share our common inheritance.

As we look, we see that the fabric of our history as a species is woven with conflicts between people seeking a rightful place. Whether it was Hebrews who struggled with Egyptians, Greeks with Romans, native Americans with Spanish conquistadors, sharecroppers with landowners, blacks with Afrikaaners, Hindus with Muslims, Jews with Nazis, women with men, rich with poor, or children with parents, we have been terribly clumsy in allocating a rightful place to all the children of creation. All of us need a place of safety; we all seek refuge. Our hearts all ache for home.

Even the story of Christmas, one of Christianity's most familiar tales, tells the story of a child who was denied a place to be born:

> And Joseph also went up from Galilee, to be enrolled with Mary, his betrothed, who was with child. And while they were there, the time came for her to be delivered.
>
> And she gave birth to her first-born son and wrapped him in swaddling cloths, and laid him in a manger, because there was no place for them in the inn.

The world made no room, and so the infant Jesus was born a refugee in a food trough for farm animals, homeless among his own people. Later in his life, Jesus would speak about the kind of belonging the world provided for him: "Birds of the air have nests, and foxes have holes," he said, but he was given "no place to lay his head."

Safety and belonging are not freely granted by the world. Millions of homeless people in our cities testify to the enduring truth of Jesus' pronouncement. Hundreds of thousands of refugees in Africa, Latin America, and the Middle East reveal our inability—or perhaps our unwillingness—to provide a homeland for all our children.

Any child in pain claims kinship with all others who live in exile from true belonging. We share a powerful communion with all who suffer and ache for love. Can't we see that this is our family and we are not alone? Simply by being born, we inherit a rightful place in the human family. Accepting this family as our own, and claiming our place in it, is a critical step in our healing. For those of us who have felt emotional exile and isolation in our childhood family this kinship is difficult to feel, hard to imagine. But it lies at the heart of our journey.

The Larger Work, the Deeper Promise

When we doubt our own belonging, we grow desperate, and we learn to grab almost anything—a job, a sexual partner, a lifestyle—and make that our place of belonging. In our desperation we lose both our serenity and our sensitivity to the needs of others. If I need your company to feel that I belong, then I am more concerned with how I impress you than I am with your particular needs and desires. You become merely a vehicle for my belonging, an agent for my comfort, no longer a child of God with your own hopes and dreams. As I approach you, it is not you that I touch, it is my own desperation.

Yet no other human being can provide that belonging for us. They are not in charge of granting us a place here, our place is already given. Our challenge, our work, is to honor our place in this moment, to breathe deeply in the unconditional gift of home.

The search for a home is an ancient spiritual metaphor. In the Hebrew story of the Exodus, the Hebrews, enslaved and abused in Egypt, groaned under their bondage. In the midst of this suffering, God said to Moses, "I have seen the affliction of my people. I know their sufferings, and I have come down to bring them up out of that land to a good and broad land, a land of milk and honey." The promised land of belonging was given to the Hebrews unconditionally. No matter how unfaithful or sacrilegious they proved to be along the way, no matter how much they complained about the difficulty of the journey, the gift of belonging was never taken away. They were not given the land as a reward for their performance; they were given the land because they required a home. Because you are the children of the earth, said their God, you may live upon the earth with my blessing.

Jelaluddin Rumi, the thirteenth-century Sufi poet, speaks beautifully of the unconditional nature of the gift of belonging:

Come, come wherever you are,
Wanderer, worshipper, lover of leaving;
Come, ours is not a caravan of despair.
Though you've broken your vow a thousand times,
Come, come again.

The invitation to belong is made again and again, but we must be able to hear the promise and accept the gift. The Hebrews, in order to find their place of belonging, first had to leave their home of fear and servitude in Egypt. It requires great courage to leave behind our fears and habits, our familiar strategies, and our great performances designed to impress others.

It is hard to believe we have been unconditionally granted a real place, a place where we truly belong, and it requires no small courage to feel we are worthy of such a gift.

Of course, the journey to our new home need not always lead to a separate country or place. Sometimes it leads us to a still, small voice within our souls, a place of belonging as sure and quiet as our very breath. The Hebrews used the same word, *ruach,* for breath and for spirit. When there is a place for breath in our body, there is a place of belonging for our spirit.

We may begin to feel our belonging in the breath—here we may take sanctuary, here we begin to feel our place in creation. Taking refuge in each breath of our life, in each beat of our heart, we find a quiet place of belonging. This refuge, this sanctuary, is neither given nor taken away by the chaotic demands of an unpredictable world. This place belongs to us, and we to it. It is where we make our home.

Belonging begins in that deep, quiet place where our spirit lives within us. "Take sanctuary in me," says the voice of God. Do not depend on circumstances to create or sustain your place of belonging, but rather make your home in the unchanging breath of the spirit that lives within. Claim your home, claim your belonging with each breath. You have been promised a place where every breath you take will be shared by all creation. The kingdom of God is within you.

The spiritual teachings of all the saints remind us to seek refuge in a place that cannot be easily shaken. In Buddhism, students of meditation begin their practice with a vow to "take refuge in the Buddha." To take refuge in the Buddha is to take refuge in the qualities of love and compassion, wisdom, and fearlessness that the Buddha embodies. Here we make our home in the seed of enlightenment that is within ourselves.

Students, then, take refuge in the *dharma* (the teaching) and the *sangha* (the community). Thus, at the onset of meditation we take our place of belonging in the heart of the Buddha, his teachings, and the community with whom we sit. Together, we belong in this moment, in this breath. We are home.

Whether we take refuge in the Buddha, make our home in Jesus, or find sanctuary in our own breath, we are gently inviting an awareness of belonging in our hearts. It may be just an instant, between the inhale and exhale, a place of grace, or a merciful moment when we rest in simply being. Here there is nothing to figure out, nothing to work for, nothing to earn. Here, we may rest.

Kabir, the fifteenth-century Indian poet, urges us to seek God within ourselves:

Are you looking for me? I am in the next seat.
　　My shoulder is against yours.
You will not find me in stupas, not in Indian shrine
　　rooms, nor in synagogues, nor in cathedrals:
Not in masses, nor kirtans, not in legs winding
　　around your own neck, nor in eating nothing but
　　vegetables.
When you really look for me, you will see me
　　instantly—
You will find me in the tiniest house of time.

Kabir says: Student, tell me, what is God?
He is the breath inside the breath.

EXERCISE
Watching Our Experience of Belonging

As you move through your day, be mindful of how you feel about where you are, who you are with, and what you are doing. A dozen times a day, stop yourself for just a moment, and quietly become aware of your breath. What does it feel like? Allowing it to be as it is, note if it feels quick, slow, deep, or labored.

As you watch your breath, silently ask yourself these questions: Do I belong here? Do I feel like I belong in this place, with these people, in this moment? Do I even want to belong here?

Notice the quality of belonging (or nonbelonging) you feel in these moments. Sometimes you will feel you belong wherever you are. Other times you may feel uneasy, uncomfortable, or isolated. Notice which people or situations seem to invite a sense of belonging. Notice where you feel afraid, or want to leave, or hide. Allow either feeling to be true, allow it to simply teach you about yourself, without judging how you are "supposed" to feel.

Sometimes you may feel uncertain, thinking, "I don't know if I want to belong here or not." Let that ambivalence be as it is. Notice what it feels like to be unsure of where you belong. Allow the ambivalence to percolate within you, allow it to be your meditation for that moment.

Let this simply be an experiment, an interesting exercise that shows you how you feel about belonging. Do not push yourself to belong. Be aware of the fear, the uncertainty, or the caution, honoring each feeling as it arises.

Allow your awareness to be gentle and compassionate, acknowledging yourself and your feelings of exile or belonging simply as they are.

With this exercise, we are not pushing ourselves to belong anywhere. We are simply watching our experience. Let that be enough for now.

Meditation
FINDING OUR BELONGING IN THE BREATH

Begin by going to the place of refuge you have made for yourself. In front of your table, find a comfortable sitting position on the floor, a pillow, or a chair. Try to arrange your back, neck, and head in a relatively straight line. Let your hands rest easily in your lap or loosely at your side. Arrange yourself so that you can sit comfortably in this position for fifteen minutes.

Close your eyes. Begin by gently focusing your awareness on the breath. The point is not to think about your breathing but to experience the physical sensation of the air as it enters and leaves your body. There is nothing to do, no place to go. Simply become aware of the sensations of the breath.

Feel the path of the breath as it moves through your nostrils, throat, chest, and belly. Experience the natural tides of the breath as it comes and goes. Without trying to control or change it, just allow it to be as it is. Let the breath breathe itself, without comment. If it is slow, let it be slow. If it is shallow, let it be shallow. If it is quick or deep, simply let it be. The point is not to change the breath but to become more fully aware of its texture, temperature, shape, and color—all of the qualities of each breath as it moves in and out.

Let your awareness inspect each sensation as it accompanies the breath. Notice the space between the inhale and the exhale, observing the intention to inhale again; moment by moment become more aware of the quality of each breath.

Find a place in your abdomen, just below your rib cage, that rises and falls as you breathe. Bring your awareness to this point. Every time the abdomen rises, silently think "rising"; every time it falls, note "falling." Rising . . . falling . . . rising . . . falling. If thoughts arise, gently let them go, returning your attention to the breath. Let all other thoughts drift by, gently keeping your attention focused on the breath as it rises and falls. Don't lose heart. At first the mind will wander frequently. Each time it does, simply note that it has wandered, and then return to the breath. Bodily sensations or discomforts may also distract your attention. Just as you did with your thoughts, gently shift your concentration back to the rising, falling, rising, and falling of the abdomen with each breath.

As you become intimately familiar with the sensation of your breath in your body, allow yourself to begin to feel a sense of belonging within the breath. As you feel the sensation of breathing, the air in the nostrils, the rush in the lungs, and the rise and fall of the abdomen, you may begin to feel that your breath belongs in your body, that there is a natural place for your breath. Feel the shape of that place, be aware of where your breath makes its home in you. On the exhale, feel the relaxation that follows the breath throughout the body.

Imagine making your home in the breath. Be aware of the sense of belonging in that place where the breath resides in your abdomen. Feel that space in your body open and receive the breath as it makes its home in you. After a while you may, on the exhale, silently allow the word home to accompany your breath. Notice when you feel a sense of home; note how the sense of belonging arises and falls away.

The breath is an anchor amid the tides of endlessly changing circumstances and emotions. Your breath is your constant companion, something that will be with you for every moment that you live. When you make your home in the breath, you take refuge in the eternal spirit that lives within you. No one can take this place of belonging from you. It is yours. This is home. This is where you live.

You may find that if you practice this meditation every day, even for only fifteen minutes, you will gradually feel more comfortable, familiar, and secure in experiencing your home in the breath. Here you may always find refuge, taking your place in your sanctuary of deep, inner belonging. You are home.

CHAPTER FOUR

Scarcity and Abundance

Once during a retreat, Marty began to feel very sad. Growing up with a father who was loud and domineering, Marty had developed a habitual reluctance to express his feelings. Yet his wife had recently left him, and at that moment Marty was beginning to feel the sadness of missing her. I went over and placed my hand on Marty's chest and asked him to breathe slowly into his heart. He began to cry. I asked him to give voice to the feelings there. As the tears came, he said, "It feels like there's never going to be enough for me." When he spoke those words, it seemed he was telling me the truest thing he could say about his life. I asked him to repeat those words a few times. With each repetition, he opened more and more, touching that painful sadness, feeling the desperate grief of a child who never had the love he needed.

Raised in fearful desperation, we are convinced that sufficient love and care lie forever beyond the boundaries of our life story. A deep sense of scarcity infected our hearts; just as we learned to fear that there would be no place of belonging for us, so did we also learn to fear there would never be enough loving care. Regardless of how loving or generous our parents intended to be, it sometimes may have felt to us as if there were never enough to go around—not enough care, not enough attention, not enough touching, safety, playfulness, or love. We came to believe that even care was in short supply. It was something used sparingly, not to be wasted, nothing we could count on.

As children, we first learned about scarcity and abundance in the marketplace of family affection. Raised with the belief that there would never be enough for us, we calibrated our dreams according to what we assumed

50

we would never have. We simply stopped asking for love, care, and affection. There was just too little available for us.

Here we have a pivotal dilemma as children: If there is not enough care to go around, then we must choose—who gets to be cared for, you or me? If there is so little love, who gets to have it? In a family where care is rationed like water in a lifeboat, who drinks first from the cup? And who decides?

When love is scarce, it feels impossible for everyone in the family to be cared for. If I take it myself, I will feel mean and selfish, hurting everyone else. On the other hand, if I give the love to you, I may not feel cared for. Thus we give birth to the scarcity contract: I will care for you if you promise to care for me. We pass a thimbleful of care back and forth forever, never being filled, rarely feeling loved.

When we grow up feeling that love is swiftly depleted, any caring relationship inevitably requires us to choose—which of us will be cared for? We have no sense that there is enough for everyone, no memory or experience that teaches us there is enough to fill the hearts of all who ask, enough to fill us up to spilling over. Care is never something shared—there is not enough for that. Love is either given or taken. And we all keep score.

Our fearful sense of scarcity sometimes drives us to latch onto anyone or anything that comes our way, just so we will have something in our lives. Barbara, raised in an alcoholic family, stayed with her husband for ten years, and even though she was miserable in her marriage, she was convinced she would never find anything better. "I just want too much," she would tell me. "I can settle for this, I know I can." For her, happiness was a dream, and she felt unworthy of wanting more than she had. "To want more than this is just stupid," she told me.

Our feelings of scarcity become so chronic and habitual that they influence the way we approach major decisions in our lives. Confronted with important choices, we fear the wrong turn will bring disaster, cutting us off even further from any possibility of care and abundance. Every new choice invites the possibility of getting even less than we have now, so we must be very careful to make the right decision. But if we begin to let go of fear, we come to see that regardless of which path we choose, either one may lead us to care, to abundance, to God. The spirit of love and creation is not so scarce that we will be forever lost if we make the wrong choice. Whatever we choose, wherever we go, there will be some doorway, some opportunity, some person or situation that may bring us what we need.

What Is Enough?

Jesus spoke often of abundance:

> Ask, and it will be given to you; seek, and you will find; knock, and it will be opened to you. For everyone who asks receives, and whoever seeks finds, and to whomever knocks it will be opened. Who among you, if your child asks for bread, will give them a stone? Or if they ask for a fish, will give them a serpent?
>
> If you then . . . know how to give good gifts to your children, how much more will God give good things to those who ask?

Parents know how to give the gifts of bread and fish to their children when they are hungry. But there are times when a child needs more than bread or fish; when the child aches for love, or kindness, or safety—things difficult to name, impossible to ask for. What of the deep yearnings of the tender heart for those things that never came, things our parents could never provide? Where do we knock, how do we seek what we were never given? And what can we ask for without feeling selfish?

When we are convinced how little is available for us, we feel confused about how much is enough. How much can we ask for, what can we hope for? When we resign ourselves to a life where love and joy will never come in abundance, we reduce the depth and breadth of what is possible for us, making our lives small and sparse. "Ask and you shall receive" rings hollow in the heart that has grown to expect less and less. There will never be enough for us; why bother asking at all?

As we reduce the perimeter of our dreams, we become less able to name what we truly need. Are we truly able to ask for what we really want, or can we ask only for what we can expect to receive? Our requests are tempered by our belief in scarcity: Since there is so little to go around, we learn to do without. But this is not a serene acceptance of whatever we are given. Underneath it all we are angry and hurt, we feel cheated and deprived.

Some of us try to rectify this feeling of scarcity by becoming more aggressive in asking for what we want, trying to create abundance by demanding that we get what we deserve. When we were small, there was not enough to go around, so we gave our part away: Now that we are getting stronger, we want our part back. But this strategy, while moderately effective, can still have an edge of desperation behind our request that reveals a lingering conviction that there is still not enough to go around. We have not come to believe in abundance, we have simply changed our response to scarcity: Instead of giving what little there is to you, I am going to keep it for myself.

This is not an act of abundance, it is still an act of fear. Learning to ask for what we want—while giving us a sense of power in our lives—can subtly mask the fact that we have yet to believe that there really is enough for us. Rooted in a theology of scarcity, we still have not touched that place where we truly believe there is enough care, nurture, and love for everyone.

Many healing therapies understandably begin by helping us to practice listening to the quiet needs within us, needs that have remained unnamed and unspoken. Then we learn to speak those needs and desires in the company of others, asking for what we need and want. As we name those inner needs, advocating the desires of our heart, we begin to heal ourselves, correcting the old injustices and negotiating for what we never received.

But getting everything we want is not the culmination of our healing, nor does it necessarily spring from a sense of abundance. The mind, given free reign, will perpetually generate a lifetime of wants and desires, always wanting more and more, and is never fully satisfied. An experience of abundance is not dependent upon the number of things we can accumulate. It does not matter how many jobs, lovers, compliments, dollars, or houses we manage to acquire to prove to ourselves there is finally enough for us. The practice of abundance is not about how much we can get; the experience of abundance arises when we feel that whatever we have is enough.

Brother David Steindl-Rast, a Benedictine monk who has studied Oriental and Western spirituality, says that abundance "is not measured by what flows in, but by what flows over. The smaller we make the vessel of our need . . . the sooner we get the overflow we need for delight." Many of us shape the "vessel of our need" out of fear and habit. We rarely examine with mindfulness and care what we truly need to be happy and serene. When we are raised in scarcity, our impulse is to heal ourselves by wanting and getting more and more. If we can have now what we couldn't have then, perhaps we will be fulfilled.

However, when we begin to examine the nature of our wants and needs, we find we may increase the possibility of feeling abundant by actually allowing some of our desires to fall away. The Buddha said that our endlessly multiplying desires are the source of all human suffering: The more we want, the more we experience suffering when it does not happen. We all have wants and needs; but if we expect those wants to be always satisfied, we will inevitably be disappointed. As we carefully check the proliferation of our desires, inviting the "vessel of our needs" to gently become smaller, we open ourselves to abundance. G. K. Chesterton said:

"There are two ways to get enough. One is to continue to accumulate more and more. The other is to desire less." Henry David Thoreau put it another way: "I make myself rich by making my wants few."

When Jesus said "I have come that you might have life, and have it abundantly," he was not promising his followers that they would always get everything they wanted. He was speaking of the abundance that comes when we can recognize what is available to us with different eyes, with an open mind and heart. If we hold onto the frustrated wants of childhood, still aching for the love that mother or father or family never gave us, then we endlessly postpone our capacity to be filled in this moment.

Many of us still wait at the doorstep of childhood for the understanding, acceptance, love, and approval that never came. Whatever we were given was not enough, not what we needed, not what we hoped for. Yet as we endlessly wait for our childhood wants to be fulfilled, we miss the abundance of this breath, this living instant. What of the care the earth has for us now, the beauty available in the light of morning, in the sunset, in the color of the sky? There is great care available in the feel of grass beneath our feet, deep nurture in the water that cools our lips, tremendous nourishment in the air that fills our lungs. As we sit with the habitual yearnings of an unfulfilled childhood, waiting for Mom and Dad to finally care for us in the way we dreamed they would, we can feel only the scarcity of what we have lost forever. But if we can begin to let go of the disappointments of childhood, we are free to wade into an ocean of care, nurture, and love that may be available to saturate every moment of our life.

Abundance can blossom as we shift our perception. "If your eye is full of light, your whole body will be full of light," said Jesus. Love and abundance arise when we pay attention to what we have already been given with freshness and curiosity. When we are always looking at the places where love never came, we tend to feel an overwhelming scarcity. But when we open our eyes to the fertile garden of the present moment, we may feel the earth itself hold us in her love, as in this poem by Wendell Berry:

> Like a tide it comes in,
> Wave after wave of foliage and fruit,
> The nurtured and the wild,
> Out of the light to this shore.
> In its extravagance we shape
> The strenuous outline of enough.

Sometimes when we sit down to eat a rich meal, nothing tastes quite the way we like it, and we feel dissatisfied. Other times, at the end of a fast or a long meditation, a small piece of bread and a sip of cool water can taste like a feast. Which is abundance, the grand meal or the bread and water? Or is it the mindfulness we bring to what we are given that helps determine our wealth?

Thich Nhat Hanh, a loving Vietnamese Buddhist master, suggests we can use our shifting perceptions to shape our experience of wealth and poverty:

> A human being is like a television set with millions of channels. If we turn the Buddha on, we are the Buddha. If we turn sorrow on, we are sorrow. If we turn a smile on, we really are the smile. We cannot let just one channel dominate us. We have the seed of everything in us, and we have to seize the situation in our hand, to recover our own sovereignty.

What Belongs to Us?

Our feelings of scarcity and abundance are complicated by the concept of ownership. We are taught to believe that certain things belong to us and other things do not. This piece of land, this spouse, this child, and this food belong to me. Those other things belong to you. What belongs to me I call "mine"; what belongs to you, I call "yours."

But what if nothing really belongs to any of us? Mahatma Gandhi said that when we buy and sell anything, we are simply contributing to the illusion of ownership. In the Old Testament, God instructed the Hebrews to observe a Sabbath day of rest and contemplation, a day to think about the multitude of gifts and blessings they had received from God. The Hebrews were also required to take a Sabbath *year*—a year when no one could plant, sow seed, or harvest crops. During this year, everyone had to rely on whatever food grew in the fields on its own. This was to remind the Hebrews that it was not their work alone but God and the earth that fed them.

Further, every seventh Sabbath year—every forty-ninth year, the Year of Jubilee—all lands that had been sold or confiscated were returned to their original owners, and all debts were canceled. It was just like the end of a game of Monopoly, when everyone gave everything back and had to start over. This way, the Hebrews would be reminded that nothing really belonged to anyone. It was all on loan from God.

Many spiritual traditions recommend owning as little as possible. After the death of the Buddha, it was decided that monks would be prohibited from keeping food overnight. Each day they had to beg for that day's food, reminding them to be dependent on whatever came from God. Similarly, when the Hebrews were in the desert on the way to the promised land, God fed them with food from heaven called *manna*. It was forbidden to keep *manna* overnight, inviting them to trust that God would feed them anew each day. One day's food was all that was needed; to demand more was to mistrust God's care.

Many years ago an American tourist paid a visit to a renowned Polish rabbi, Hofetz Chaim. He was amazed to see that the rabbi's home was completely empty, a simple dwelling furnished only with a few books, a single table, and a bench.

"Rabbi," asked the tourist, "where is your furniture?"

"Where is yours?" the rabbi responded.

"Mine?" asked the puzzled American. "But I'm only passing through." The rabbi smiled.

"So am I," he said.

We cannot measure abundance by what we accumulate. Abundance is an experience of the heart, a wind that blows through us like a flute. There is nothing to hold onto—who can hold onto music? It floats in the air. Our treasures are in the eye, the ear, in the heart that feels the wonder of things. "Where your treasure is," said Jesus, "there will your heart be also."

A few years ago I was visiting with Padre Pedro Ruggiere, a Maryknoll priest working with the poor in Pamplona Alta, a barrio on the outskirts of Lima, Peru. He was showing me around the village, and all the children ran to greet us and grab our hands as we walked, shouting, "Hola, Padre" and laughing with delight. Everyone loved this priest who had lived and worked beside them through illnesses and childbirths, poverty and oppression.

Padre Pedro and I walked to Mass one Sunday morning, through the dusty streets, past the open sewage and refuse that filled the byways of the barrio. The church was a half-demolished concrete shack with broken glass on the floor and a single table in front for the altar, and no other furniture. People from the village crowded in, singing and playing Peruvian pipes and drums. When everyone was settled, Padre Pedro shared the parable of the mustard seed.

"The kingdom of God is like a grain of mustard seed," he began, "which, when sown upon the ground, is the smallest of all the seeds on the earth; yet when it is sown it grows up and becomes the greatest of all trees, and puts forth large branches, so that the birds of the air can make nests in its shade." Pedro continued, "A mustard seed is so small that if you are not careful, you may drop it, even lose it. We must take care of the small things, for they may grow to be the most wonderful."

Pedro had lived with these people for a long time, and he knew their poverty and their despair. But he also knew about their courage and their joy, and he knew that the well of spirit from which they drank was deep and rich. He also knew that in spite of terrible poverty, injustice, and want, there lived in that community, in that makeshift church, a tremendous sense of abundance.

As I was leaving to come back to the United States, a young boy presented me with the cross from around his neck. He said I should have it, because I had come from such a long way to be with them. I wept as I thanked him, feeling unworthy of the gift, humbled by the generosity of one who had so little.

What is enough for us? How will we know we are cared for, what do we seek as a sign? Many of us feel that since we were not given enough as children, it is up to our parents to somehow tip the scales by giving us more love, or a full apology, or some reparation for what we never received. But there is love available for us here and now, in the smallest of things, if we would only look. If we hold our parents hostage, refusing to feel loved until it comes directly from them, we may miss the gifts that are possible in our lives in this very instant.

Thus, we begin to cultivate a practice of abundance as we empty ourselves of the unfulfilled wants of childhood. There are other seeds, other places where we may seek love, grace, and sustenance. Our parents were never meant to be the only source of our care and abundance. There is a passage in Ecclesiastes that says, "Keep sowing your seed morning and night, for you never know which will grow—perhaps it all will."

The Larger Family

While abundance is not necessarily measured by what we possess, still, millions of children and families experience a very real scarcity of basic human needs. Forty thousand children, the equivalent of a midsize city, die of hunger and hunger-related illness every single day. Many die for lack of ridiculously inexpensive vaccines. For these children, scarcity is a genuine, tangible source of suffering.

When those of us who live more comfortably are plagued with feelings of scarcity, we are tempted to take more than we need, to hoard more than we can use, and spend billions to protect ourselves from loss. For example, what we in the United States spend on weapons in one day would support all the United Nations hunger programs for a year. If we can begin to heal our own fears about scarcity and abundance, we may be free to more fully attend to the needs of all people in need.

Gandhi said that God inevitably comes to the hungry in the form of food:

It is good enough to talk about God whilst we are sitting here after a nice breakfast and looking forward to a nicer luncheon, but how am I to talk of God to the millions who have to go without two meals a day? To them God can only appear as bread and butter . . .

We are not always aware of our real needs, and most of us improperly multiply our wants, and thus unconsciously make thieves of ourselves. If we devote some thought to the subject, we shall find that we can get rid of quite a number of our wants.

By simplifying our needs, we may become more conscious of the needs of those around us. If we feel a desperate scarcity in our lives, then everyone else is a competitor, an opponent on the battleground of survival. But if I am filled by whatever I have received, everyone else is my sister or brother. There is enough for everyone, and my practice is to help them be fed.

We truly need little to feel abundant. When we are paying attention, a single breath can fill us to overflowing. The touch of a loved one or a moment of sunlight can bring delight to our hearts. The simple gesture of someone's hand resting in our own, a single word of kindness, or a small gift of appreciation can be all we need to feel a tremendous sense of care and well-being. We need so little to feel loved; all we need to do is begin to notice the multitude of tiny gifts and small miracles that punctuate each day we are alive.

Many of the world's religions were born in the desert, a place with very little food or water. Yet generations of women and men have found that through spiritual practice and mindful attention to the exquisite gifts of the earth, even in the midst of the desert they may experience a rich spirit of abundance. As Isaiah sings, "The wilderness and the dry land shall be glad, the desert shall rejoice, and blossom as the rose. It shall blossom abundantly, and rejoice with joy and singing."

Brother David says, "Fullness flows into us in the measure we become empty." By opening our hands and allowing the fearful holding of childhood scarcity to fall away, we may learn to drink from a limitless reservoir of care—care we can feel and taste, care that fills and sustains us. The poet Kabir writes:

Thou hast made me endless
    such is thy pleasure
This frail vessel thou emptiest
    again and again, and fillest
    it ever with fresh life.
Ages pass and still thou pourest,
    and still there is room to fill.

Meditation
CULTIVATING A SENSE OF ABUNDANCE

The experience of scarcity and abundance is influenced by what we feel is "enough" in any given moment. When we become trapped in "wanting," we find ourselves propelled into fear and scarcity, and we desperately look for that person or thing that is going to make everything work for us. If only we had the right job, the right relationship, more money, more time, less pain in our body . . . then we would be okay.

The "wanting mind" brings us much suffering; it is a self-perpetuating habit that prevents us from experiencing the fullness of where we are and what we have in this moment, driving us to grab desperately for something else, something different. It teaches us that when we are here and now, we are somehow incomplete, and that what we already have could never be enough. We are cut off from the abundance of the moment.

In these meditations, as we mindfully investigate our wants and desires, the way we constitute what is "enough" begins to shift. When we observe the endless play of desires without identifying with them, we may begin to sense a whole new inner spirit of freedom, and the experience of abundance becomes more available to us.

Part One
Observing Our Desires

For approximately ten minutes, sit comfortably in your quiet place of refuge, arranging your body in a meditation posture. Begin once again by letting your awareness rest on the breath. Allow a few moments for your attention to become clear and focused. As your concentration settles on the sensation of the breath as it rises and falls in the abdomen, gently shift your attention to the arising of wants and desires in your mind. For these ten minutes, notice each want, each desire as it arises. They may appear as pictures, words, feelings, or sensations in your body.

Let your mind be blank like a clear sky, and wait carefully for each desire, like a cat waiting at a mouse hole. They may hide a bit when you are first watching, but they will come.

When a desire arises, make a silent mental note of it: "wanting, wanting." Turn all your attention to the investigation of that desire. Whether it is a desire for food, or to move your legs, or to finish some project, to go to sleep, or to be a better meditator, try to see the desire as clearly as you can. Notice what kinds of things you find yourself wanting. Are they material things, changes in your life, emotional states? Silently note each desire as it arises: "wanting to move," "wanting to eat," "wanting to go to the bathroom." How does it feel in your body? What does it feel like in the heart? Continue noting each "wanting, wanting" until it naturally recedes. Then gently return to the breath, until the next desire arises.

Pay meticulous attention as you await the next desire. Some wants come as soft whispers, others arrive with a loud and demanding voice. Note each one and observe its nature until it subsides and the sky is clear again. After ten minutes, relax and take a short break.

Part Two
Cultivating a Sense of "Enough"

Rearrange yourself in the meditation posture. Allow your mind to become quiet as you focus on your breathing.

For this period, visualize the breath flowing directly into the heart. As you inhale, fully experience the complete nurture and sustenance of the air as it flows into your body, precisely nourishing each and every cell. Feel it soften and open your chest cavity, allowing the muscle tissue to gently relax and open. As you exhale, feel the relaxation move through your body. As the breath-spirit flows out, softly note, "enough."

With the inhalation, experience the fullness and completeness of this moment. With the exhale, noting "enough, enough," allow yourself to sink ever more deeply into a sense of complete fulfillment. In this moment, in this breath, there is enough for you. All that there is, all that you need, is here for you in this moment. Allow the fullness of the sense of "enough" to flood your heart and body. Gently soften, drinking from the care that is provided for you in this breath, in this moment.

Now and then, wants and desires may arise. As before, silently note, "wanting, wanting," and return to the breath. On the exhale, allow the word "enough" to flow out with the breath. What do you notice? What does it feel like to say "enough"? How long does it last? What takes its place when it goes? Take several moments to use the breath as a tool to explore what the sensation of "enough" might feel like in your body. Then you may gently open your eyes.

As we expand and deepen our ability to experience a sense of "enough," we may find a reservoir of nurture and peace open within us, bringing a sense of gentle abundance. In this one moment, in this single breath, there is enough for us. Nothing else is needed. All we need is here, now. Enough.

CHAPTER FIVE

Judgment and Mercy

"You are ugly. You are stupid. We are all ashamed of you. You never do anything right. You are dirty. You are nothing but trouble. Go away." In the middle of a circle sat Beverly, listening to the members of her therapy group call out malicious judgments about her. One by one they shouted hurtful things, condemning her talents, her intellect, and her appearance, criticizing everything about who she was. "You don't deserve to be here. You're a fake. You're not good enough." Beverly wept as she took it all in.

In this exercise, members of the group were repeating what Beverly had told them to say. They were merely speaking aloud the chorus of voices that inhabited Beverly's mind. "I hear them all the time," she told the group. "They tell me I am ugly, stupid, no good—it just goes on and on. The way you all sound right now, that's what my mind is like. It never seems to stop."

As a young girl raised in an abusive, chaotic family, Beverly had absorbed countless insults, criticisms, and judgments. These voices had found a home in her psyche, and for most of her life they had served as her intimate companions. As we sat parroting the judging voices of her mind over and over, we could hear how unforgiving and relentless they were. After a while, the repetitive intensity of the voices began to sound ridiculous and impossible to listen to. All of a sudden Beverly started to laugh; soon we, too, were all giggling as we felt the absurdity of it all. How could she take them seriously? Beverly was a good mother and a loving wife, an active member of the community, a talented artist, and generous with her friends and family. For an instant some of the persuasive authority of

61

Beverly's judging mind fell away and became a little less potent in the face of her playful, freeing laughter.

The greatest barrier to our own healing is not the pain, sorrow, or violence inflicted upon us as children. Our greatest hindrance is our ongoing capacity to judge, to criticize, and to bring tremendous harm to ourselves and others. If we can harden our heart against ourselves and meet our most tender feelings with anger and condemnation, we simultaneously armor our heart against the possibility of gentleness, love, and healing.

Unfortunately, children raised in pain learn to trust what is painful. In families where things were painful or unpleasant, people often spoke eloquently and often about exactly how unpleasant they were: Dad's job was not good, it made him miserable; Mom was dissatisfied with Dad; the children were not bright enough, did not work hard enough, and were not respectful enough. The family was not happy because there was something wrong with somebody: If it were not for the children, Dad wouldn't drink; if it were not for Mom's moods, the family would have more fun; if it weren't for this or that problem, school grade, neighbor, or event, we would all be happy.

Our family catechism was clear: Suffering happens because things go wrong. So we learned to cultivate a judging mind, a mind that could dissect every moment and ferret out those things, people, or events that stole the family happiness. We felt if we could uncover and name everything that was wrong, imperfect, broken, or unsatisfactory in our lives, we could somehow make everything better. We even learned to feel relief when we uncovered some defect or malignancy in ourselves, for by discovering all that was wrong with us, by eradicating all our defects, perhaps we might eventually earn the right to be happy.

We judged ourselves in the hope that we would be more perfect and more acceptable to our parents, to God, and to ourselves. We learned to judge everything about ourselves—our pain, our joy, our abilities, our intellect, our appearance, our worthiness, our imperfections. We sought out everything that was human, fragile, or tender about us, and assaulted it with anger and impatience. If only we were better, less broken, more perfect, we might finally feel welcome, we might finally be loved. But, in a futile search for acceptance, the violence of our judging mind tore at our hearts and brought little happiness to anyone.

We also learned to judge ourselves as a tool for self-defense: If we could root out our defects before our parents discovered them, if we could rid ourselves of fault and error, perhaps they would be less angry and disappointed with us. We criticized ourselves with cleverness and enthusiasm in the hope that we could prevent others from judging us even more harshly.

Most children who grew up in family pain know this voice: "We are broken, we are not good enough, we are phony, we will never make it, we don't have what it takes to be successful, we don't even have what it takes to be fully human." After a while, the most painful judgments feel the most reliable, the most believable. We are quick to believe in what is broken or in need of repair, and much less likely to take seriously any strengths or gifts we may possess.

We relentlessly judge ourselves for who we *should* be, and rarely accept ourselves just as we are. Whatever we are feeling in this moment is judged against some mythical ideal of how we "should" be feeling, what we should be doing, and who we should be. If we feel hurt, we think we should have been healed by now; if we feel frightened, we think we should be stronger; if we feel sad, we think we should be happier. Every moment, every breath of our lives is subtly judged as unacceptable. Measured by the standards of who we should have been by now, we constantly fall short.

But what if the feelings that arise within us every day—even the sad, hurt, or uncomfortable sensations of our hearts and bodies—have their own value and carry something to teach us? If we are not "supposed to feel" sad, and we touch that sadness with anger or impatience, then we are unable to listen to what our sadness may be teaching us. Refusing to allow our sadness to be true, we see our sadness as a mistake, something broken, something to be gotten rid of. But what if the sadness is not evidence against us, not a condemnation of how slowly we are healing but simply a moment of sadness, an instant of sorrow that has arisen in our body? What if that sadness holds a seed of something forgotten, something wanting our attention? Who will listen? How can we allow ourselves to be human, to feel at times tender and broken, and not touch it with judgment and violence? Can we hold our pain and touch it instead with mercy and care?

The judging mind insists that we become other than who we are, and we fall victim to the violence of that requirement. If we are never who we are supposed to be, not feeling what we should, then we must always be doing something wrong. As a young boy, Tom was criticized frequently by his father. His father constantly told him he was wrong, never good enough, a continual disappointment. His father would yell at him for every little mistake, sometimes using a belt to punctuate his criticism. As a child, Tom could never get angry at his father for the way he was treated—that would only provoke another beating. So he learned instead to turn that violence against himself, constantly criticizing and verbally beating himself up. He had learned to treat himself the way his father treated him: judging himself and his feelings as defective and unacceptable.

When he first came to see me, Tom held a great deal of fear and anger in his body. "I always feel like I am screwing up," Tom told me. "At work, with my friends, even when I am by myself, I feel stupid, like I'm just not doing it right." He felt these judgments as a knot in his stomach and a tightening in his throat. When the judgments were in full force, he felt he could hardly breathe, choked by the incessant criticism and fear. "I'm so afraid I will never be good enough."

My Fault

In India, they say that when a pickpocket meets a saint, the pickpocket sees only the saint's pockets. Similarly, when we look at ourselves and the world through eyes of judgment, seeking only what is wrong or broken, we see only a small fraction of whatever is before us. When we are attuned to catch the sound of a particular frequency, we miss the symphony of who we are and who we have become. The judging mind is not interested in exploring the whole truth, nor is it designed to measure the richness of all we have been given. On the contrary, our judging eyes habitually mutilate those parts of ourselves that are tender, light, playful, and kind. We focus exclusively on those parts of ourselves that we dislike and often render the more gentle and loving contents of our hearts and spirits irrelevant.

Indeed, we may feel confused when we encounter people who offer us tenderness and love. When we hear someone speak with gentleness and mercy, when they approach us with an open heart, we feel suspicious and mistrustful. Perhaps they are after something, or maybe they are just in denial about their true feelings. In our past, words of care almost inevitably concealed some danger or criticism just below the surface. True affection was rare, and is still difficult to accept.

Raised in family pain, we find it hard to let go of our judging mind. When we want to find out what is most true, our first impulse is to look for what is bad or broken, what is dark and troublesome, what is defective. Letting go of the judging mind feels like letting go of knowing what could hurt us, surrendering our most potent weapon for survival. If we stop judging ourselves and everyone else so rigorously, how will we know what is true? How will we protect ourselves from harm?

When Sandra came to see me, she felt trapped in her marriage. She said she no longer loved her husband, but did not want to hurt him by leaving— and she especially did not want her three children to suffer. If she followed her own needs and desires, she would ruin everyone's life, and it would be all her fault because she was incapable of love.

We talked at length about her childhood, and spent a great deal of time exploring her relationship with her father. He had abused her sexually when she was quite small, and she felt that that, too, must have been her fault. She should have protected herself somehow, she should have been able to prevent it from happening. She was convinced she should have been able to stop him.

Sandra judged herself mercilessly for being abused. Whenever we spoke of it, she adamantly refused to consider the possibility that it might not have been her fault. "I know it doesn't make sense, but I know it was my fault. I feel like I've never done anything right. I should have been stronger as a little girl, I should have been able to make things turn out right. And now, because of how messed up I am, my whole family is going to be ruined."

Her mind had fixed itself upon her childhood abuse and used it as a judgment against her entire life. The more I tried to explain that a five-year-old girl was powerless over a thirty-year-old man, the more her judging mind tightened its grip on her spirit. Many sessions would end with her adamant as ever about where the blame for her suffering belonged; "Nothing you tell me will ever convince me that I did not do something wrong."

Then, toward the end of one session, I asked her about her children, a son and two daughters whom I knew she loved very much. Her daughters were three and seven years old. "What if your daughters came home one day and told you a big man had fondled them and then made them do things they didn't want to. Would you punish them, would you yell at them for letting it happen? Would you tell them it was their fault?" A look of horror crossed her face. "Of course not! How could . . . they are so young, just children, it could never be their fault. I would hold them and protect them and fight for them, of course it couldn't be their fault . . ." And Sandra, in that moment, feeling a rush of sadness and mercy fill her heart, began to cry for her children, for herself, and for all the violence and judgment she had carried so long.

Letting go of the judgments against herself, Sandra began to feel more deeply all the things that were true about her childhood. She was hurt badly, her father was violent, her mother did not protect her, she could not protect herself, and she carried great sadness that ached to be grieved. But she was also strong, insightful, and creative, and worthy of care, mercy, and love. And while her judging mind had condemned her inability to love, in fact she was quite capable of love, and it was her tremendous love for her children that enabled her to break free.

The Sin of the Self

Love is the ingredient that gives birth to mercy. Thomas Merton said that the heart of spiritual practice is "a search for truth which springs from love." To heal, we must first know where we are wounded, uncovering all the places inside us where we feel broken or incomplete. But rather than touch those places with violence and judgment, we may learn to meet ourselves with gentleness and love. As a child of God, as a member of the family of the earth, we stand in need of care, and are worthy of kindness and love. The poet Rainer Maria Rilke said that "what is going on in your innermost being is worthy of your whole love."

Unfortunately, when we feel broken or incomplete, these are the moments we feel most unworthy of love. We feel that our pain, confusion, or fear is clear evidence that we must be doing something terribly wrong, and we must frantically struggle to make ourselves acceptable before we may earn the right to be loved. But in fact we have got it backwards: It is precisely when we feel broken that we are in the most need of love.

Unfortunately, many of us learn to love ourselves slowly and reluctantly. Betty would spend the first half-hour of her visits with me apologizing for having come. "I know I probably shouldn't need to be here," she would say. "I can't believe I still feel so afraid. I must be really screwed up." This woman was terribly hurt as a child by parents who were emotionally disturbed. Now, in her thirties, she was ashamed that she still felt tender and confused about her life. "It was all really no big deal. I should be stronger, I should just get on with my life. Why am I so weak, why do I still hurt so much?"

Some of us feel our sorrows are evidence of some sin or some imperfection, convinced that if we were better, stronger, or more perfect, we would not be suffering the way we do. Interestingly, the original Greek word for "sin"—*hamartia*—is simply an old archer's term meaning "to miss the mark." Since the very act of being human means we will periodically "miss the mark," we are all by definition "sinners." But there is no judgment implied in the term—only an indication that as a point of attention, it invites a focus to our practice. If we are merciful with ourselves, if we meet our shortcomings and imperfections with mercy and lovingkindness, we feel a profound permission to use our "missing" as part of our learning to grow. We need not perfect ourselves to earn the right to be loved. Love and mercy are not prizes for good behavior; they are the ingredients that allow us to heal and to become more fully human.

Truth, Mercy, and Nonviolence

Mercy is a quality of mind that lovingly accepts ourselves as we are, without judgment or violence. With a merciful heart, we are able to accept our successes and failures, our gifts and imperfections with love and compassion. We can touch our most tender places with kindness, gentleness, and nonviolence. With eyes of mercy, we are free to explore the sadness, the clumsiness, the joy, the playfulness, the confusion, the tightness, the hunger, the laughter, and to touch it all with unconditional love. The more we meet ourselves with love instead of violence and judgment, the more available and open we are to being seen, being known, and being intimately cared for by ourselves and others.

When we are merciful, we accept the totality of who we are with unconditional love. We embrace ourselves without judgment, without condition, and with complete forgiveness. We see ourselves and others, as Stephen Levine says, with "soft eyes." Not with eyes that distort or deny, but with eyes that attend more gently to the full spectrum of what is true.

When we judge, when we hate, when we harden our eyes and hearts, we perpetuate great harm to ourselves and the world, and we lose the way to peace and healing. The practice of mercy opens a path of healing rooted not in violence but in peace, love, and truth. When Jesus taught his followers not to judge themselves or others, he was not simply saying they should be "nice." He was speaking to the subtle violence we invoke in our own lives when we judge, and was also alluding to the deep healing that may arise within us when we walk a path of nonharming. Judgment inevitably gives birth to cruelty; mercy and nonviolence bring healing and peace.

In Sanskrit there is a word, *ahimsa*, which may be translated as "nonharming" or "noninjury." For Gandhi, *ahimsa* was the cornerstone of his campaign of nonviolent resistance to the British in India. When he began his campaign for Indian independence, he called it the "nonharming truth movement." This *satyagraha* movement was predicated on the belief that one could see the deeper truth in people and events only through the eyes of nonviolence and compassion. He knew that if they met violence with violence, the war would go on forever. In the face of such violence, only a passionate commitment to the practice of nonharming could bring true peace and freedom for all. In light of his unshakable commitment to *ahimsa* above all else, it was clear that Gandhi was less interested in political victory than in meeting friend and foe with respect, gentleness, and mercy.

So it is with our own healing. Genuine healing and the development of true loving kindness are impossible unless we first undertake a practice of *ahimsa*, of nonharming. Nonharming is an essential ingredient of mercy. Through the practices of mercy and noninjury, we refuse to judge, to hate, or to condemn ourselves or our deepest feelings. Before we can heal, before we can learn to love, we must first stop the war within ourselves.

In Buddhism, the practice of *ahimsa* is one of the central spiritual precepts. We are all of one family, all of one community, all interdependent with everything that lives, in a deep ecology of body and spirit. As a way to honor our kinship with one another and in recognition of how precious all life is, Buddhists take a vow to practice nonharming, to treat all sentient beings with respect, love, and care. They believe that as children of creation, each of us is one of those precious beings worthy of care, affection, and loving kindness.

How may we cultivate such nonviolence in our own hearts? We may begin by recognizing the harm that all judgment creates in our hearts and spirits. Whether we are hurtful toward ourselves or others, the residue of that violence lingers in our body and heart like a virus, choking our healing and imprisoning our spirit.

Whether we bring hurt to others or to ourselves, the result is inevitably the same: We unwittingly perpetuate the violence that brought us suffering as children. Any violence we commit against ourselves merely gives birth to more violence on the earth; rather than healing the sufferings of childhood, we are adding to them. In the same way, any violence we consider against others inevitably contributes to the reservoir of hurt we carry within ourselves. When we are filled with hate for someone else, how do we feel? What does our body feel like? Whenever we judge another, when we name some quality or behavior in someone else as "enemy," we usually tighten in aversion and hatred. We carry the tremendous pain of our own anger, we are closed and hard, and we hear only the echo of hurt and anger in our minds as it replays itself over and over. We feel internally battered each time the hatred or judgment arises within us. Our anger and judgments of others, said Thomas Merton, only invites more and more sorrow into our own hearts. "The weapon with which we would destroy the enemy," he said, "must pass through our own heart to reach them."

Our grandparents brought their sorrows to bear on our parents, and our parents in turn carried their pain into our family. How long will we hold our own anger, impatience, and violent judgments in our hearts and minds? When will we find the courage to be gentle and the wisdom to take a path of nonharming, so that we and our own children may begin to learn the ways of kindness, healing, and peace?

Gandhi said that "nonviolence is not a garment to be put on and off at will. Its seat is in the heart, and it must be an inseparable part of our being." Whether in the Bhagavad-Gita of Gandhi, in Jesus' prescription to love our enemies, or the vow of nonharming taught by the Buddha, each teaches that the way to healing and peace begins with gentleness and nonviolence toward ourselves or others.

We may begin to heal the violence of our judging mind by trying to practice nonharming. For a certain period of the day, we may dedicate ourselves to watching how many times we judge, criticize, or belittle our feelings or actions. Each time you notice that you are critical or judgmental in some way, consciously remake the vow not to use violence in any form. Watch how many times and in how many ways we bring harm to ourselves and our feelings.

Jamie, who was particularly adept at judging and criticizing herself, said she would try to take a vow of nonharming toward herself for an entire week. When I next saw her, she said she was amazed to see how often she was hurtful and unkind toward herself. "It was the busiest week I've ever spent," she said. "I had no idea how much I get on my case about everything. But it was such a relief to notice it, and to try to let it go. Every once in a while, I could really just stop the war in my head, and it would get quiet and peaceful in here. It was great."

Cultivating nonharming toward ourselves is a tremendous step toward allowing healing love into our broken hearts—especially for those of us who, feeling the sting of physical or emotional pain as children, have internalized much of that judgment and violence in our souls. We are so in need of mercy and care, and so clumsy in allowing it to be born in our own lives.

In the same way, as we work to cultivate a practice of nonharming toward others, we need tremendous courage to confront the atmosphere of violence that permeates our culture. Walter Murray, a friend and colleague, was the first black Affirmative Action officer at Vanderbilt University. When Walter and I were studying Gandhi's *satyagraha* movement and its effects on the struggle for civil rights in the United States, he told me the following story:

One day we were preparing to join a civil rights march through Birmingham, Alabama at the height of the conflict between civil rights workers and the Birmingham police. We had prepared to march nonviolently through the city, but Bull Connor (the commissioner of public safety) had readied his men and dogs for a confrontation with the marchers. I took my place in line. Standing next to me was a close friend, a big football player, who marched next to his girlfriend, a small young woman who fit under his arm.

We started to march. As we walked, crowds gathered to shout at us and harass us. The crowds got bigger and started to become mean, and many of us were frightened of getting hurt, even killed. But we were committed to doing this without violence, no matter what happened. So we kept on marching.

Suddenly the police and the dogs were told to attack, and billy clubs were swinging everywhere around us. Right next to me and the football player, a policeman rushed up with his club and smacked the young woman in the head, and she just fell to the ground. The football player, who watched his girlfriend fall, looked straight at this cop. His eyes just looked deep into him for what seemed like a long time. And then this big football player, with his massive arms, reached down to pick up his girlfriend, take her in his arms, and kept on walking.

It was incredible, the strength and commitment he had. That was how we had to be; we knew we had to remain nonviolent. It was our only hope for change.

Mercy is one practice capable of effecting real change in a violent world. The gentle movements of truth and healing blossom only in the hearts of women and men dedicated to love, mutual respect, and nonviolence. Saint Francis, who dedicated his life to peace, taught his followers to attend to the quality of peace in their own lives as they worked for the healing of others. "While you are proclaiming peace with your lips, be careful to have it even more fully in your heart," he said.

The Sufis say that real truth is always spoken with love, and that every word we speak must first pass through three gates: "At the first gate we ask ourselves, 'Are these words true?' If so, we let them pass on. At the second gate we ask, 'Are they necessary?' At the last gate we ask, 'Are they kind?' "

So must we ask ourselves, are we kind? Can we approach ourselves with kindness, may we be loving and gentle with ourselves, with our clumsiness, with our slowness to change, with our habits, with our tender hearts? Mohandas Gandhi, who dedicated his life to healing and peace, fervently believed that kindness, mercy, and nonharming were the only paths capable of healing the cause of violence itself—namely, the hardened, broken hearts of women and men:

My optimism rests on my belief in the infinite possibilities of the individual to develop nonviolence. The more you develop it in your own heart, the more infectious it becomes, till it overwhelms your surroundings and, by and by, might oversweep the world.

EXERCISE
Investigating the Judging Mind

This exercise has two parts. In the first, we will investigate the ways in which we are violent with ourselves. In the second part, we will begin to cultivate a practice of nonharming.

Plan to undertake this exercise for an entire day. You can do this any time, even on a day when you are at work, at home with your family, or on a trip. From the beginning of the day to the end of the evening, you will simply explore the ways in which you criticize, judge, or bring harm to yourself.

Beginning with the moment you get up in the morning, take the first half of the day to note every time you judge or criticize yourself for anything at all. Watch how often you judge yourself for being late, for how you look, or how you feel. Listen for how you criticize your performance and judge yourself in word and deed. Be aware of all the critical voices as they appear. You may silently say to yourself, "judging, judging" as each critical thought arises. How do they make you feel? Do they make you softer or tighter? Pay attention to what happens in your body when they are present. At this point, our purpose is not to eliminate these voices but to understand them with open, mindful attention.

Notice how often you judge yourself, even for the smallest things. Do the criticisms come a few times an hour? Every few minutes? Be aware of any periods without significant judgments. What happens to your body and heart when they are quiet?

You may begin to feel some discomfort or agitation as you become more aware of the litany of judgments that sometimes fills your waking hours. You may find yourself becoming angry, you may even experience some nausea as you become aware of the violence of such incessant abuse. This is the way you treat yourself every day. Listening to these judging voices without pushing them away, you can become aware of the extent of the constant criticisms that relentlessly bombard your heart and body.

After half the day has passed and you become familiar with the quality and frequency of these judgments, you may begin to cultivate a practice of nonharming. Take a moment to silently promise yourself that from this moment on, you will begin to practice nonharming in word, thought, and deed. Take a vow that you will cease to use any judgment or criticism to harm yourself in any way. If you discover yourself judging, simply stop, get quiet, take a breath, and retake the vow of nonharming. You may say, "I will not judge or hurt myself with thoughts or criticisms. I will now treat myself only with loving kindness."

You may need to retake this vow a hundred times during the day before experiencing some relief. Be careful not to judge yourself for criticizing yourself—this simply keeps the judging mind occupied. Each time you notice a critical voice, simply reaffirm your promise of nonharming.

Pay attention to the quality of your experience each time you promise not to harm yourself. How does the promise affect your body? With every reaffirmation of the vow, do the periods between the judging voices gradually lengthen? As you practice inner nonviolence, what do you notice about your feelings toward yourself? What do you notice about how you feel toward others?

Cultivating nonharming is one of the most gently effective steps on a path of mercy, healing, and liberation. As the cacophony of judging voices slowly begins to recede, we make peace with ourselves, inviting a merciful compassion into our hearts, bodies, and spirits.

Meditation
CULTIVATING MERCY
(A Loving Kindness Meditation)

This meditation may be practiced at any time, and takes only a few moments. It is based on the Buddhist practice of metta, *which is used to send loving kindness to all beings who inhabit the earth. With this exercise, we will practice sending loving kindness to ourselves.*

Begin by arranging yourself in front of your table, in your place of refuge. Take time to relax and find a comfortable position, then gently close your eyes. Allow your awareness to rest in the breath, feeling the sensation of the rising and falling of each inhale and exhale. Use the breath to help you settle into your body, finding a place of belonging, a place you may rest inside.

Then gently say these words to yourself, or make a recording of these words and play them back:

> *May I dwell in the heart.*
> *May I be healed.*
> *May I be filled with love.*
> *May I be free from suffering.*
> *May I be happy.*
> *May I be at peace.*

Repeat each phrase slowly, using each breath to deepen the heart's ability to listen, to hear each word. Allow yourself to soften, to receive the nurture and the warmth of loving kindness. Cradling yourself in your own care, you may whisper these phrases again and again, until you begin to feel a genuine sense of mercy and love for yourself.

This meditation prayer of loving kindness can become a part of your daily practice. With it, you may expand your practice of nonharming and cultivate a meditative awareness of yourself as a child of creation, a precious being receiving the gifts of mercy and love.

CHAPTER SIX

Grandiosity and Humility

Many of us hold tightly to the belief that we are terribly broken. Because we were hurt in some way as children, we feel especially singled out for harm, especially wounded. It feels like no one could ever know how badly we hurt. Our wounds made us special—unique victims of terrible injustice—and we felt isolated, unique, somehow different from everyone else.

But at the same time we were especially sensitive to the subtle dynamics of our family suffering, and so may also have felt specially gifted, uniquely able to heal what was broken, somehow chosen to fix what was wrong. We could see what no one else could see and felt specially charged with the responsibility to do something about it. Consequently, we learned to see ourselves as set apart from the rest of the world, both by the unique gifts and by the terrible sufferings that were given to us.

As we journey toward freedom and healing, we are often reluctant to let go of our deep conviction that we are special. Regardless of whether we feel specially gifted or specially wounded, our being "special" feels like a birthright, something to be secretly proud of, knowing no one will ever be or feel quite like us.

But if we are unlike anyone else, then the healing available for others— belonging and sanctuary, abundance and mercy—will remain forever beyond our reach. Whatever relief that is possible will never be possible for us, for our wounds are special, different, terminally unique. Holding onto the particularity of our suffering, we place ourselves, our gifts, and our wounds outside the circle of the rest of humanity. As a special case, we are not susceptible to the treatments and miracles that work for "normal" people. And so we feel condemned to suffer alone.

Grandiosity and Importance

We learn our first lesson in being special as a small player on the family stage. The child's world is built on cause and effect: When the child smiles, Mom and Dad smile; when the child drops a bottle, Mom or Dad picks it up. When the child cries, someone inevitably comes to find out why. The child naturally feels that they create the world around them through their actions and desires, and they begin to feel very powerful.

This is the grandiosity of the child. We came to believe that what happened in our family happened because of what we did or didn't do, what we did or didn't say. Feeling ourselves at the center of the family drama, we felt that if we suppressed our wants and desires, we could create peace. If we soothed Mom's anger, things would not get out of control; if we made Dad happy, he would not be so depressed and wouldn't drink. If we pleased Mom and Dad, we could prevent a family fight at dinner. We felt powerful and important, charged with the responsibility to somehow keep things together. We felt it was our actions and behavior that turned the family wheel, and we felt singled out as the one who saw what no one else could see.

But if everything happened because of what we did, then how could we explain when things went terribly wrong? Whose fault was it when Dad *did* get angry, or Mom drank too much, or we were hit or violated in some way?

One explanation was that our parents were simply beyond our control, and that we could be hurt at any time. In our family, pain could simply happen at random. But for children completely dependent on the family for food and care—even for life itself—the idea of such a totally dangerous or unpredictable environment was much too terrifying. So the preferred explanation, the one that gave us a sense of control, was that family pain happened because of something we did. If suffering happened because of who we were, then we could fix ourselves, thus making sure we would never be hurt again. We cultivated the illusion of control by deciding we were the primary architect of our family experience.

Feeling an exaggerated sense of our own importance, we assumed everyone was responding to what we did and watching how we behaved. As we grew, we began to feel responsible for how everything around us turned out—the happiness and suffering of our parents, our spouses, our friends, our colleagues, and our children. One of the reasons we learned to judge ourselves so mercilessly is that we held ourselves to a much higher standard than the rest of humanity. Others were allowed to fail, to falter, to seek the help of others; we, on the other hand, were required to do it all perfectly, by ourselves, without a mistake, without the aid of anyone else.

Bill was a psychiatrist with a very busy practice. He worked long hours as a consultant for a variety of treatment centers and was committed to being a good provider and a loving husband and father. But he said there was little joy in his life, as he felt choked by his responsibilities. There were so many who wanted so much, and there was so little left for him. Even though he felt overwhelmed, he never asked his family or friends for help; it felt as though he had to do everything by himself. When he first came to see me, he said he felt exhausted.

As a child of an angry alcoholic, Bill had learned to figure everything out himself. He felt it was his job to do everything right, never ask for help, and make sure everyone was taken care of. In the process, he learned to feel extremely important—so important that he could not allow anyone to share his burden.

During one session, I asked him to close his eyes and quietly scan his body for any strong sensations. He said he could feel his heart beating strongly, working hard. "Tell me what your heart is saying," I asked. "If you could give it a voice, what would it say?"

He was silent for a moment, listening to the voice in his heart. Then he spoke: "I am tired. I feel that I am always beating, I must always keep working, or everything will die. I can never rest. I feel like I am straining to keep everything alive. Everything depends on me. I cannot let them down. I can never stop." Bill began to sob.

With his eyes still closed, I asked him to imagine a color that would soften the tension in his chest, and to breathe that color into the chambers and vessels of his heart. "Allow the heart to soften, to rest. Feel the sensation of softening as it touches the cells and muscles of the heart. Allow it to feel rest." As he let the healing breath open and expand the tension around his heart, his breathing became slow and steady. He seemed more relaxed.

After the meditation, he told me he had recently been to a doctor because his heart had developed an arrhythmia—it would periodically skip a beat. They suggested he take medication, but he was reluctant to do so, and he now saw that the condition of his heart mirrored the condition of his life. "It feels like when my heart skips a beat, it is the only time it can rest." He saw clearly the strain he had put on himself—and on his heart—by taking on such a tremendous sense of responsibility. His insistence on being the source of all life for everyone around him had brought serious emotional and physical costs. After a few weeks of our meditations together, his arrhythmia disappeared.

Bertrand Russell once said that "one of the signs of an approaching nervous breakdown is the belief that one's work is terribly important."

When we take on the mantle of "special," we invariably delude ourselves with the measure of our own importance. Seduced by the notion that our work is indispensable to the continuation of the species, we invariably feel tired, frightened, and alone, holding onto a deeply private suffering that no one can touch. Only by letting go of our inflated sense of importance may we begin to find the companionship and healing that comes with being simply human.

Grandiosity and Woundedness

A second, more subtle form of grandiosity arises within our experience of feeling broken. When we enter therapy, when we go to workshops and read books and talk to friends, what we most often bring is our brokenness. Our wounds and hurts, our pain and suffering become our offering, something we carry like a gift to the altar. When we were hurt as children, nothing seemed as real or as sacred to us as our pain. We feel convinced that we have been handicapped by our childhood sorrows.

Doug is in his mid-thirties and afflicted with albinism. His hair, which he wears to his shoulders, is snow white, as is his beard His skin is extremely light in color, and his overall appearance is striking, even handsome—although Doug feels more shame than pride about his appearance. With his skin color, he could easily get burned if he stayed too long in the sun. Nevertheless, when he was a child, his father would regularly take him to the beach and make him stay there to "toughen him up." Kids in school often beat him up because of his looks; when he told his parents, they never seemed to do anything about it. He was in great pain, and no one would listen.

As Doug and I explored the hurts of his childhood, he said he was afraid nothing would give him relief, given his physical condition and childhood pain. His affliction was so obvious, everyone stared at him, and there was nothing he could do about it. He felt his particular problems were too unique, too special to be alleviated by therapy.

"Actually, Doug," I said to him one day, "I find you to be quite ordinary." At the mention of the word *ordinary,* Doug became enraged. "You have no idea how much I suffered, how hard it has been. I *am* different—just look at me! People stop to stare at me, I can't go outside in the summer, and I was beat up almost every day as a kid. I have problems that nobody can ever understand."

Doug had transformed his wound into something sacred and important. His wound had become his most intimate companion, the lens through which he looked at his life. His wound identified him and set him apart.

It is hard for any of us to let go of feeling broken. As long as we take a certain pride in how wounded and misunderstood we were as children of our family pain and dysfunction, the more tenaciously we hold onto our conviction that we are special. But what if we are no longer sick, no longer handicapped? What if we have simply become addicted to the *idea* of being especially ill—to the point that when someone accuses us of being *ordinary*, with no special needs or problems, we feel slighted?

For several weeks I playfully accused Doug of being the most ordinary person I had ever met. One day he came in and said to me, "You know, I have been trying on the idea of being 'ordinary,' and at first I felt small and afraid, angry that no one was paying attention to me. But when I stopped working so hard at being special, I realized no one *was* paying attention to me, and I could just be who I was. I started to feel relaxed, even calm inside. Even when it lasted only a few minutes, I felt incredibly free."

Nobody Special

"In our everyday life," said Zen master Suzuki Roshi, "our thinking is 99 percent self-centered. 'Why do I have suffering? Why do I have trouble?' " This kind of thinking makes us attached to how important we are, how important our suffering must be. Suzuki Roshi goes on to say, "It is just you yourself, nothing special."

When we were small, our family members rarely (if ever) spoke openly of their tender, human feelings. So when we felt sad or afraid, we assumed we were alone in feeling those things. But unknown to us, everyone in our family was in some pain; each of our parents, our sisters, and brothers felt fear, sadness, loneliness, and confusion from time to time. Although they went unspoken, painful feelings were shared by everyone in our home.

Since our feelings were kept secret, we felt our wounds set us apart from those we loved. We quietly took possession of sadness and fear as *our* sadness, *our* fear, belonging to us and to no other. What we could not know was that every child born experiences these very same feelings. The way pain came to us need not set us apart. On the contrary, it may invite us into a deeper communion with all living beings. Our pain does not make us a victim; our gifts do not make us important. We are simply human— nobody special.

Many of us suffer from what Walker Percy describes as "the great suck of the self." When we feel the world has conspired to cause us suffering, we undoubtedly overestimate our relative importance in the planetary scheme of things. For some of us, this suggestion may feel like an insult, but it may also give us great freedom. If we are not so important, we are no longer

responsible for living up to the imagined expectations of a universe infatuated with our every move. Instead, we are set free to live each moment
listening to what is true in our body, heart, mind, and spirit without
scrutinizing our every move for signs of greatness.

In the second century A.D., a number of monks who came to be known
as the Desert Fathers and Mothers set up spiritual communities in the
Egyptian desert. Abba Or, one of the Desert Fathers, said, "Either flee
from people, or laugh at the world and the people in it, and make a fool of
yourself in many things." When we stop taking ourselves so seriously, we
are set free to more playfully engage the world in which we live. We are free
to explore our boundaries and to experiment with what is possible. When
we begin to be "nobody special," there is nothing to defend; we are free to
be whomever we are.

Humility

Chuang Tzu said:

> The man of Tao
> Remains unknown
> Perfect Virtue
> Produces nothing
> "No self"
> Is "True Self."
> And the greatest man
> Is Nobody.

Kurt Vonnegut once described human beings as "sitting up mud." The
word *humility* comes from *hummus,* which means earth or mud. To be
"humble" is to feel ourselves as part of the earth—made from dust,
returning to dust. The Hebrew creation story says God created humans by
mixing dust and spirit. Thus, even the word *human* reflects our sense of
oneness with the earth.

There have been times when I found myself wanting to show someone
what a marvelously insightful teacher and healer I turned out to be. I want
whoever is with me to be impressed with my wit and wisdom as a
counselor, and I subtly hold them hostage until they are suitably moved by
my skillfulness and magic. I play the Wizard of Oz—complete with lights
and smoke and booming voices—when all the while I am simply a frightened little boy, pulling levers and pushing buttons, hoping it all works,
hoping no one pulls back the curtain, hoping I won't get caught.

But I am already caught—caught in wanting them to feel sorry for my pain or to be impressed with my life. Either way, I have turned them into objects of my game rather than subjects of my heart. When I need people to see me as special, I focus primarily on my need and cannot hear the depth and breadth of who they are in that moment. In my rush to be special, I do not honor the common humanity that binds me to others.

In truth, none of us is more special than anyone else. Each of us was given a particular combination of wounds, gifts, talents, and imperfections that merely gives texture to the quality of our experience. Our wounds and gifts do not set us apart, they are simply human qualities that unite us. Joseph Campbell describes this humanness as a doorway to love and understanding: "The umbilical point, the humanity, the thing that makes you human and not supernatural and immortal—that's what's lovable."

Perhaps we may learn to approach life as a beginner. If we are not under continual pressure to prove how extraordinary we are, we can begin each day with the mind of a novice. None of us are experts in being alive. We are simply human, players in a life where sometimes we succeed and sometimes we don't. When we pretend to be more knowledgeable, talented, or successful than we really are, we cut ourselves off from the wonder of our own curiosity and the discovery of new experiences. "In the beginner's mind there are many possibilities," said Suzuki Roshi. "In the expert's mind there are few."

We are all human beings who are born, trying to survive, learning to love, and preparing to live and die with some dignity and peace. No more, no less. To learn humility is to honor that your hurt and mine are one, that my life and yours are cut from the same cloth, and that we share the gentle communion of being human.

Just as we took refuge in being special, we can learn to take refuge in being ordinary, not being in charge, not being the center of the universe. Indeed, perhaps the first step in our healing is to be able to admit a certain level of ignorance and powerlessness in our lives. How many of us really know what we are doing? How many of us truly feel we are experts in the practice of life, that we have it all together? Rumi playfully reminds us:

Do you think I know what I'm doing?
That for one breath or half-breath I
    belong to myself?
As much as a pen knows what it's writing,
Or the ball can guess where it's going next.

Humility and Accomplishment

Some of us try to create an illusion of our own importance through our accomplishments in the world. We seek to elevate our worth by demonstrating how much work we can do and how well we can do it. By accomplishing more and more, we eventually give the world no other choice but to recognize our special gifts and talents. We may even take some secret pride in how much more effectively, creatively, or efficiently we accomplish what others have been unable to do before.

But those of us who seek to feel important through our accomplishments must be particularly careful. As we strive to accomplish more and more, we tend to take ourselves and our work very seriously, until over time we feel increasingly tired, unappreciated, overwhelmed, and isolated. The more we are convinced our work is specially important, the less we feel able to ask for the support, sustenance, or company of others. Tara Tulku Rinpoche, a Tibetan monk, once cautioned that "the intensity of our sorrow will vary in direct proportion to the intensity of our feeling that 'I am important.' "

In some cultures, those who build, lead, teach, or heal are certainly seen as important but are given no more importance or special treatment than anyone else. Working hard and doing good work are simply parts of the ordinary practice of being human and require no special reward. Dr. Richard Katz, the Harvard anthropologist, writes of his experiences among tribal leaders, teachers, and healers in a Fijiian community: "Becoming a healer in Fiji does not bring economic rewards or increased social status. On a variety of economic and social indicators, healers are the same as nonhealers. They are given no special privileges in order to perform their healing."

The practice of humility invites us to consider that while there is much important work to be done in the world, our work does not make us important. Our importance, our value, and our worthiness rest in having been born as a child of God on the earth. Nothing more is required. We, like all people, deserve to be fed, clothed, sheltered, and loved, not because we are special, not because we have accomplished what no one else could do—we deserve belonging and care simply because we are human.

Kip Tiernan is a charismatic, dedicated community organizer who founded Rosie's Place, a shelter for homeless women in Boston. One day she came to a meeting where several of us were discussing the urban poor and how we could help them. She began by sharing her early experiences working in Roxbury, a struggling neighborhood in Boston:

I first moved to Roxbury in the late sixties. I went with tons of files, assuming that somewhere in all of them were all the answers for the problems of Roxbury. The people of Roxbury treated me with tender concern. They laughed at my seriousness and said to me "It's okay, Kippy, nothing much is gonna change because you're here. But we're glad you're here." It was one of the greatest lessons I hope to learn about myself.

We make the mistake of thinking that the problems of the entire world are on our shoulders, and it's up to us alone to solve them. Well, we don't. I must remind myself that I am part of the struggle and that is all that is really expected of me . . . to celebrate small victories, to have fun on the run.

The words *humility* and *humor* share the same root. When we see ourselves in a lovingly humorous light, it becomes more difficult to see ourselves and our accomplishments as the measure of all things.

When someone makes an obvious mark on our world—someone like Gandhi, for example, who, through a timely combination of insight, creativity, and devotion, accomplished a great deal on the human stage—history often judges them as somehow special, set apart from the community of humans from which they came. But history often confuses success and accomplishment with importance. For, while Gandhi's talents were certainly admirable and unique, he himself taught that his gifts rendered him no more important than anyone else involved in the struggle for freedom. Gandhi placed no more value on his own life than he did on the parents who gave him birth and raised him, on the farmers who grew the food that fed him, or on his followers who did so much of the work. "I claim to be no more than an average person with less than average ability," he wrote. "I have not the shadow of a doubt that any man or woman can achieve what I have, if he or she would make the same effort and cultivate the same hope and faith."

Gandhi believed that he was simply another pilgrim on the common path of peace. Similarly, each of us who reads Gandhi's writings and tries in our own way to change the world in which we live is, like Gandhi, a child of the earth, capable of great success and failure, able to give and receive, able to touch the divine spark deep within ourselves—ordinary human beings, blessed with the tremendous gift of life.

Thomas Merton speaks of the rewards of approaching our career, vocation, work, or spiritual practice with this same measure of humility:

The more you are able to work in a spirit of detachment, the closer you come to working for God rather than for yourself, the less strain there is on your nerves. You do not worry about things so much, and therefore you do not get too confused, so mixed up, so tired.

In fact, you learn to recognize that your self-love, your pride, is trying to take over the work by your reactions. When you are exhausted and upset and haunted by work that seems to be going badly, it means you are working for yourself, and are taking the consequences.

But when you are free you work with an ease that amazes you. Half the time, without any necessity for special thought on your part, God seems to remove obstacles and do half the work for you. When God wants a thing done, the speed with which it achieves completion and success almost takes your breath away.

EXERCISE
The Practice of Being Ordinary

This exercise is simply about noting how often we feel special, different, or somehow set apart from those around us. It is an exercise that you can practice frequently as you go through your normal daily activities.

Several times a day, wherever you are, take a moment to examine your relationship to the people around you. Whether you are driving down the road, sitting in a meeting, in line at the supermarket, or with a group of friends, notice how you see yourself in relation to everyone else. Do you feel special, somehow different from everyone else? In what way? Do you feel more intelligent, more complex, harder to understand? Are you more introspective, more sensitive, somehow deeper than everyone else in line at the bank? Perhaps you feel more wounded, more insightful, or maybe you just feel you have more (or less) potential than everyone else.

Notice how often, and in which particular ways, you feel qualitatively set apart from your fellow humans. What feelings arise as you notice your "specialness"? How does it feel in your body? What are your impulses? Does it make you want to hide or go away, or does it make you want intimacy, or to somehow make contact?

Once you have examined the sensation of being "special," take a moment to imagine the possibility that you may, in fact, be quite ordinary; that you are, in fact, nobody special. Imagine saying to the person next to you, "I am just like you. We are exactly the same. There is nothing special about me that sets me apart from you. I am as ordinary as they come."

How easy (or difficult) is this to say? Where do you get caught? Ask yourself this question: What would I have to give up in order to be ordinary, to be just like everyone else? Which unique or sacred gift, which special wound or talent do I use to prevent myself from truthfully admitting that I am not really special at all?

Watch yourself experiment with feeling ordinary. Notice the resistance, the discomfort, the fear, or uncertainty that arises. As you imagine being ordinary, nobody special, what possibilities arise? If you were in fact nobody special, what would you do today? If you were released from the burden and responsibility of being exceptionally unique, and could simply be an ordinary human being, how would you feel free to act? What normal, unexceptional activities would you enjoy today?

Allow yourself to play with the freedom that comes from being ordinary and nobody special. The pressure is off. You can relax. Nothing special is expected of you. Nobody is watching. Why should they? You are just an ordinary child of the earth. Perfectly unexceptional, perfect just as you are.

CHAPTER SEVEN

Drama and Simplicity

In our search for intimacy and trust with those we love, whether spouse, lover, friend, or family, there are really only two basic communication skills required of us. The first is that we are able to share information; the second is that we are able to exchange care.

When we skillfully share information, we are able to name our wants and needs; we can speak what is in our heart in a way that can be heard; we can exchange thoughts and feelings with someone else and expect to be understood; we learn to speak clearly and precisely not only about what is precious but also about what is difficult; and we share a common commitment, along with our friends and partners, to listen together for what is true and necessary.

When we exchange care, we name our love for one another without fear. We listen for what is painful or difficult, and work together with those we love to make adjustments that will bring healing and peace. We may listen to another's heart without always feeling that our own needs are being slighted, and we may express our genuine concern and affection for another's well-being in a way that allows them to feel that our care is trustworthy.

Yet, in our families, the exchange of both information and care was often accompanied by high drama and theatrical presentations of emotion. In families where people are not skilled in listening attentively to one another, things tend to escalate until only the biggest, loudest displays get noticed.

Consequently, meaningful attempts to genuinely communicate our thoughts or feelings were often met with great resistance, confusion, or anger. Any moment of genuine affection or simple communication could be quickly sidetracked by someone's fragile self-esteem, their quickness to feel slighted, or their emotional hair trigger, all of which enabled a simple statement of feeling or fact to instantly escalate into betrayal, rage, isolation or depression. Our tendency toward grandiosity, our clumsiness in speaking and listening to what was simply true, and our inability to act in a simple, caring manner with one another all combined to provoke an atmosphere of high drama. Whenever we felt unheard or unloved, we resorted to theatrics, manipulations, and dramatic escalations. Instead of exchanging information, we learned to make points and win arguments; rather than exchange care, we learned to evoke sympathy for ourselves and our causes. Through dramatic outbursts, everyone tried to manipulate information and feelings in a way to come out in their favor. But in the process, real care and true feelings were obscured by our family theatrics, and we rarely felt listened to or cared for.

Anger, for example, was rarely a simple matter of a difference of opinion. More likely, it was accompanied by dramatic threats, loud arguments, flying objects, or harsh punishments. Mark told me that his father would yell at him for half an hour if he forgot to take out the garbage. Ellen remembered a time when her father, upset with something her sister said at the dinner table, turned the table upside down and stormed out of the room. When we fear we will not be heard, we invoke higher and higher levels of drama to get our point across.

Many have memories of family fights ending in violence, of children being bundled up and carried off in the night, of painful divorces, dramatic reconciliations, and grand promises about things that were never to happen.

Even love would be professed with great drama. Anna told me that her mother sat her down every night before she went to bed and said, "Anna, you are going to be the greatest dancer in the world." It was not enough to simply support her child's love for dance; she must be the "greatest," the "best." Sylvia was told by her mother that she was "much better than all the other children" in her class. These were the same mothers who could fly into a rage whenever their daughters brought home bad grades from school. Both love and criticism were inevitably delivered with inflated, disproportionate emotionality.

When these loud arguments, threatening judgments, and tearful confessions incessantly punctuate the family story, our ear becomes more attuned and receptive to high drama. Only when life escalates into outrageous proportions are we able to listen; our ear has become accustomed to attend more carefully in those moments for what is important and meaningful. Consequently, as we grow older, we find ourselves precipitating one crisis after another, perfecting our ability to sift out some meaning from the rubble of each successive emotional earthquake. We learn to provoke dramatic confrontations, postpone our tasks and responsibilities until they reach crisis proportions, and fan the flames of volatility in our love and work relationships. The most painful and dramatic episodes become our most reliable and intriguing teachers, while the still, smaller voices of our spirit are ignored and unheeded.

Our habitual fascination with drama can infect the way we experience our own unfolding. As we write the story of our lives, we litter our stage with inflated tragedies and injustices that mirror the rich, conflicted theater of our childhood. Every infatuation becomes a great and wonderful love; every disappointment becomes a horrendous and insufferable catastrophe. If all the world is a stage, those of us addicted to drama play our part with gusto and enthusiasm.

Drama and Complexity

For many of us, childhood was not only dramatic, it was also very complicated. Simple acts and phrases were often meant to conceal complex messages, and we quickly learned to decipher all the levels of meaning behind the words and gestures of those around us.

For example, if our mother said that our father was not an alcoholic, it sometimes meant, "Dad is an alcoholic and we all know it, but I am too afraid to talk about it." When someone told us, "Don't worry, everything is fine," it could just as easily mean something was terribly wrong. When they said, "Let's just have a good time," it usually meant everyone was miserable. Everything meant something else. The truth was not found in what was said but embedded *within* what was said—or even what was *not* said. We heard the words that were spoken, but what did they really mean?

We became quite adept at figuring out the complexity of things and seeking out hidden meanings. Reading the intricacies of a given moment, we learned to divine ulterior motives and intentions behind every act: Why did they do this, what did they really want, what did they mean by that? Our eyes scanned for what was not apparent, as nothing was ever what it appeared to be.

In these families, a misplaced toy could be interpreted as an attack on parental authority; a forgotten pail of garbage became a terrible betrayal. Feelings were couched in complex language, and painful truths were camouflaged in secret emotional family codes. Since no one spoke the truth directly, everything was shared through symbolic language: If you did

A, it really meant B; if you said X, you probably meant Y. Each family developed its own code.

On her way home from school, Susan would check if the window shades were open or closed before she went in the house. If they were closed, it meant someone inside was either drunk, hung over, or fighting; if the shades were open, the coast was generally clear. Bill learned to tell by the way his dad hung up his coat whether or not he was in a bad mood. Everything could be interpreted through the family code.

This secret language often remains embedded in the family story for a long time, even after everyone is grown and moved away. Paul, a man of forty-two, went home to visit his father and stepmother for the holidays. After dinner he took his plate and put it in the sink, intending to wash it later that evening. When his stepmother found his unwashed plate in the sink, she flew into a rage. "How dare you leave that plate in there for me to clean? I've always known you never respected me! And apparently you never will!" Here we are not fighting about dishes. The dishes are merely a symbol pointing to something else, some unspoken, unresolved hurt that has remained buried in the family psyche for generations. And as long as we continue to communicate in complex family codes, our hurts and fears will probably remain unspoken and unhealed as they sit hidden in a dirty sink.

Another element of our complex family drama was its unpredictability. Usually, once we had learned the codes of communication, we learned to predict from Dad's moods, Mom's behavior, or the tone of the dinner conversation exactly what everyone was feeling and how the evening was going to go. But occasionally we would stumble upon a phrase or behavior we had never encountered before, and it would spring like a booby trap, taking us completely by surprise. Something we thought was an innocent comment would suddenly provoke tremendous anger or rebuke. We learned quickly to file away any new data, vowing never to repeat the same mistake again. Thus, we developed an encyclopedic categorization of words and gestures that seemed like one thing but actually meant something else. We came to feel that everything in the world needed to be translated, that every appearance had to be uncovered to reveal its true meaning.

We become accustomed to seeing the world as a symphony of signs and symbols that are important only to the degree that they reveal what is masked or hidden away. The act of making tea, for example, is significant only if we can discover why it is being made, who is making it, and who it is for. Is it a reward or a punishment; is it the good tea or the inexpensive tea; is it a gift or a bribe; and what will they want in return?

As our mind desperately searches out the intricate levels of intention and meaning surrounding the teamaker, we miss the cup of tea. We miss the sound of the water flowing into the cup, the image of steam gently rising, the aroma of fresh herbs steeping in hot liquid, the rich color, the soft, comfortable soothing of the throat. As we rush to probe the deeper, hidden meanings, the delicacy of these simple moments is lost.

In Search of Simplicity

When we become habituated to seeking out high drama, intrigued by the infinite complexity of things, we often overlook the simple power of a single action, a simple word, or an uncomplicated gesture. We feel that nothing of importance is ever obvious, and the value of any truth lies in how difficult it is to find. We take pride in the complexity of our minds, drawing comfort from our ability to look past appearances and seek out the real, hidden truth. We gradually adopt a hierarchy in our perception of reality: The more complex or dramatic an event, the more we believe in its intrinsic value. But as we constantly elevate the levels of drama and complexity in our lives, we become blind to the gifts and blessings that may arise when we approach the world more simply.

Once a young Anglo man wanted to share the wonders of civilization with his adopted Navajo father, who had never seen a paved road or a skyscraper. One day he showed his father a picture of the Empire State Building. As he went on and on about the building's architectural intricacies and other exceptional qualities, his father interrupted him to ask, "How many sheep will it hold?"

The young man, caught up in the exhilarating complexity of architectural accomplishment, missed something that his Navajo father saw instantly. It is the Navajo way to gauge the value of things in the simplest terms. Neither distracted nor impressed by dramatic details, the old shepherd sought first to know how well it would hold sheep.

Raised in drama and complexity, we lose our ability to see with a simple eye. We are quickly bored with people and events that do not involve some great intrigue or spectacle. Companions that fail to provide us with grist for our melodrama soon appear dull and uninteresting. Ensnared by the tyranny of high drama, our hearts begin to lose interest in what is plain and unadorned.

Yet the things that are simple—the touch of a child's hand on our cheek, the color of the sky at sunset, the smell of rain in the summer, the taste of a fresh piece of fruit—in a moment of awareness, these things can vibrate with something deep and true in our hearts. Many spiritual practices are grounded in the wisdom and beauty of this simplicity. In Buddhism, for example, students of meditation are taught to become aware of the rising and falling of the breath. Nothing more dramatic or complex than this is necessary to begin cultivating deep mindfulness. Watching the breath, attending to the sensations as it rises and falls within our body, we may experience tremendous peace and serenity. Similarly, in Christianity, the very center of practice is the act of Communion, which consists of sharing with others a small piece of bread and a sip of wine. Many of the highest sacraments are acts of extraordinary simplicity.

Yet our hearts mistrust simplicity. When love is given only with secret conditions, the mind of the child learns to analyze every gift for its hidden meaning. Every act is a Trojan horse, every word wears a disguise. As our eye seeks to expose the hidden complexity of every moment, how can we learn to see with an eye that is simple and clear?

The Difficulty of Simplicity

Even if we decide to let go of complexity and high drama, we may find we have become quite attached to how complicated we are. Not only have we learned to see the *world* as complicated, but we take some pride in our *own* complexity. Our self-esteem is bolstered by how difficult we are to understand, how complex and subtle our problems are, how our particular lives are exceptionally intricate and difficult to unravel.

We take comfort in our complexity, seeing ourselves as *especially* broken, *exceptionally* wounded, *unfathomably* troubled. We use our high levels of internal complexity to grant ourselves permission to take a great deal of time with our own healing—for how can we be expected to change or get well when our problems are so complicated and difficult to understand? The practices and solutions that work for others will certainly fail in our case, because our dilemmas are far more complex than everyone else's. Theirs are simple; ours are intricate, delicate, and in need of special attention.

Frances's parents divorced when she was quite young. She lived with her mother, but her father would regularly visit, often taking her to the park for the afternoon. Since her dad suffered from a variety of mental distresses, the visits often ended badly; inevitably there would be something that would anger or upset him. Then, he would order Frances back into the car and drive her straight home, leave her on the front porch, and drive away without a word. Frances, who loved him very much, would be left feeling hurt and confused.

As an adult, Frances felt uneasy about who she was deep inside, and said she was afraid she would never be able to figure herself out. Love, safety, affection, trust—it was all so complicated. The exchange of care seemed so complex, it was almost impossible. In despair, she would often just give up trying and retreat to her apartment, feeling sad and lonely for days at a time.

We worked for several months on the painful residue of her childhood, analyzing the messages she received from her father, and trying to listen for the ways she thought about love. There came a point in our work where I suggested she might begin to meditate. I suggested she use the practice of mindful breathing to begin to let go of some of these old, complicated stories and to start to make a loving home for herself in her own body. To my surprise, tears came to her eyes at the suggestion, and she said she felt terribly hurt.

"When you ask me to try to meditate, it feels like you aren't seeing me, that you don't see how painful and delicate my problems are. How can I make you understand that these aren't normal problems, they are much more subtle than that? I thought you could see how complicated and difficult my feelings are, but when you tell me to just meditate, it sounds too simple. It feels like you don't see me at all."

Frances had learned to find some comfort and solace in the difficulty and complexity of her life. Even though she felt lonely and isolated in her pain, the complex nature of her distress had become an ally, a companion on her journey. Things as simple as a caring touch, a safe family, or a father's love were unimaginable to her; things were more complicated than that. She did not believe anything so simple could heal her, and she mistrusted anyone who suggested that it could.

So we wait for a healing that, if it comes, will be dramatic and complex, one that matches the complicated nature of our distress. A single word or touch, a healing breath, the simple honesty of a loving moment—these feel impotent and inadequate. In the face of our inner complexity, we feel powerless; things about us are just too complicated. We cannot be held responsible for our distress; try as we may, it is just too large to be healed. Thus we wash our hands of our own destiny.

"Perhaps if you just gave me a lobotomy," Joseph said to me, "it would be so much easier." Whenever we would reach a tender place in our work together, Joseph would kiddingly suggest a lobotomy. His life felt so complicated and difficult to figure out, it seemed like an excellent solution to his problems. One cut of the knife and all would be well.

Ironically, this was not an unusual request. Many others besides Joseph had jokingly requested a "lobotomy" over the years, particularly when the process of their healing seemed slow or painful. What strikes me about the "lobotomy" approach is that it is inherently theatrical, using high drama as the ultimate cure. "What I have," each seems to say, "is not merely pain and discomfort. What I have is a powerful, incurable, rampantly complex, and invincible toxic emotional malfunction that is totally out of control. It will require special surgery, powerful magic, all the skill of Western medicine, and a few miracles to put me back together, because what I have is especially, terribly complicated."

At some point we must ask ourselves, are we willing to be healed? Seduced by the infinite puzzle of our own pathology, we often resist any healing available to us that utilizes the simplicity of common words, colors, and gestures. Yet if we continue to take pride in the uniqueness of our individual drama, we may be destined to wander in isolation, frustration, and disappointment. If we can surrender our addiction to complexity, perhaps we may be persuaded that we are simply human beings and we all have pain, we all have sorrow, and we all hurt.

Sometimes we become infatuated with the stories we weave around our sorrows: We hurt because of this, and then that happened and that hurt me, and then I hurt because of this next thing, and on and on. When someone speaks to me in this way about their pain, I often stop them and ask that they just say, "I hurt." Nothing more, no explanations, simply, "I hurt." So many times when we speak this simply, the tears come freely and easily. Released from the stories and interpretations we have grafted onto our pain, when we say "I hurt," there is nothing in the way, no complications, just simple sorrow. It feels like such a relief, such a blessing. Even pain can feel like a blessing when it is shared simply and clearly.

There is a song about simplicity that comes from the Shaker community. Many of us learn it as children:

'Tis a gift to be simple, 'tis a gift to be free,
'Tis a gift to come down where we ought to be.
And when we find ourselves in a place just right,
We will be in the valley of love and delight.

The Problem of Meaning

Another hindrance to the practice of simplicity is our belief that everything of value must be infused with many levels of meaning. Raised in family distress, we learn to look for the reason behind every gesture: Why were the blinds down, why did he hang up his coat that way, why did she say that, and what did she mean? Everything anyone said or did held some secret meaning, and we would not feel better until we found out what it was.

We easily become trapped by the desperate "whys" of our childhood. Carol, for example, had grown up in an alcoholic family, and she had done some very good work healing the wounds and making peace with her childhood. Still, she would occasionally find herself caught in some struggle or problem, and would come to me and say, "I am so disappointed in myself. I thought I had all this stuff figured out—and here I am, back at the beginning. Why do I do this? How come I keep getting caught in the same places? What is wrong with me? Why can't I ever figure this out for good?"

Each time she felt stuck, Carol would beat herself with endless "whys"—why did I, why am I, why can't I? I would gently remind her that pain and sorrow would probably always be a part of her life, that they were just part of the deal. The fact that she felt hurt, stuck, or angry might not *mean* anything about her, her family, or her childhood. It might simply be pain, fear, or anger—ordinary human feelings arising in an ordinary human being. These were simply her shares in the sorrows of being human, feelings she had observed in herself a thousand times before.

After a while, Carol could allow herself to let go of questioning and blaming, and we would both laugh at how easy it was to get caught wanting to know "why" before we could let anything painful or unpleasant fall away. In our quest for the meaning of every little blip on the screen of our life, we often find ourselves trapped and mired, wandering about in endless, meaningless detail, searching for the elusive "why" that will lead us to freedom.

Once a man sought the Buddha to ask him a number of questions about the meaning of life. Namely, was the universe eternal or not; was it finite or infinite; was the soul the same or different from the body? and other such things. He said, "If the Buddha can explain these to me, I will stay and follow him. If he cannot, I will see that he is not the Blessed One, and I will leave."

The Buddha heard of this, and called the man to him and told him a story. "Suppose a man is wounded by a poisoned arrow, and his friends bring him to a surgeon. Suppose the man should then say: I will not let this arrow be taken out until I know who shot me; what his name and family may be; whether he is tall, short, or of medium stature; whether he is black, brown, or golden; and from which city or village he comes. I will not let this arrow be taken out until I know the kind of bow with which I was shot; the kind of bowstring and arrow; what type of feather and with what kind of material the point of the arrow was made." The Buddha said to him, "Surely that man would die without knowing any of these things." Whatever one believes about these problems, said the Buddha, you will still have birth, old age, death, sorrow, and pain. If you insist on knowing the reason "why" before you begin, you will surely die. Knowing why is not always useful. Sometimes we must just begin our practice—learning to remove the arrow—so that we may be set free.

This clarity of action is illustrated by a famous Japanese haiku:

> Old pond.
> Frog jumps in.
> Plop!

As adults, we rarely allow a frog to jump in an old pond. We have to know why it jumped, how it got there, what else happened, and what it all means before we feel comfortable letting the frog jump into the water.

Similarly, in the process of personal growth and childhood exploration, we often insist on deciphering all the problematic levels of our lives before we allow ourselves to be healed. We hold our childhoods hostage, waiting to wring from them the many levels of meaning, all the answers to the riddles of our lives, before we claim the right and the courage to live freely and abundantly. Thomas Merton once said that many of us waste precious time exploring the complexity of who we are, and who we have been, before we allow ourselves to be healed. "There are no levels," he said. "Any moment you can break through into the underlying unity which is God."

The Seeds of Simplicity

In order to develop a simple eye, we must shed our belief that only things that are dramatic have real value, and that the true meaning of things lies within their complexity. Only then can we begin to discover that simple things can have great power. One small measure of yeast can leaven an entire loaf of bread. A single mustard seed can grow into a tree of grand proportions. Suzuki Roshi stresses the value of simple attention: "For Zen students a weed, which for most people is worthless, is a treasure. With this attitude, whatever you do, life becomes an art."

William Blake echoes this call to attend to the smallest details:

> To see a World in a Grain of Sand
> And a Heaven in a Wild Flower.
> Hold Infinity in the palm of your hand,
> And Eternity in an hour.

Simple acts can become seeds planted in the garden of our lives. Everything that grows requires a seed of some kind. The seed starts the process, inviting the miracle of growth to come to full flower. The seed is simply a teacher; by itself, it cannot make anything grow. It also needs earth, air, sun, and water to blossom and bring forth fruit. The power of the seed is that it has the information; it knows the story. It knows the story of this plant, this organism, this being—and it can teach that story to the earth, the air, the sun, and the water. The seed serves as a patient storyteller, and, having heard the story, the four elements galvanize and repeat the story, again and again, cell by cell, slowly, patiently, until the story comes true— tangibly, improbably, inexplicably true.

Like the planting of a seed, the repetition of a single act can give birth to a new way of life, a new way of being. At the height of the campaign for Indian independence, Gandhi took a spinning wheel and began to spin. He said that if everyone began to spin their own cotton, the simple act of industry and creativity could spark the dreams of a nation. That spinning wheel became a seed that blossomed in the hearts of an entire people.

A solitary act like the spinning of cotton, the repetition of a short prayer, or the making of a cup of tea can become a seed of great healing. When we spend a few moments attending to something as uncomplicated as the rising and falling of our breath, our attention becomes more focused, we become relaxed, and our minds feel clearer. By attending to the experience of the simple acts of breathing, speaking, touching, and walking, we allow new experiences to take birth in our lives and hearts, experiences far less dramatic and complex than those of our childhoods.

Every act we perform with mindfulness and care may plant a seed of awakening. The Buddhists say that even chopping wood and carrying water can lead us to healing and enlightenment if we bring them our full and loving attention. As Mother Teresa has said, "We do no great things; we do only small things, with great love."

The Practice of Simplicity

On a trip to South America I was blessed with an opportunity to study with Gustavo Gutierrez, a Peruvian priest who is deeply loved and honored for developing a theology of liberation for the poor and oppressed in Latin America. Sitting at the Catholic University in a room filled with eager, young Peruvians anxious to serve those in need, I listened to Father Gutierrez speak about Jesus' beginnings.

"The experts all said, 'Nothing good will ever come from Galilee.' Galilee was small and rural, much too primitive a place to give birth to anything of great significance. They all insisted that the Messiah, when he came, would come from a place of glory, a family of honor and sophistication. This is why, when Jesus was born in a manger and raised in tiny Galilee, no one recognized that God had been born in their midst.

"So, too," he continued, "they now say that nothing of value can come from the poor of Latin America, of Africa, of Asia. But do not let them discourage you—for the spirit of God is everywhere."

When our eye is attuned only to things dramatic, sophisticated, or spectacular, we may miss the birth of something strong, simple, and beautiful right in front of us. We are shrouded in detail, protected from direct contact with the spirit of life. But as we learn to watch the breath, the seed, the cup of tea, or the newly born, we begin to appreciate the tremendous power of the spirit that takes form in all life.

When we begin spiritual practice, some of us expect dramatic transformations and dream of exquisite experiences of enlightenment. In one Buddhist monastery there is a sign near the kitchen that announces: "Pots and pans are Buddha's body." This reminds us that each and every object, every act of lifting, washing, drying, and cleaning, however small or insignificant, is a part of our practice, a path of enlightenment. Jesus echoed this teaching when he said that the one who is mindful in the small things will be mindful also of the greater things.

It is not easy to undertake a practice of simplicity. We tend to want our journey to be more glamorous, our meditations exhilarating, our progress showy and impressive. Even while we are meditating we are considering how well we are doing; while praying, we often secretly critique our spiritual growth since the last time we prayed. Sujata said: "A saint is a very simple person: When they walk, they walk. When they talk, they talk, and that's all. They don't think while listening, daydream while walking, see while touching.

"That is very hard. That is why they are saints."

There is a story of a Zen Roshi who always taught his students to practice simplicity of action and attention: When you eat, just eat; when you walk, just walk. One morning, a student found him at breakfast, eating cereal and reading the paper. The student was confused, and confronted the Roshi.

"You always tell us to act simply, to pay attention: When you eat, just eat; when you walk, just walk. Why are you here at the breakfast table right now, eating cereal and reading the paper at the same time?"

The Roshi smiled at the young student and said, "That, too, is simple. You see, when you eat and read—just eat and read."

The practice of simplicity asks that we pay attention. As we walk, eat, move, and speak, we simply bring our awareness to each moment. If we fully attend to the act of grasping a cup of tea, or speaking a single word of kindness, it can help us to become awake in this moment. If we are alive in this instant, it is much harder to view this moment through the lens of our childhood. If we spend our time *thinking about* this moment, we can get caught analyzing how this moment reflects our childhood. But if we simply *experience* this moment, noting the experience of walking, breathing, and touching, then we are free of our history, more fully alive.

Ralph Waldo Emerson wrote: "Whenever a mind is simple, it is able to receive divine wisdom; old things pass away; it lives now and absorbs past and future into the present hour." In the simplicity of the present moment, he asserts, all things take on new life, all things become powerful, rich, even sacred.

"Go confidently in the direction of your dreams," urged Henry David Thoreau. "As you simplify your life, the laws of the universe will be simpler." Every moment we may try to simplify our lives. With each conversation, with every thought, every plan, every step, we may try to become aware—are we moving toward complexity or simplicity? What can we let go, how can we live more simply? What can we do to engage others more directly, how may we approach our day with more attention to the simple moments of being fully alive?

Thich Nhat Hanh teaches his students the practice of simplicity of attention by encouraging them to notice every step they take. Is it quick or slow? Hard or gentle? Tentative or sure? Attentive or thoughtless? Here he describes the simple Buddhist practice of walking meditation:

> Place your foot on the surface of the earth the way an emperor would place his seal on a royal decree.
>
> A royal decree can bring happiness or misery to people. It can shower grace on them or it can ruin their lives. Your steps can do the same. If your steps are peaceful, the world will have peace. If you can take one peaceful step, you can take two. You can take one hundred and eight peaceful steps.

EXERCISE
Walking Meditation

In this exercise we use walking as a way to practice simplicity of attention. Normally when we walk, we are trying to get from one place to another, using our walking to help us accomplish some task. Perhaps we are rushing to an appointment, walking through a store as we do our shopping, or perhaps we are jogging to keep ourselves fit. For now we will walk simply to walk, to experience the sensation of walking.

You may do this meditation inside or outdoors. Begin by finding a place to stand quietly, centering your attention in the body. After a moment, begin walking very slowly, at a fraction of your normal walking speed. Allow each step to take a few seconds. Find a comfortable pace that is not so slow that you feel off-balance, yet not so fast that it is difficult to focus your attention on each step. The object is not to get somewhere, but to observe what it feels like to be walking.

Let yourself become aware of three distinct movements contained in each step you take. The first movement occurs when you lift your foot up from the earth. As your foot rises off the ground, note silently to yourself, "lifting." The second movement is "moving," when you move your foot through the air as you step forward. Again, as this happens, note "moving." Last, as you place your foot on the ground and complete the step, note "placing."

As you walk slowly forward, allow your eyes to rest on a spot a few feet ahead of you. The object is not to look from side to side as you would when you took a stroll in the park. The point of this meditation is to experience the many sensations that arise when you simply use your body to walk, one step at a time. Walking mindfully straight ahead, after about fifteen feet you may slowly turn around, noting "turning," and return back to your original point. If the mind wanders, gently return your attention to the sensations of lifting, moving, and placing. You may repeat this cycle as many times as you like.

Be aware of the unique qualities of each movement. Feel the simplicity of each action as you lift, move, and place your foot on the ground. Feel the sensations that arise with each movement. What do you notice? Do this exercise for fifteen minutes. Notice what happens to the quality of your concentration. Later, you may extend the practice to half an hour.

When you have become comfortable and familiar with the walking meditation, you may expand the practice to include other bodily movements you use every day. Choose a simple, regular activity that you usually perform on "automatic pilot." Resolve to make that particular activity a meditation for the week, a reminder to wake up, to cultivate simplicity of attention. For example, you may choose making tea, washing the dishes, cleaning the house, or taking a bath. Before each activity, pause for a few seconds and resolve to perform this act with full attention, noting each simple movement as it arises: pouring, wiping, rubbing, drying. Allow the simplicity of each gesture to hold its own integrity.

Here, we begin to value each act not because it gets something done, but because the simplicity of the act itself reveals an intrinsic beauty. In this way we begin to invite a deep appreciation for the simple things that grace our everyday lives.

EXERCISE
Exploring a Life of Simplicity

Arrange for some time to sit in your place of refuge, in front of your table. Allow yourself to become calm and quiet, using the breath to settle yourself into your body and heart.

Then, in a simple way, review your current life. Bring to mind each of several major areas, including your work, your relationships or family life, your finances, your leisure activities, your possessions, your goals, and your spiritual life. One by one, as each area comes to mind, ask yourself the following questions: What would it be like to simplify this part of my life? What could I let go, what could I do to make this part of my life more quiet and simple?

Allow the images and responses to arise in your mind. Continue to sit quietly, reflecting on the choices before you. Notice which feel immediately comfortable and which feel difficult or frightening. The object is not necessarily to change anything immediately. In this moment you are just noting where you desire more simplicity in your life and becoming aware of which changes you may consider to make room for that simplicity. Take as much time as you need with each part of your life, becoming aware of whatever steps you might take. Then make a resolution to begin making mindful changes in each area.

CHAPTER EIGHT

Busyness and Stillness

In his poem "Keeping Quiet," Chilean poet Pablo Neruda invites a moment of stillness:

> Now we will count to twelve
> and we will all keep still.
>
> For once on the face of the
> earth,
> let's not speak in any language
> let's stop for a second,
> and not move our arms so much.
>
> It would be an exotic moment
> without rush, without engines;
> we would all be together
> in a sudden strangeness . . .

Wait for a moment, says Neruda; let us listen. Our lives are infected with a chronic, continuous rush to movement, a habitual and constant busyness. We are forever speaking too much, moving our arms about, filling time and space. We are saturated with busyness; our lives spin faster and faster, keeping pace with the accelerating world around us. Let us stop a moment, he says, let us rest a while in stillness. Let us explore ourselves and one another in the quiet. Perhaps we may hear more clearly the still, small voices of our souls.

As children, when we felt overwhelmed by our family pain, we learned to run from that pain. We learned to move faster, to hide ourselves from intimate contact, to make ourselves moving targets, harder to hit. We even used high drama to shield ourselves from the quiet hurts that punctuated our lives together. Remaining still, we felt too vulnerable and exposed; motion became a defense, our strategy to protect ourselves from the assault of family suffering. The faster we moved, the less we could be seen and known, the more invisible we were, and the safer we felt. We took refuge in speed, productivity, and busyness; camouflaged by relentless activity, we never lingered in one place long enough to be caught.

In our families, moments of stillness and silence were rare. When things were quiet, it would often portend some sleeping crisis that was brewing beneath the surface. In a moment of quiet, when we were unoccupied with some diversionary activity, any of our latent family sorrows, festering disputes, or lingering discomforts were liable to erupt in some kind of fighting or drama. So we all ran from the stillness; it felt too unpredictable, too dangerous. We learned to quickly fill those quiet moments with expedient activities to distract ourselves and everyone else from the kinds of feelings that could arise in stillness. We made ourselves busy with some task, diversion, or drama, immersing ourselves in planning, thinking, arranging—anything that would muffle the tender voices, fears, and sorrows that occupied our hearts.

Rare were the moments when our family could sit together quietly, listening to the gentle, quiet serenity of simply being family. More likely, we would find ourselves in the middle of some potential catastrophe that would send us all scurrying around in frenzied reaction, strategizing, or defensive maneuvering. As activity and busyness became our primary vocation, we gradually lost our ability to listen carefully to the deeper, gentler truths about ourselves. Our speed and activity deafened us to the delicate yearnings of our hearts and spirits.

Our desperate activity could also mask fear or emptiness. We were afraid to stop, to listen too closely to our own insides. We were frightened by the stillness, wary of those moments when we were alone with ourselves, empty and quiet. Maybe we were afraid we would be confronted by something dark and terrible within ourselves—or, even worse, perhaps we would discover what was missing, some dark hole, some ache deep inside that could not be filled. And so, rather than get quiet and listen, we learned to keep moving.

Some of us also used speed and productivity in our campaign to justify our worth. We learned to work very hard to earn our place, to be allowed to belong somewhere, and, as adults, we frantically continue to accomplish more and more, seeking elusive approval from all the surrogate parents and siblings that populate our busy lives. We fear we have not yet accomplished enough to deserve our place, so we push ourselves harder and faster, taking on additional projects and responsibilities in a desperate drive toward acceptability.

And so we find it hard to settle into quiet. When we approach a moment of stillness, our first impulse is to run, to generate activities, to explain ourselves, to point to some accomplishment, to distract ourselves at any cost. As we explore the practice of stillness, we inevitably encounter two distinct forms of restlessness: The first is a restlessness of the body, and the second is a restlessness of speech.

Restlessness of the Body

We lead very busy lives. Whether we are doctors, laborers, artists, teachers, waitresses, priests, cooks, or counselors, we all like to feel that what we do is valuable and good. Each of us does our best to be reliable, productive, and helpful to our families, friends, and neighbors. But in our desperate rush to be productive, we may take on more and more, until our work becomes overwhelming and our enthusiasm and vitality become stifled by a frantic busyness that threatens to choke our spirit.

"There is more to life," said Gandhi, "than increasing its speed." Many of us believe that speed will actually set us free: The more we can impress and satisfy others, the more we get done, the better we will feel. The more we accomplish, the more we will feel like we deserve to be here and the closer we will feel to a sense of serenity. But of course we are never quite done. We refuse to rest, claiming there is too much to do, too many people to see. Our work is so important and our responsibilities so critical that to leave anything at all undone would be irresponsible and unthinkable.

One of the dangers of busyness and overwork is that we lose the capacity to listen closely to what our work is really about. In our rush of movement, we forget our gifts, we lose touch with our talents and intuitions, we become deaf to our genuine, inner wisdom. Thomas Merton says that when we succumb to this busyness, we are actually giving birth to a subtle form of violence:

There is a pervasive form of contemporary violence . . . [and that is] activism and overwork. The rush and pressure of modern life are a form, perhaps the most common form, of its innate violence.

To allow oneself to be carried away by a multitude of conflicting concerns, to surrender to too many demands, to commit oneself to too many projects, to want to help everyone in everything, is to succumb to violence.

The frenzy of our activism neutralizes our work for peace. It destroys our own inner capacity for peace. It destroys the fruitfulness of our own work, because it kills the root of inner wisdom which makes work fruitful.

Brother David Steindl-Rast reminds us that the Chinese word for "busy" is composed of two characters: "heart" and "killing." When we make ourselves so busy that we are always rushing around trying to get this or that "done," or "over with," we kill something vital in ourselves, and we smother the quiet wisdom of our heart. When we invest our work with judgment and impatience, always striving for speed and efficiency, we lose the capacity to appreciate the million quiet moments that may bring us peace, beauty, or joy. As we seek salvation through our frantic productivity and accomplishments, we squander the teachings that may be present in this very moment, in the richness of this particular breath.

In the Book of Ecclesiastes, there is a proverb: "Better one hand full of quiet than two hands full of striving after wind." Unpracticed in the art of quiet, we hope to find our safety, our belonging, and our healing by increasing our levels of accomplishment. But our frantic busyness actually makes us deaf to what is healing and sacred, both in ourselves and in one another.

Restlessness of Speech

Just as speed can muffle the voices of the spirit, so can excess speech distract us from our inner wisdom. As children, we learned to use language as a weapon for our defense. We used language to explain, to justify, and to defend ourselves and our behavior. We used words to soothe and cajole, to manipulate and impress. We learned to listen for what our parents wanted to hear and quickly manufacture whatever words or phrases would satisfy them. We used language as a vehicle for convincing the world of our importance, our talents, and our worth.

We came to use language more often to mask the truth than to reveal it. It hardly mattered if what we said was *true,* the important thing was to get people to *believe* it was true. Our words were designed to manipulate and placate those we felt could hurt us. We wove whatever stories seemed required, using whatever speech necessary to create an acceptable impression for those around us. "Yes, I love you, Daddy," we would say, whether we meant it or not. If asked, we would fearfully insist, "No, I'm not scared"; out of our pain, we would courageously reply, "That's okay, it doesn't hurt." Language became our first line of defense against pain; only infrequently would we use it to reveal the truth.

When we habitually employ language to tailor the appearance of reality, altering and fabricating our words to satisfy everyone's changing demands, we gradually lose our capacity to hear our own truth. We manufacture so many explanations about ourselves that we can no longer discern which are fabrications and which are true.

We also use speech to keep us from feeling alone. When we speak, we are always engaged, enmeshed in the thoughts and feelings of others. As children, we learned to use speech as a vehicle to engage our parents, hoping to disarm them with our reason, our arguments, and our cleverness and wit. If we could keep them talking, we might be able to postpone any significant danger. Consequently, we usually feel most safe when we have the verbal cooperation of those around us.

In silence, we feel more alone. Keeping silent, we cannot count on the approval of others, since we are never sure what they are thinking about us. Without language, we are cut off from any external reassurance that all is well. Without this constant stream of information, we may quickly become apprehensive, worried, and frightened of the unknown.

A few years ago, Ron came to one of our retreats. As always, we asked people to spend the first morning in silence. When we emerged from this silence, Ron said: "This was the first time in my life I have ever been around quiet people who weren't angry. In my family, when everyone was quiet it meant someone was furious, or somebody was going to get hit. I couldn't believe how it felt this morning to be sitting next to everyone, eating breakfast, with nobody saying anything—and nobody was angry at me. At first I was terrified. Then, when I realized I was safe, it felt great. It was incredible."

Excess speech can serve to perpetuate our restlessness. Psychiatric researcher Dr. James Lynch discovered that the mere act of speaking actually elevates our blood pressure—from a ten- to fifty-point increase—after less than thirty seconds of everyday, nonangry, conversational speech. The simple act of speaking actually brings about a certain level of tension in our bodies, which is then reflected in elevated blood pressure. He says it appears to be "a normal reflex."

Brevity and simplicity of language can help us cultivate a place of inner stillness. Yet increasingly we find ourselves manufacturing more and more words to compensate for the stillness we feel we have lost. Someone once noted that the Lord's Prayer contained 56 words, the Twenty-third Psalm 118 words, and the entire Gettysburg Address only 226 words—while the

U.S. Department of Agriculture directive on pricing cabbage contained 15,629 words. One could easily conclude that we place a higher value on pricing cabbage than on liberty, prayer, or serenity. Nevertheless, we have certainly become drenched in a sea of words that have lost their meaning.

Stillness and Healing

As children, we used speed and activity to bring safety and relief. If we believe that healing will come through our own effort and activity, we will be suspicious of any healing that arises out of stillness. Yet many cultures and healing systems honor the power of rest, meditation, stillness, and silence to cultivate the healing process. How can we expect healing to occur if we refuse to allow for a rhythm between activity and stillness in our lives?

As busy people, our natural inclination when seeking a path of healing is to choose a method that involves a great deal of analysis and effort. We tend to gravitate toward healing practices that diagnose something dark and broken within us, something that may be exorcised only through a tremendous amount of work on our part. If we do enough therapy, read enough books, go to enough workshops, and put together an extensive therapeutic résumé, perhaps we can gather enough treatment credits to be granted some kind of healing diploma. Only by working extra hard at fixing ourselves do we feel we can earn the right to be set free of our suffering.

Our predisposition to busyness makes us feel much more comfortable when we can undertake some activity. We are wary of healing practices that speak of inner balance, practices that prescribe being quiet, sitting still, doing nothing. Simply sitting quietly with ourselves, we tend to feel our pain more acutely, we experience the depth and texture of our broken heart, we feel the poignant sting of tears yet to be shed. In stillness, without the distraction of being busy, we touch our inner landscape with excruciating intimacy, and we may feel for the first time the extent to which our tender feelings have been bruised.

So we are reluctant to be still. But at the same time, if we will allow our hearts and minds to surrender into a quiet stillness, we may discover that all we have been seeking is already here within ourselves, within our spirit. If we have been looking for peace, we may find peace; if we have been looking for healing, we may find healing; if we have sought God, we may find the kingdom of God alive and well within our very hearts. Perhaps there is nothing to do, no place to go—everything we seek is already here.

The last place we tend to look for healing is within ourselves. The longer we sit with ourselves and the closer we get to the root of our sorrow, the more dangerous it feels. We are ashamed of who we are and frightened of who we may be, so we use a smoke screen of activity to mask our insides.

But perhaps our greatest healing comes only when we listen quietly and carefully to ourselves and our sorrow. Maybe there is nothing for us to take out, nothing to fix, nothing to do but mindfully touch our heart and spirit with quiet, loving attention. Merely by sitting still, we may feel the love that God already has for us, even explore the love we have for ourselves. Here, we may taste of the grace that already fills our being, and drink from the strength that already exists in the tenderest places of our heart.

Thomas Merton writes:

> Be still
> Listen to the stones of the wall
> Be silent, they try
> To speak your
>
> Name.
> Listen
> To the living walls.
> Who are you?
> Who
> Are You? . . .

Who are we? Desperate for an answer, we rush to discover and define ourselves through analysis, therapy, activities, accomplishments, and successes. Yet when we allow ourselves to be still, we invite a different kind of knowing, we allow our intuition to uncover those small and secret truths that lie deep within us. Most of us spend our lives carrying a host of questions and problems around with us—questions that, in the quiet wisdom of our deepest heart, may already have been answered. In stillness, we can hear the accuracy of our intuition; in silence we can hear the still, small voice of our spirit, teaching us what is true, reminding us of what is necessary, what is healing. There rests deep within us a clear voice that knows our deepest heart. Confusion arises only when we are too busy or distracted to listen. "Be still," says the psalmist, "and know that I am God."

"Who is there that can make muddy water clear?" asks the Tao Te Ching. "But if allowed to remain still, it will gradually become clear of itself." Many spiritual traditions speak of a time in our healing when there is nothing left for us to do, nothing more we may accomplish with our own will or our own strategies. Here, we must surrender to the healing teachings that arise only when we become still and silent. This is the moment when God inevitably "leads us beside the still waters, and restores our soul." "Still water," says Chuang Tzu, "is like glass . . . it is a perfect level. If water is so clear, so level, how much more the spirit of man. The heart of the wise man is tranquil, it is the mirror of heaven and earth . . . Emptiness, stillness, tranquility, silence, nonaction . . . this is the perfect Tao. Wise men here find their resting place."

In stillness we may recover our strength and wisdom; in the quiet of nonaction, we are led to what would give us spiritual nurture. Meister Eckhart, the fourteenth-century Christian mystic, said that "nothing in all creation is so like God as stillness."

Sharing and Silence

How do we overcome our fear of quiet? Addicted to busyness and activity, we fear stillness and silence the way we fear death—we feel terrified of letting go, surrendering into unknown emptiness and sorrow, afraid of what will arise out of the quiet formlessness.

First of all, we need not choose between activity or stillness. It is not one or the other, not a decision to have a life of speech or a life of silence. Rather, our task is to attend to the rhythm between the two. There is a balance in our lives between action and stillness, between speaking and keeping quiet. When we are sensitive to that rhythm, allowing it to guide us, we are able to gain tremendous healing from sharing the contents of our heart—while we may also benefit from being still and silent. "There is a time for every purpose under heaven," says the preacher in Ecclesiastes, "a time to be born, and a time to die; a time to keep silence, and a time to speak."

The Desert Fathers and Mothers, fleeing the orthodoxy of the larger church, adopted simple styles of living, and their spiritual practices consisted of prayer, service, and quiet contemplation. They believed that the soul was kindled with heat from deep within us, and so one should try not to dilute the inner fire with excess speech:

When the door of the steam bath is continually left open, the heat inside rapidly escapes through it; likewise the soul, in its desire to say many things, dissipates its remembrance of God through the door of speech, even though everything it says may be good.

Thereafter the intellect, though lacking appropriate ideas, pours out a welter of confused thoughts to anyone it meets . . . Timely silence, then, is precious, for it is nothing less than the master of the wisest thoughts.

Interestingly, many contemporary treatment communities have come to associate healing not with silence but with speech. Programs that treat childhood and family dysfunction correctly stress the need for speaking from our heart, for sharing our story and our hurts with others. Children whose feelings were ignored or repressed need to feel encouraged to name safely the delicate and tender scarrings of their heart. When silence has been enforced by terror, as we speak the truth of our childhood our wounds begin to open, to breathe, and to heal. We feel less alone, less ashamed, and more part of the human family when we share our deepest feelings in communion with others.

But at the same time, as we rush to rectify the silences of the past, emphasizing the healing properties of "sharing," we sometimes relinquish the power of stillness and quiet as a vital part of healing. In our contemporary culture, "sharing" is prescribed as a cure for all ills. We are taught that all our feelings, emotions, and quiet stirrings of the soul are only valuable when they are shared with others. Expressions such as "thanks for sharing this with me" or "it was good to share that with you" show that the door to our steam bath is expected to be open most of the time. Thus, our current model of enforced sharing may prove as hurtful and tyrannical as the model of enforced silence. When we were told we had to hide our feelings, we felt imprisoned from within; if we are now forced to always share our feelings, we may feel imprisoned from without.

Right Speech

When we do speak, how much do we share, and how often? Must we be speaking all the time, and must we tell everything we know? How may we speak what is deep and true with others, yet not be overcome with a busyness of speech that distracts us from our deeper, quieter wisdom? The Lankavatara Sutra, an ancient Buddhist text, says that if we are not careful, we may find ourselves "stuck in words like an elephant in the mud."

The Buddha taught that when we do speak, we should choose our words carefully, speaking only what is most loving and true. He instructed his disciples to practice "right speech," that is, to refrain from using language to tell lies, to harm another, to create disharmony, or to engage in useless babble. Right speech is benevolent and gentle, meaningful and useful. One should not speak carelessly, said the Buddha. We should speak only at the right time and place, and if what we have to say is not useful, we may keep "noble silence."

Once there was a man who was very sick, and his friends and family were gathered around him. They had been attending to him for a long time, taking him to see all manner of physicians and healers, all to no avail. By now, they had given up hope of a cure; they were simply caring for him until he died.

One day a Zen master entered the village, and a crowd of people emerged to greet him. In the crowd was the sick man—his friends had brought him before the master. They asked if he could heal this man. The master looked at him and was silent for a moment. Then he said, "Yes, I can," and he leaned over and spoke a few words to the sick man. He looked up and said to those assembled, "Soon this man will be well."

In the crowd was a close friend of the sick man, someone who had tended to him night and day and knew the desperate nature of the man's condition. He became impatient with the Zen master, uncomfortable with this stranger who would treat this poor man's grave illness with such a simple display. "How can you do this?" he asked. "This man is terribly ill—how can you possibly heal him with just a few words?"

At this, the master turned to the man and scowled. "You know nothing of these matters. You are nothing but an ignorant fool!" he said. Hearing this, the man became furious and filled with rage. His love for his friend and his anger at this stranger brought up tremendous hatred; he turned red in the face, and was about to strike at the master. Just then the Zen master held up his hand and said, "Wait. Look at yourself, and what change has come over you. If a few unkind words from me could bring about such a powerful change in you, could not a few kind words also bring much healing?"

The Practice of Silence

Right speech is born out of mindful silence. When we are still and quiet, we hear more clearly what is true, we appreciate the colors of things, and feel the weight and texture of what we hold in our hands. We feel our steps on the earth, we hear the sound we make as we walk. In silence we are free to expand beyond the habits of childhood, to grow beyond what is already in our thoughts, and to speak more than what is already in our mouths. When we are constantly speaking, we hear only what we have already concluded about ourselves and the world. Silence allows us to discover things about ourselves that we have not yet begun to imagine.

Silence is not simply the absence of speech. Silence has its own integrity, a tangible fertility in which new thoughts and images may arise within us. Our inclination when presented with a problem is to do something about it—to figure it out, to analyze it, to take it apart and work with it. But as you have undoubtedly begun to discover in your quiet meditations, the practice of silence may allow the problem itself to shift, to evolve, to slowly take shape in a new way, allowing a resolution to emerge out of the stillness itself. How many of us have wrestled endlessly with a particular problem, only to have the solution pop into our mind unannounced when we weren't thinking about it at all? Our challenge is to trust in the wisdom within ourselves, to feel there is a trustworthy ally in the deep stillness of our soul. As Seng-ts'an, the third Zen patriarch, explains: "The more you talk about it, the more you think about it, the further from it you go; stop talking, stop thinking, and there is nothing you will not understand."

In silence, the Buddha became enlightened:

> Siddhartha listened. He was now listening intently, completely absorbed, quite empty. Taking in everything. He felt that he had now completely learned the art of listening. He had often heard all this before, all these numerous voices in the river. But today they sounded different.

In silence we hear the "numerous voices in the river." As we learn to listen, we are able to hear more voices, more possibilities, more frequencies. Our ear can receive new sounds, sounds beyond those we grew accustomed to in childhood. When we are quiet, we begin to hear that we are more than just a wounded child, not just wife or husband, son or daughter. We are a crystal with many facets, and in silence we may begin to notice each one more clearly. Only as we allow ourselves to listen quietly can we appreciate the rich abundance of all we are.

As we learn to keep silent, we begin to feel our kinship with the divine spirit within us and to hear the voices of God as they teach us of strength and healing, compassion, peace, and love. Mother Teresa explains:

> We need to find God, and God cannot be found in noise and restlessness. God is the friend of silence. See how nature—trees, flowers, grass—grow in silence; see the stars, the moon and sun, how they move in silence? The more we receive in silent prayer, the more we can give in our active life. We need silence to be able to touch souls.

It is difficult for us to refrain from speech. We use our words so habitually that they are often out of our mouths even before we have thought of speaking. There is a story about four Zen pupils who vowed to observe seven days of silence:

> On the first day they were all silent, and their practice went quite well. But when night came and the lamps were growing dim, one of the pupils could not help exclaiming to a servant, "Fix those lamps."
>
> The second pupil was surprised to hear the first one talk. "We are not supposed to say a word," he remarked.
>
> "You two are stupid. Why did you talk?" asked the third.
>
> "I am the only one who has not talked," concluded the fourth pupil.

The Practice of Stillness

How do we invite stillness into our busy lives? In the Hebrew Bible, the practice of keeping the Sabbath (Shabbat) was designed to establish a rhythm between busyness and stillness, to have one day each week in which we allow our work to fall away and attend to the quieter things of the spirit. According to one Hebrew writer, the Sabbath served

> . . . to disconnect us from our normal attitude of making, doing, and changing . . . To experience the world free from the need to interfere with it is a transformative and liberating experience. But it can't be achieved in the midst of a day filled with getting, spending, speeding, and making.
>
> So we take one solid period of time, twenty-four hours, to change our relationship to the world—to refrain from acting upon it and, instead, to stand back and celebrate the grandeur and mystery of creation . . .
>
> The *Shabbat* has a joyful feeling . . .

In the Christian and Buddhist traditions, followers periodically go on retreat, allowing the cares and responsibilities of daily life to fall away so that they may listen more carefully to the healing, grace, and wisdom born of silence. With each day, with each breath, in prayer and meditation, they quietly attend to the gifts and truths that only germinate when the heart is still.

Others, including many Hindus and Muslims, go on pilgrimage, undertaking a journey to a shrine or holy place. The journey itself becomes a meditation, a time for quiet reflection. With each step, the distractions of daily busyness fall away as they walk a path that takes them ever closer to the Beloved.

We need not wait until we have time for a lengthy retreat or a great pilgrimage. For many of us, a few moments of quiet each day may give birth to a new texture in our lives. As one of the Desert Fathers explained, "There is but one method; to be still with the attention in the heart. All other things are beside the point."

How many quiet moments do we habitually fill with some activity or speech? We may begin to notice isolated moments that arise from time to time, moments in which there is absolutely nothing we need to do or say. We may be sitting on a bus, or standing in line, or find a few unexpected minutes between appointments. Instead of rushing to pick up a magazine or start a conversation, can we simply allow the moment to become silent and still? Perhaps we may close our eyes, or allow our gaze to rest easily on some point in front of us. Then, simply rest in the quiet, observing all the thoughts and sensations that arise. What do we notice? What are the images and feelings that arise? What deeper sensations or thoughts begin to appear after a few moments; which questions or solutions present themselves after only a short period of quiet?

Can we learn to allow the silence, can we feel at ease doing nothing? Notice how often we generate activity for its own sake, how often our speech consists of mindless chatter, how often we use words simply to be included in a conversation or to keep away uncomfortable silences. As the poet Nanao Sakaki wryly remarks,

> If you have time to chatter,
> Read books
> If you have time to read,
> Walk into the mountain, desert and ocean
> If you have time to walk
> Sing songs and dance
> If you have time to dance
> Sit quietly, you Happy Lucky Idiot.

In stillness and silence there is tremendous possibility. Our eyes and ears are more receptive to the voices of the spirit, the teachings that are alive and present in our heart. In this spirit, Pablo Neruda ends his poem, "Keeping Quiet":

> If we were not so single-minded
> about keeping our lives moving,

and for once could do nothing,
perhaps a huge silence
might interrupt this sadness
of never understanding ourselves
and of threatening ourselves
with death.

Perhaps the earth can teach us
as when everything seems dead in winter
and later proves to be alive.

Now I'll count up to twelve
and you keep quiet and I will go.

EXERCISE
The Practice of Mindful Speech

Often we use speech to keep ourselves busy and distracted. We maintain a smoke screen of verbal activity to protect us from the world and to insulate us from our inner feelings.

For one day, we will observe and restructure our habits of speech. First, resolve that for this day you will ask yourself these three questions before you begin a conversation with anyone: Are my words true? Are they necessary? Are they kind? In addition, when you are in conversation with someone, resolve to try not to speak of any person who is not present—in other words, refrain from gossip. If every word you speak must be true, necessary, and kind, you may find yourself speaking far less often.

Observe your impulses to speak. What things are you tempted to talk about? What are some of the hardest things to not *say? What do you notice about how you use language? What does it feel like to keep silent when you normally would have spoken? What feelings or emotions do you notice in the quiet?*

The point of this exercise is not so much to maintain silence but to notice the quality of your speech, how busy it is, and often how unconscious. Undertaking a practice of noticing our speech may lead us to a more mindful use of language. We have a reflexive, immediate impulse to fill our lives with the busyness of speech. As we allow that impulse to recede, we may discover a subtle quieting of the mind and experience a heightened awareness of our inner voices.

Meditation
EXPLORING STILLNESS IN THE BODY

Arrange to have an hour when you will be able to remain alone and undisturbed. You may want to be at home or you may want to be outside, in nature.

This exercise will be used to explore the practices of stillness and silence. Resolve that for one hour you will not speak, read, write, or communicate in any way. You will not do any work, run errands, or get anything done. Your only task is to listen, to observe, and to experience your life without distraction for an entire hour.

You may begin by sitting still. Look around you. What things do you notice about your immediate environment? Are there any objects, shapes, or colors that attract your attention? What do you notice about how your eyes move around the room? Is your gaze searching and deliberate, or more flowing and easy? As you settle into the quiet, what feelings do you notice? Be aware of both the pleasant and unpleasant sensations that arise. What desires do you notice? What impulses do you have, what things do you feel compelled to do? How easy or difficult is it to let those desires go for this moment and relax into the stillness?

After some time, assume a comfortable meditation position and close your eyes. Allow your awareness of the breath to guide you gently into your body. Let the breath show you where you are tight and where you are relaxed. Allow yourself to receive the many sensations of pressure, temperature, texture, speed, and peacefulness that move through you. When a particular sensation becomes predominant, inspect the quality of each feeling: Is it hard or soft, hot or cold, tight, relaxed, or tingling? Notice what happens as you observe it. Does it get stronger or weaker, larger or smaller? Does it begin to dissolve? Make a mental note of the sensation, noting "pressure," "tightness," "pain," etc., until the sensation recedes. Then return to following the rising and falling of the breath. Each time a new body sensation arises, attend to it until it recedes, and return again to the breath.

Notice any impulses to get moving, to get something done, to get up and run. Allow yourself to sit with this meditation for twenty minutes. Then, if you like, you may open your eyes. You may now get up and walk slowly. What do you notice about your body as it moves? How do you decide which direction to turn, where to walk next? Pay attention to how your mind, heart, and body work in concert to propel your body over the ground. With each step, keep listening for any feelings or sensations that arise within you.

At the end of the hour, you may resume your normal daily activity. Be aware of the shift from stillness to movement, from silence to speech, being aware of the changes that occur in the body as you begin moving and speaking. Try to remain aware of the stillness within yourself throughout the day.

EXERCISE
A Day of Silence

Some of us, as we deepen our practice, may wish to spend an entire day in silence. This may be difficult for many, yet it may also expand our capacity to listen more closely to the still, small voices within. This will be a day where you may walk, observe, eat, meditate, and rest if you like. It will be a day to refrain from most other activities, including writing, reading, watching television, drawing, or listening to music.

Because you will not be speaking for the entire day, some advance preparation will be required. Ideally, this day should be spent alone at home or at some retreat setting. If your household circumstances require you to be at home in the presence of other people, arrange with them beforehand to allow you to remain undisturbed by requests for speech or activity. Make sure all your external obligations have been taken care of, acquiring whatever simple food you will need during the day. Feel free to disconnect the telephone.

When you awake on the day of silence, begin your mindfulness even as you get out of bed. Let your normal morning activities, such as washing, brushing your teeth and hair, and getting dressed, become the focus of your awareness. You might try slowing down each activity to observe the process more precisely. Use simple, silent labels to keep your attention focused in the present moment, such as "washing, washing," "dressing, dressing," "eating, eating," etc.

As the day progresses, you will undoubtedly encounter moments of restlessness. Without judging or condemning, observe the sensation of restlessness as it arises in your body. You may feel an overpowering desire to move, to go do something, to get something to eat, to preoccupy yourself with some activity. Temporarily postpone this movement, and observe how it feels to momentarily deny the impulse to become busy. Let yourself sit a moment in stillness before unconsciously jumping up to do anything. Allow any urge to arise at least three times before mindfully acting on it.

Periodically throughout the day, you may wish to meditate in your place of refuge with the breath meditation. Other times, you may simply sit quietly and listen to your body. Let yourself listen for the subtle changes, thoughts, desires, and feelings that wash through your heart and mind as you sit or walk quietly. What do you notice? Your perceptions may reveal new and interesting details about yourself or your home that you normally pass by every day.

Take the time to explore whatever arises in your eyes and ears, in your touch, smell, and taste. When you eat, eat slowly, noting the sensations as you prepare the food, as you chew and swallow your meal, and as you clean up after the meal is finished.

As your usual routine has been slowed considerably, you may become aware of a sense of fatigue. This might in fact be a genuine need for rest, as you finally listen to the tiredness in your body—in which case you may wish to take a short nap.

However, fatigue may also signal a resistance to an unpleasant or painful state of mind or body: You don't wish to feel something unpleasant, so you become sleepy. If you recognize that the sleepy mind is actually a deep reluctance to feel something inside, you can take a few deep breaths, sharpen your concentration, and explore whatever seems to lie beneath the surface of your awareness.

The practice of silence allows one to become quiet and mindful, giving your wholehearted attention to yourself in this moment. This may at times fill you with a sense of joy or well-being, or a feeling of peace. As you become still, you begin to drink from the fullness of your being.

At the end of the day, you may wish to offer a prayer or meditation of thankfulness for the rich fabric of experiences that you received through this time of stillness and silence.

CHAPTER NINE

Disappointment and Nonattachment

We first learn about disappointment when we wish for something that does not come true. When we were small, we may have wished for a new toy or a best friend, a longer summer vacation, or a wonderful adventure. Some of us may have hoped for a different kind of family—for parents who were younger or more playful, or a family that was warmer and more loving. But when our wishes didn't all happen the way we wanted—when our toys, adventures, or parents didn't turn out quite the way we dreamed they would—we felt sad, let down, and disappointed.

As children, we tended to have definite ideas about how things should be: Parents shouldn't fight, mothers should be reliable, fathers shouldn't yell or hit us, families should be caring and happy. We had a powerful sense of what was fair, and we insistently believed that everyone should be kind, that our parents shouldn't be mean, and no one should be angry. The more we experienced our family's hurt, anger, or impatience, the more tightly we held onto our expectation that we should all be more loving. Even as the fabric of our family unraveled in fighting, drinking, or divorce, we secretly continued to expect that somehow everyone would snap out of it and become the warm, loving family we never had.

But we were inevitably given less than we expected: Beth wished for a mother who didn't go off and leave her alone for hours at a time; Don wanted a father who didn't hit him; John expected his father to be more understanding; Mary dreamed of the day her father would tell her he loved her; Rick wished for a mother who would not need to ask his advice about everything; Laurie wanted a mother who wouldn't drink and then make Laurie stay up with her and talk all night; Carole wished she had a brother that wouldn't fondle her; Diana ached for a mother who hadn't committed suicide. Every time we expected more than we were given, with every heart's desire that never came true, we became more and more disappointed.

We carried a picture of our perfect family in our mind's eye, but the world around us never matched that picture. Every time Mom drank or Dad yelled, after every fight or violation, a small piece of our heart would break, and we would begin to feel a sense of hopelessness that perhaps the needs of our hearts would remain forever unfulfilled. As our tender dreams and wishes were shattered again and again, some of us eventually began to suspect that we might spend our entire lives wishing for things that would never come true.

Of course, there would always be an occasion, a special moment on a particular day, when things did turn out the way we hoped they would. There would be a day when things were light and happy in our family, a time when Dad did take us fishing, or Mom helped us with our homework, or we all laughed together and played a game, or took a walk and everyone had a good time. But even when a moment of happiness spontaneously arose, we still found ourselves feeling cautious and watchful, waiting for the moment when the happiness would end. Even as we tried our best to enjoy whatever happiness came along, we had eventually become so accustomed to being let down by the broken promises of our family story that we soon learned always to look behind the happiness, probing for the inevitable suffering, the hidden catch, the certain disappointment that was to come.

We were so accustomed to unmasking the illusion of happiness that even when everyone seemed to be having a good time, we suspected they were only pretending, obscuring their true sufferings. We saw the playful moments as a façade, a fragile veneer beneath which the deeper, more uncomfortable truths were hidden. Gladness seemed like a denial mechanism, destined to crumble under the weight of painful feelings yet to be uncovered. A smiling face was likely to mask darker things—and so, over time, we learned to equate the dark side with the truth. Pain and sorrow had come in so many ways and in so many forms, eventually suffering began to seem more real, more honest than happiness.

We concluded that the people who seemed happy were those who just couldn't see what we saw, who were too dull or ignorant to see the "real" painful truth about things. We even took pride in our ability to find suffering where there appeared to be gladness; it was a mark of our intelligence and sensitivity that we could discern the flaws in the pretty story. We saw everything through the lens of our broken hearts.

As we grow older, we continue to hope for things we do not have. While the things we wish for may change—instead of a new toy we may wish for a new car, a better career, a larger home, or a more compatible spouse—still, when these things do not come exactly as we anticipated, we experience disappointment. And as each new frustration resonates with our childhood memories, then our disappointment—worn deep and wide through the repeated regrets of childhood—becomes like a hammock to which we quickly retreat in comfort and familiarity.

This dance of expectation and disappointment follows us wherever we go. If we pay attention, we find we always want something other than what we have. When we are in the city, we dream of the country—and in the country we miss the stimulation of the city. When we are alone, we ache for company, and when we are busy with our family, we wish we had more time for ourselves. We are suffocated by our ever-changing desires and preferences. Relentlessly pursuing our mercurial wants and desires, we try to minimize our suffering by trying to make the world just the way we want it to be. Yet each time, in spite of our best efforts to arrange it all just right, it somehow turns out to be unsatisfying: It doesn't last long enough, it lasts too long, the right people aren't there, something is not quite right—and again we are disappointed.

Disappointment and Despair

Each family had its own reservoir of regrets, of opportunities lost, unfortunate relatives, unsatisfying jobs, or bad marriages. As children of these families, we became used to uncovering whatever darkness and disappointment lay hidden beneath the surface. Later, as adults, we may have felt the additional disappointment of unsatisfying jobs, lack of success, or failed relationships. After a while, we learned to protect our hearts by altering our expectations to fit the shape of our childhood scars: Rather than expect the best, we begin to expect the worst. Over time, these chronic disappointments generate a sense of despair.

By cultivating the expectation that we will inevitably encounter failure, pain, and sorrow, by seeking out disappointment and regret before they take us by surprise, we feel somehow more safe, more in control. We feel less vulnerable to being caught with our hearts exposed, less open to being hurt by our shattered dreams. If we expect the worst, we will never again be disappointed.

How many times during a day do we find ourselves considering what might go wrong? How much time do we spend trying to predict how this job, relationship, or project might blow up in our faces? Even when things are going smoothly, how many hours do we waste wondering when the other shoe will drop, waiting for the moment when it will somehow turn from good to bad? Because our hearts have been broken so often, because so many dreams have wasted away, failure and disillusionment begin to seem more trustworthy and more durable than happiness and delight. We actually anticipate the inevitability of disappointment, feeling some relief when the other shoe falls, when the muck hits the fan, when all that appears to be well is finally revealed to be ruined.

Erik Erikson, in his early work as a child analyst, observed young children who were exhibiting clear symptoms of despair. These girls and boys seemed to actually court failure—destroying toys or ruining friendships with playmates the instant it appeared that something might go wrong. Then they would retreat into despair when everything did turn out badly. Erikson noted traces of triumph and satisfaction on the faces of these children as the inevitable failure of their situation played itself out. But he also realized that their retreat into despair was a defense, a protection. Their fear of failure was so strong, they would actually invite disaster just so they could get it over with. But, said Erikson, in their hearts "these children loved and wanted to be loved, and they very much preferred the joy of accomplishment to the triumph of hateful failure."

Henry, a lawyer and a recovering alcoholic, came to me feeling depressed. He was raised by his mother and grandmother, both of whom had lost their husbands. Both women were sad and tired, and felt their lives were over. Henry remembered sitting at the kitchen table and feeling the weight of his family's disappointment. He heard his grandmother tell his mother how tough her life was going to be, that she had had her chance for happiness and had lost it, and that she better get used to it. "There will never be another chance for you," she said.

Little Henry sat quietly and absorbed their regret, taking their despair as his own. Small wonder, then, that as an adult Henry had found himself mired in depression and despair. He had long ago decided that things were never going to work out, so why bother trying?

Some of us may have recognized a similar despair in our own parents, watching as they surrendered to the discouraging inevitability of what fate had dealt them. We watched their hurt, their disillusionment, and the sense of defeat that drenched their lives. Many of us took on our parents' suffering as a map of our own destiny, using the level of their regret to calibrate the limits of our own happiness. Moved by love and pity for our parents, some of us made a secret, unconscious vow to never allow our happiness to exceed that which Mom and Dad managed to gather for themselves. If we were to be too lighthearted and too free, it would feel like we were stealing their happiness; there was so little joy, to want more would be terribly selfish. Accepting their sorrowful inheritance, we felt somehow more loyal and loving as their sons and daughters.

This is not a choice we ever make consciously but rather a decision we make from a place deep within us, a place bound by a powerful kinship with those who gave us life. By choosing unhappiness so that our parents might be happy, perhaps we felt we were giving them a precious gift, sacrificing our joy on the altar of their sorrow. But it was, of course, a gift that would benefit no one.

We never receive any real satisfaction from choosing despair. Like Erikson's children, we have become so terrified of what will happen when things go wrong—so frightened of the pain, the exposure, and the grief— that we desperately armor our hearts by readying ourselves for the worst. But as we devote all our attention to preparing ourselves for sorrow, we slowly strangle the possibility that we will ever know real joy.

The Practice of Nonattachment

How do we free ourselves from this cycle of expectation, disappointment, and despair? We may begin by acknowledging that we will never be totally free from hurt and sadness. When we lose the job or the promotion we worked so hard for, when we find ourselves in financial difficulty, when our spouse asks for a divorce, when we lose a good friend to cancer, we will inevitably feel the sadness and grief that accompany any loss.

If we can never escape the pain of being human, how, then, can we heal ourselves of disappointment and lingering despair? We are trapped between two old patterns of thinking. On the one hand, we still carry our passionate childhood belief that the world should change and that everyone should stop dying or leaving or being mean. People should simply come together and rebuild the world the way it was supposed to be in the first place. While this is a beautiful dream, and something to which we may dedicate our lives, simply holding a wish in our heart does not necessarily make it come true.

The alternative, however, is to expect the worst. Many of us who repeatedly experience disappointment become cynical, smugly quoting Murphy's Law when something goes wrong. But while learning to expect disaster may make us feel less vulnerable to disappointment and hurt, our fatalism casts a long shadow deep in our soul, and murders any possibility of joy that may arise in our spirit. As we perfect our ability to predict what is dark and painful, we gradually lose our ability to recognize what is vital, beautiful, and alive.

If anticipating the best brings us disappointment, and expecting the worst leads to despair, then we feel damned whichever way we turn. How do we imagine we can ever find peace? How can we ever be happy?

One method is to experiment with the idea that we may allow *all* our expectations—the bad ones and the good ones, the big and small ones—to gradually hold less importance, to recede into the background of our lives. This is a very difficult practice. Our lives are drenched with expectations for every situation. We cling to a set of old, tarnished blueprints, maps for safety and protection we drew up when we were small and afraid. Then we stumble from place to place, urging the world to perfectly match these blueprints, terrified the world will not turn out the way we want, and disappointed when it turns out the way we feared. Only when we free ourselves from the prison of our expectations are we able to meet the world afresh and to see with new eyes. If we allow our attachments to recede, even for an instant, we are more free to appreciate what we have been given and to see more clearly the fullness of who we have become.

We may begin this practice by becoming more aware of the quality of our expectations. What are we expecting in this moment? What do we assume will happen an hour from now, or tonight, or tomorrow morning? Whenever we are driving around town, or taking the bus to work, or sitting in a meeting, or preparing to go on a date with a friend, we may pause for a moment and take inventory of all the hopes and plans we are carrying in that instant. No doubt we are already planning for how the bus ride will go, what we will say at the meeting, or how wonderful our time with our friend will be. As we use up the fullness of every moment by worrying and anticipating how the next encounter will go, we suffocate our spirit in a sea of plans, presumptions, and calculations.

Of course, it is impossible to live completely without expectations and preferences. Some of our expectations come from deep in the heart and seem quite reasonable. It seems perfectly normal, for example, for a child to wish for a happy family, or to expect to be treated with affection. But regardless of how simple and reasonable it may seem to wish for love, there will be a moment when that wish becomes an expectation, a feeling that we *should* be loved, or that somehow we have *earned* love, and feel we have a right to get it. As soon as our wish becomes an expectation, the instant we *assume* that love will come, we are preparing ourselves for a moment in the future when we will be disappointed by someone who will love us too little, too hard, too soft, or too late. And then, unable to receive whatever care is offered, we will measure what little we are given against how much we expected. This is the basic recipe for disappointment.

The mind ceaselessly generates thousands of tiny expectations every day, expectations that subtly color the lens through which we perceive our world. A few weeks ago, I was awakened at six in the morning by my four-week-old son Maxwell. He wanted the usual attention required by an infant—some food, a change of diaper, a moment of rocking on my chest. Since my wife Christine had gotten up with him during the night, I was glad to spend this time with our new son.

This particular morning, however, his need for rocking seemed greater than before. We ended up sitting in the rocker for almost an hour as he fidgeted and fussed. I found myself getting hungry, so I decided it must be time for my breakfast. As soon as I made that decision, I began to rock a little more deliberately, trying to get Maxwell to fall asleep so I could eat. Of course, as I got hungrier, Max became fussier.

After about ten minutes I had worked myself into a dilemma: When was I going to get breakfast? I became impatient, frustrated by Max's inability to just let go and go to sleep. After all, I had to eat too! This lovely moment—sitting peacefully with my son in the early morning, gently rocking ourselves together—had become a moment of disappointment, frustration, and impatience.

What had changed? Max was still my newborn son, the rocker still quietly rocking. The only difference was that I had begun to *expect* that I would soon get breakfast. That tiny expectation had turned a moment of grace into a moment of distress. In that instant I had a choice: Either I could keep rocking—all the while thinking, "breakfast, breakfast"—or I could let my attachment to breakfast temporarily fall away, and think instead, "rocking, rocking." As soon as I let go of the concept of an immediate breakfast, the moment again became gentle and easy. I could sit, I could watch Maxwell's eyes, and feel his body warm and soft against mine. There would be breakfast for everyone sooner or later.

How many gentle moments do we poison each day when we cling to our expectations? When we are imagining breakfast while we rock the baby, we miss the joy of rocking, we lose a precious moment with the baby—and we still miss breakfast. When we simply rock when we are rocking, and then eat while we are eating, we become more open to the blessings available in this moment.

Some expectations are extremely difficult to relinquish. Some of us still expect our parents, friends, or spouses to finally become the loving people we always wanted them to be. We think of how it might have been if only the right person or career had come along. Some of us are still so attached to these hopes that we have not yet really begun our lives in earnest. We are still patiently waiting for the world to match our perfect picture before we start. How much longer can we wait?

Our challenge is to learn to meet whatever is in this moment without condition, without comparing it to what should have been. Practicing nonattachment, letting go of our expectations and meeting the moment face to face, we are free to appreciate whatever is set before us, to drink deeply from what is alive and beautiful in that instant. Unencumbered by our holding onto what should or shouldn't have been, we are free to be surprised by life, to experience the wonder of our life just as it is, with our sorrows and joys simply providing the color and texture. When we don't know what to expect, we may approach even sadness with curiosity and an open heart. When we loosen our grip on our expectations, everything becomes a surprise.

However, as children of family pain, we learned to dislike surprises. Surprises often disrupted our intricate schemes for coping with the family drama. Surprises usually brought with them some unfortunate, painful event; whatever came unexpectedly usually came with some pain or problem. A surprise usually meant something had gone from bad to worse; pleasant surprises were rare. So our overall strategy for safety depended on our ability to avoid surprises.

Nevertheless, says Brother David Steindl-Rast, "the wisdom of the joyful heart begins with surprise." If we cultivate nonattachment to our expectations, if we can savor this particular moment just as it is, then we are free to be surprised by our lives. The world provides us with many unanticipated moments of wonder, beauty, and grace, moments we may appreciate only when we are willing to be surprised. We may find ourselves delighted by an unanticipated gesture of care, startled by a pleasant feeling in our body, or captured by a particular view of the city we had never really noticed before. As when a rainbow suddenly appears in the sky after a summer's rain—even though we understand how a rainbow is made and we could have expected it—since we did not expect that particular rainbow at that particular moment, we are absolutely surprised and delighted at its coming.

The Problem of Happiness

One of the rewards of these spiritual practices is that after a while, without warning, we may stumble upon a moment when we realize we are beginning to *feel* lighter and more playful, more present and easy in our life. Slowly, gently, as our healing takes shape in our lives, it begins to dawn on us that we might actually feel happy.

Now, for many of us, disappointment and regret have become so much a part of our lives that the idea of happiness can be confusing, even a little disturbing. Our disappointments have kept us safe; happiness is just too unpredictable, too fleeting, too untrustworthy. The possibility of impending happiness, the invitation to crawl out of our cocoon of disappointment and embrace more fully the richness of our lives, can at first seem frightening: We feel so exposed, so vulnerable. Interestingly, we now find ourselves confronting a disquieting ambivalence about our own happiness.

We are unprepared for happiness; perhaps we feel unworthy to fully accept it, or guilty for receiving more than we should, or perhaps we can't even decide if we are *really* happy or if we are just inventing a more sophisticated form of denial. Should we trust it? How long will it last? Our chronic fascination with failure and disappointment makes it extremely difficult for us to enjoy the simple blessings of the moment.

Sometimes it is easier to trust a period of happiness when we bring our attention to the body and the physical experience of letting go. How does our breath feel? Do we notice any relaxation? Where do we feel it? Where do we feel the release, in our neck, back, face, or hands? Where does it begin, how does it move through us? When we anchor our awareness in the body, we are less able to talk ourselves out of a moment of lightness or joy.

Just as we learn to practice nonattachment, letting go of our endless expectations, so must we also learn to feel comfortable with joy. We are far more at ease with sorrow and disappointment; when we bump into the possibility of happiness, we feel clumsy and stiff, awkward and afraid. Part of our healing is made possible when we make as much room in our hearts for joy as we have made for sadness and fear. For what purpose do we undertake healing, to what end do we embark on spiritual practice, if not, in part, for joy? Joy, Teilhard de Chardin has said, "is the most infallible sign of the presence of God."

The Experience of Joy

> From joy springs all creation,
> By joy it is sustained,
> Towards joy it proceeds,
> And to joy it returns.
>
> —Mundaka Upanishad

Many traditions speak of joy as one of the fruits of spiritual practice. A joyful heart deepens our ability to love ourselves, to love the earth, to love one another, and to love God. The ninety-eighth Psalm urges us to "make a joyful noise unto the Lord, all the earth; break forth into joyous song."

"Know the nature of joy," say the Hindu Upanishads. "Where there is joy there is creation." The Christian scriptures say that the angels announced the birth of the infant Jesus by saying, "Behold, I bring you tidings of a great joy, which shall be for everyone."

We invite the possibility of joy through a gradual letting go, sinking gently into the love of the divine. But how can we welcome joy when we have so much fear, so little faith that we will be cared for? How will I know I will not be hurt? Can I allow myself to believe that I can be happy? This is our dilemma, and also that of the frightened child. Jesus would often say "be not afraid," because he knew that as soon as we surrender into the life of the spirit, all our fears quickly arise to block our path.

Because we are so attached to our fears and disappointments, we must use a variety of techniques and devices to loosen our fearful grip on despair. For some of us, letting go of expectations helps us remain soft and open to the joys of the moment. Some may find it easier to find joy in the company of others. Often when we are isolated and alone, we begin to feel tight and afraid; when we gather together with others to sing, dance, or share our stories, we unlock those places where we get hard and stuck, trapped by the inertia of our hopelessness.

At one of our retreats there was a woman named Jean who was raised in a particularly painful alcoholic family. She was an exceptionally responsible person and had a great deal of trouble allowing herself to relax. She was so frightened of letting go of her need to care for everyone else that she rarely felt any happiness herself. At the end of the retreat we usually spend a period of time praying, sharing a sacred meal, and singing Hindu chants or old gospels. At this retreat Jean was particularly moved by the spirit of the group as she allowed herself to become a part of the celebration. Slowly the music, the singing, and holding hands began to melt away some of her fear, and her face appeared soft and open. It was as if she realized for the first time that she could feel safe and welcome enough to allow herself to feel happy. Not because she was useful, not because she had done good deeds, but simply because there was joy in that place in that moment, and she was welcome to share in it.

When the singing ended and we were preparing to leave, Jean came up with tears in her eyes. "I get it," she said to me, "I finally get it. I can just be happy. It's all right just to feel good. This is what you were trying to tell me about all along. I can hardly believe it—I actually feel happy."

For the past few years in Santa Fe we have gathered to worship at a service called "Celebrate the Heart of Healing." The service is for people living with AIDS, their families, friends, and loved ones. For a few hours we join together to sing, pray, share stories, and light candles. Although we have the opportunity to share our sorrow, the point of this particular gathering is rather to celebrate the tremendous gifts that have been born in the lives of all those who have been affected by the HIV virus. We speak of hearts opening, lives being changed, relationships being healed, and families gathering in love as they struggle with the immediacy of life and death.

When the idea of a celebration service was first discussed, some felt that a ceremony of gratefulness would be insensitive to the profound grief of so many who had felt deep loss in their lives. After all, AIDS is a terrible, incurable disease, they said, and we should not be light and playful about it. Their expectation was that if we gathered around AIDS, it should be a sad and maudlin affair.

But the people living with AIDS were grateful—dozens of people instantly volunteered to help. Many of them said, "We are so tired of going to memorial services, it is so refreshing to be able to laugh and honor everything we have been given." One of the local physicians who specializes in AIDS concurred. "We laugh more with our AIDS patients than with anyone else," he said. "We are all so clearly aware of what is important and what is not, we can much more easily attend to what is precious."

When it came time for the service, much to our surprise, more than a thousand people had filled the church. When the singing and chanting, the meditations and prayers and candles were done, all the people with AIDS and their lovers, friends, mothers, and fathers held one another in a large circle. We all cried, laughed, and celebrated with full hearts the joyful gift of being alive.

Our expectation is that a life-threatening illness would bring only grief; we are surprised when we find there is also joy, laughter, healing, and love. One of the reasons we gather together in song, around tables in twelve-step programs, in churches, and in healing circles is to remind one another in the company of other beings that sadness is not all we are given. Isolated in our disappointment, we may spend our time remembering only our sadness and pain. Yet when we gather together, we may become less attached to our despair and become mindful of the tenacity and trustworthiness of a joyful heart.

The Attachment to Happiness

Often, when we stumble upon a moment of happiness or joy, we become so afraid of losing it that we try to capture it and hold it forever. Perhaps we try to replicate the same circumstances, doing exactly the same thing just the way we did it before, using the same words and gestures, hoping to invoke the identical feeling of well-being again and again. This is the mind of the addict, desperately repeating the same act, hoping it will produce the same result. Yet the more we try to hold onto joy, the more quickly it withers away. Because joy arises not out of holding but out of letting go. As William Blake observed,

> He who binds to himself a joy,
> Does the winged life destroy,
> But he who kisses the joy as it flies,
> Lives in eternity's sunrise.

One can't become attached to joy; joy is a quality that arises out of nonattachment. Joy is a surprise, a gift, an experience born when we are looking somewhere else. The less we plan, the less we expect, the easier it becomes for happiness and joy to find a place in our hearts.

Still, it is difficult not to grab for happiness. We clutch at our models, tightly gripping our strategies for happiness: "If I had a happy childhood I could be happy now," or "If only I can find a really good therapist," or "As soon as I get my career together, life will be really sweet." Every condition we set on the intervention of spirit and grace in our lives reduces our capacity to be surprised by happiness and growth wherever we are. If we can reduce our demands on ourselves, on the world, even on God, we make some space for happiness. Seng-ts'an, the third Zen patriarch, opens his "Discourse on the Faithful Mind" by saying, "The Great Way is not difficult for those who don't cling to their preferences."

Nonattachment and Gratefulness

The Buddha said that in our lifetime we would experience ten thousand joys and ten thousand sorrows. Those of us who were given many sorrows at an early age find ourselves reluctant to surrender into the joys that are also possible. While we must allow our hearts to grieve fully the sufferings we were given, can we also celebrate joy when it comes? Are we open and attentive to the sweet moments when sorrow abates and joy arises?

Part of the practice of letting go, of nonattachment, is cultivating a sense of gratefulness for whatever has been placed on our table. Gratefulness is a practice that makes joy possible. Many of us mistakenly believe that we can only feel grateful when things work out exactly the way we planned, when everything turns out right. Happiness, then, is reserved only for people who have no worries, for whom everything goes their way. Joy is the privilege of rich people, people who live on the beach, people who have no worries, nothing to be afraid of, people who never had a painful childhood. But Brother David says we make a big mistake when we equate happiness and gratefulness with a problem-free life:

> We tend to misunderstand the link between joy and gratefulness. We notice that joyful people are grateful and suppose they are grateful for their joy. But the reverse is true: Their joy springs from gratefulness.

> If one has all the good luck in the world, but takes it for granted, it will not give one joy . . . it is not joy that makes us grateful, it is gratitude that makes us joyful.

As children, when we insulated ourselves from the pain of family sorrow, we also diminished our capacity to receive almost anything at all, regardless of how pleasant or unpleasant. Since we have allowed so very little to come in, since we rarely allow ourselves to receive anything, we are inexperienced in being thankful.

Some people think that being grateful consists primarily of learning to grudgingly accept whatever we get. But gratefulness is a practice that touches our deepest reluctance to be awake and alive, teaching us to embrace even what we cannot change or control, and even to be able to give thanks for what has been given. This is the true heart of letting go. For who knows what teaching, what gift is concealed in this moment, in this unexpected event, in this unanticipated change of plans?

"Rejoice always . . . and in all things give thanks," wrote Saint Paul. How can we learn to give thanks in all things? Gary Snyder, the Zen poet, suggests we begin simply by offering thanks on a daily basis for our lives, our food, our friends, and our breath. "Grace is the first and last poem," said Snyder. By learning to give thanks, we clear our eyes and prepare our mind to accept that whatever we have been given may, indeed, be a gift. As Meister Eckhart, the devoted mystic, said, "If the only prayer you say in your whole life is 'thank you,' that would suffice."

The prescription of gratitude is not given lightly, for many of us have experienced terrible tragedies, and it would seem heartless indeed to suggest that we must give thanks for our abuse, our cancer, our divorce, or our AIDS diagnosis. Yet at the same time, even in the jaws of a life-threatening illness, there are people who feel they have much for which to be grateful. When we can give thanks for our breath, even as it moves through a body racked with pain, we open ourselves to great healing.

Accepting Joy

> The gloom of the world
> Is but a shadow;
> Behind it,
> Yet within reach,
> Is joy.
> Take Joy.
>
> —Fra Giovanni, 1513

Many of us, accustomed to disappointment and afraid of joy, may sometimes feel that our joy steals from the joy of others. The practice of gratefulness allows us to feel part of a deeper economy of care, a profound exchange of love as we give thanks to God, to spirit, to the earth, and to all living beings, gratefully acknowledging all we have been given. Mother Teresa said: "She gives most who gives with joy . . . The best way to show our gratitude to God and the people is to accept everything with joy. A joyful heart is the normal result of heart burning with love."

True happiness is not selfish; in fact, when we are joyful we are more likely to feel we are spilling over, filled with a compassionate love for all life. Joy marvels at the beauty of all things, celebrates life, and rejoices in the well-being of all. Thich Nhat Hanh teaches that "if you are happy, all of us will profit from it. All living beings will profit from it. Happiness is available . . . please help yourself."

The Buddha taught his disciples to "live in joy." The King of Kosala once said that he found the Buddha's disciples to be exceptionally jubilant, that his followers actually seemed to be enjoying the spiritual life. The Buddha said that *was* the spiritual life. Play is a natural by-product of nonattachment; we are less afraid about how things will turn out. Play is the joyful attitude of the children of God. When we are spontaneous and happy, we are dancing with the divine light in all things. Sasaki Roshi wrote a short poem about his life with God:

> As a butterfly lost in a flower,
> As a bird settled on the tree,
> As a child fondling mother's breast,
> For sixty-seven years of this world,
> I have played with God.

If we are to continue our spiritual healing, we cannot remain forever afraid of joy. Our sorrows and disappointments, however trustworthy and familiar they may feel, are not the only things that are true about our lives, our hearts, or our destiny. Spirit itself invites us to be joyful, to be awake, to passionately and courageously allow this moment to live within our hearts, deep and full and strong, to allow joy, to become alive, and to celebrate fervently the gifts of the children of God.

To know joy we must wake up, we must not sleep in our expectations and disappointments. Paying attention to every molecule that graces our body with warmth and nourishment, we give thanks for life itself. When we forget to give thanks, we sink into a joyless life.

When we hold tightly to our demands and expectations, we invite lives of disappointment and despair. When we allow our expectations to dissolve, we become more open to the fullness of the moment, open to appreciate the richness of our lives. And as we learn to give thanks for all life, we become more fully alive.

Reverend Eido Tai Shimano, a Japanese Zen master, speaks of an unexpected moment, a moment of surprise and gratefulness:

People often ask me how Buddhists answer the question: "Does God exist?" The other day I was walking along the river . . . I was suddenly aware of the sun, shining through the bare trees. Its warmth, its brightness, and all this completely free, completely gratuitous. Simply there for us to enjoy. And without my knowing it, completely spontaneously, my two hands came together, and I realized I was making *gassho*. And it occurred to me that this is all that matters: that we can bow, take a deep bow. Just that. Just that.

EXERCISE
Watching the Move to Disappointment

Disappointment can be like a hammock to which we instantly retreat whenever we are confronted with people and situations that fail to meet our expectations. This exercise helps us observe how quickly we move to a state of disappointment, and allows us to see how that state affects our feelings and behavior.

For one week, notice how often you feel disappointed or let down by the people or circumstances around you. Watch carefully what happens when something in your life goes in a way you didn't expect or doesn't turn out the way you hoped. Notice how the mind responds to this change. Also, observe how quickly the mind begins to anticipate the worst, noticing how you protect and armor yourself against impending disappointment.

How does the mind explain the presence of defeat or disappointment? What words, phrases, or images arise to describe the nature of things and why they have happened to you? Notice any feelings of hopelessness or defeat. As you begin to feel disappointed, what are your impulses? To go away? To isolate? To ask for care? To try something else? Take note of all your responses whenever you feel in any way let down or disappointed by those around you.

The purpose of this exercise is simply to observe our attachment to disappointment, not to change it. Try to name the circumstances in which you are especially vulnerable to disappointment. With which people or situations are you most likely to predict an unhappy outcome? What were you hoping for? Was it something you had wanted before? What kinds of things tend to disappoint you the most? Notice which expectations you feel most keenly, which you feel are most justified, and which make you most angry when they are unfulfilled.

Use this exercise to carefully observe the dance of expectation and disappointment as it plays itself out in the mind and heart. As you become more aware of your expectations and disappointments, you may begin to imagine other responses, other options. What moves are available to you besides disappointment? What other choices are possible? Which expectations are more open to change and which can be let go? Acknowledge to yourself that all things arise and pass away, that all joys and sorrows are subject to impermanence. Slowly you may begin cultivating a practice of nonattachment, allowing some of your expectations to shift and fall away, making room for a more genuine acceptance of whatever you have been given.

Meditation
A GRATEFULNESS MEDITATION

At the end of the day, sit in front of your table in your place of refuge. Take a few moments to review the day. Recall all the pleasant people and events that occurred, noting also those that were uncomfortable or difficult.

Close your eyes and allow the significant events to arise one by one. Viewing the pleasant experiences one at a time, let yourself give thanks for whatever gifts may have touched your life today. Silently name any gratefulness you may feel for each person or event, taking the time to let your heart open and receive the gift of that experience. Giving thanks for each gift, allow each image to arise and fade away until you feel complete.

Next, begin to recall any unpleasant experiences from the day. Focus your attention on one particularly painful encounter or event. Now, try to touch that memory with gratefulness. What do you notice as you practice giving thanks for something painful? What emotions arise? Does it make you soft or angry? Does it feel easy or hard? Stay with one image, repeatedly giving thanks for the fact that this person or event was a part of your day. Be thankful for whatever teaching they brought, whatever they helped you notice about yourself. One by one, touch each painful memory with some gratefulness.

Finally, give thanks for your life. Take a moment to explicitly name all the qualities of your life for which you are grateful. Practice naming thankfulness for your breath, your body, the people who care for you, your spouse, lover, or children, for the colors of the day, for your home, for your food. Reviewing as many gifts as come to mind, speak a word of silent thanksgiving for everything you have and for all that you have become.

Notice what happens in your body as you practice giving thanks. What emotions arise? You may practice this meditation every day. At the end of a week, what do you notice about your move to disappointment? What do you notice about how you perceive your life? Using the practice of gratefulness, we may begin to rearrange the habitual inertia that drives the machine of expectation and disappointment. Through gratefulness, we open the door to joy.

CHAPTER TEN

Habit and Mindfulness

As children, we learned to watch things very closely. We scrutinized whatever was happening around us; we became expert at discerning any indications of impending danger or distress, and sharpened our senses to detect any evidence of trouble. We would always watch for anything unusual, for the precise moment to advance or retreat, for the right thing to say or do. We trained ourselves in the art of observation, vigilant in noting the smallest details, receptive to the slightest shifts in the family atmosphere.

After a while, we became accustomed to watching for a few very specific, predictable situations or events. These were the moments that, when they came, seemed to bring the most suffering. Depending on the characteristics of our family, we might become especially adept at watching for scarcity or betrayal, dishonesty or withdrawal, impending violence or emotional rejection. Over time, we formed a habit of seeing everything through the lens of the most predictable dangers. We developed a subtle myopia as we learned to watch only for what would hurt us; everything else became less interesting, less relevant.

Melody was an attractive, creative woman whose generosity and good nature made her quite popular. She was well liked, intelligent, and had a good sense of humor. However, Melody's father had died when she was quite young, and she inherited a stepfather whom she felt never really loved her. So when Melody was young, her experience of feeling bereft of a loving father had convinced her that she must have been unlovable; there must be something deeply wrong with her. Why else would both her fathers have treated her so badly—one leaving her alone, and another never loving her?

134

Melody would spend a good portion of each session trying to convince me how broken she must be, how bad, selfish, and unlovable she was. She did not want to be convinced otherwise. Despite her many friends, her popularity, and her talents, the thing she felt most true about her was that she was basically unloved and inherently unlovable.

Our understanding of what is true about ourselves is shaped by what fascinates us, and our feelings and behaviors are influenced by the things that capture our attention. If our eye is always attuned to where we feel broken, we will be unable to see where we are already whole. If our eye is focused on danger, we will habitually move to protect ourselves; if we are skilled in perceiving scarcity, we will learn to hoard what we have. The way we perceive and interpret the world around us significantly alters our response to it, and, over time, creates an overall context for the experience of our lives.

If, out of fear or sorrow, we focus our attention only on those areas that brought us suffering in childhood, our understanding of ourselves and others will remain small and incomplete. Many of us used our childhood observations to put together a story about ourselves and the world, a story that we came to believe was the only real truth. The stories we put together were simple and clear: "I was never loved, and probably never will be. There will never be enough for me. I will always be disappointed. No matter how hard I try, I will never be good enough. The world will never be safe for me. I was hurt so badly, I'm beyond help. No one will ever understand me. My dreams will never come true."

After a while—like Melody—we learn to look only for those people, events, or experiences that will validate our story and provide confirmation that our limited way of seeing is accurate. We learn to see ourselves as victim, powerless and violated, and somehow deserving of our sad fate. We see the world as painful, dangerous, scarce, and unkind. We come upon a formula that explains how things work, and we use that formula to interpret everything that happens to us. Even if the story is a painful one, as long as it remains constant, we can develop strategies to cope with what we are given. Our way of seeing the world becomes an ally, providing us with tools to explain our self-fulfilling stories about disappointment, scarcity, fear, and despair.

Yet as we entrap ourselves with these habits of watching ourselves and the world in a particular way, we stifle our heart's ability to grow, to learn, and to heal.

As we get older, even though the players and the circumstances may change, we still end up in situations where the old stories always come true. We hold onto our habitual ways of seeing and feeling, taking our one truth and clinging to it, forever blinding ourselves to any new information. There is a story told by the Buddha:

A young widower, who loved his five-year-old son very much, was away on business, and bandits came, burned down his whole village, and took his son away. When the man returned, he saw the ruins and panicked. He took the charred corpse of an infant to be his own child, and he began to pull his hair and beat his chest, crying uncontrollably. He organized a cremation ceremony, collected the ashes, and put them in a very beautiful velvet pouch. Working, sleeping, or eating, he always carried the bag of ashes with him.

One day his real son escaped from the robbers and found his way home. He arrived at his father's new cottage at midnight, and knocked at the door. You can imagine, at that time, the young father was still carrying the bag of ashes, and crying. He asked, "Who is there?" And the child answered, "It's me, Papa. Open the door, it's your son." In his agitated state of mind the father thought that some mischievous boy was making fun of him, and he shouted at the child to go away, and continued to cry. The boy knocked again and again, but the father refused to let him in. Some time passed, and finally the child left. From that time on, father and son never saw one another.

After telling this story, the Buddha said, "Sometime, somewhere you take something to be the truth. If you cling to it so much, when the truth comes in person and knocks on your door, you will not open it."

Like the father who sees only the ashes of his "dead" son, many of us who experienced deep unhappiness become accustomed to seeing only our hurt, our fear, and our disappointment. We take one feeling, one story about our childhood, and place it on the altar of our lives, holding it as sacred truth, making it more true than anything else in the world. When hurt comes, we say, "Ah, there it is again: the real story of my life." When disappointment, or fear, or anger arises, we feel comfort in knowing that we are now in familiar territory. This disappointment, this fear, this anger—this is our real story.

After many years, our habitual ways of seeing ourselves become so chronic that we can hardly imagine any others. We are no longer simply a child, a human being; we have become the Unloved, the Vulnerable, the Disappointed One, the Abandoned, the Misunderstood, the Deprived, the Terribly Broken. Waking up in the morning and getting ready for the day, we put on our story like an old bathrobe and a soft pair of slippers. We are so accustomed to introducing ourselves as the victim of our story, we actually feel ambivalent about whether or not we can really change—or even want to. Our very life becomes a familiar, droning habit.

When Sonia came to see me, she would usually begin by telling me about all the wonderful and exciting things she had been up to. She was an articulate, professional woman who was respected in her field, and she enjoyed sharing her victories and adventures with me. But halfway through our time together, she would often begin to feel the weight of her life, and she would feel sad and start to cry. "I feel so bad," she would say, "I feel so alone, so hurt and sad inside."

Now, Sonia had many good friends with whom she could talk, friends who could share her deepest feelings. But whenever she felt sad, she would go off by herself and hold onto those feelings for hours at a time. As a child of an abusive father, she had often had the experience of being left alone, feeling she was unloved and unlovable. So she decided that this must be, at her deepest core, who she really was inside. In those moments, friends, victories, and accomplishments meant nothing; her lonely sadness was the deepest truth she knew. Whenever sadness would arise in her, she felt that was the "real" Sonia coming out.

Rick was a gay man who was gifted in his work. He ran many successful programs on behalf of those in need, and was respected as an administrator and supervisor. But as a child, he was frequently rejected and criticized by his father, and was burdened by the stigma of his emerging sexuality. He decided early on that he was obviously very weak, and not at all strong inside. Whenever he would speak about himself in our therapy group, he would always defer to someone else's opinion about him, asking for advice and guidance at every turn. He didn't believe he had enough strength inside to find the answer within himself. Despite his achievements as a program director and community leader, he was still convinced that he had no inner fortitude. Although he very much wished to feel strong and courageous, he feared he was destined to feel weak and wounded.

Each of these people had fallen into a habitual way of thinking about themselves. In the face of the pain and the hurt in their families, they had put together a story that wouldn't change, a story that would last, that could readily explain the rest of their lives. They had long ago decided who they were, where they hurt, and what they were really made of inside. This became their litany, their mantra, the sacred story in the scripture of their lives.

Even though an essential part of us may want desperately to be free to grow and change, another part is not quite sure we are ready to find a new story. The old strategies seem to work just fine. Rather than change our story, some of us prefer to find new people to help us share the old story in a new way; or perhaps we practice new ways to analyze and dissect the same old truths. "I know I am broken," we say, "now I just want to find out exactly how it happened." Or, "I am so sad. I need to find out where all this sadness came from."

We enjoy analyzing and exploring the same tired explanations for our lives. We have become so habituated to the color and texture of our particular problems that, after a while, we stop looking for relief. The mind creates an illusion of a static, stable person: "I am this kind of person. These are my opinions, and this is how I am. My problems are this and that, I am wounded in this way, and I will probably have to live this way and do these kinds of things." But these are just fables we make up in order to give ourselves something to hold onto. These habits, however painful, become so comfortable and familiar that it requires a tremendous leap of faith and courage to even begin to imagine that a new kind of life is possible.

There is an ancient Chinese proverb that says, "If we do not change our direction, we are likely to end up where we are going." We build our lives on the foundation of what we believe our destiny will be. If it is our emotional habit to feel hurt, sad, misunderstood, or disappointed, then we will orchestrate our friendships, careers, and marriages to reflect and support the old stories. We perpetuate the old story again and again; it begins to feel predictable, consistent, and manageable. It protects us from change; by sheer familiarity it makes us feel safe. In this piece by the poet James Tate, we hear the desperate ingenuity of the mind that has become so habituated to the old story that it refuses to accept anything new:

MAN WITH WOODEN LEG ESCAPES PRISON

Man with wooden leg escapes prison. He's caught. They take his wooden leg away from him. Each day he must cross a large hill and swim a wide river to get to the field where he must work all day on one leg. This goes on for a year. At the Christmas party they give him back his leg. Now he doesn't want it. His escape is all planned. It requires only one leg.

Fear of Change

Our habits, however comfortable and familiar, are based on our assumption that things never change: "The way they were in my family is the way they will always be." "The way it has been for me is the way it will continue forever." "Since I have studied the situation and know all the rules, I can rely on my strategies to carry me through for the rest of my life."

But the world is not immune to change. On the contrary, it is the nature of all things to change. Look at our lives, how they move and shift: Once we were young, and now we are older, friends and family have come and gone, social circles have evolved, jobs have changed, we may have moved our home many times. What we once loved may have faded, or passed away; what we now love, how long will that last? And what will arise to take its place as we walk the path of our life?

Listen, in this very moment, what do we hear? Sounds arise and fall away, thoughts and feelings come and go, tastes, smells, and memories pass through our body and mind, resting only briefly before they recede, replaced by new thoughts and new feelings. What stays, what remains the same? Where is yesterday, last week, last year? Where is our childhood? Everything changes. It all vanishes so quickly.

Even our bodies change. The cells in our body completely replace themselves every seven years, which means that we are not the same person we were seven years ago. Where did we go? Our bodies feel the effects of aging, our mind learns new things and forgets others, our heart opens and closes. We are awash in a sea of change.

The Buddha taught that each moment arises for just an instant and then, as it changes, a new and different moment appears. This is the basic law of universal impermanence. The preacher in Ecclesiastes concurs when he says "all is vanity"—that is, everything is temporary, all will change; whatever exists now will fade away. One moment will always be replaced by a different moment, each with its own life and its own time:

For everything there is a season,
And a time for every matter under heaven:
A time to be born, and a time to die . . .
A time to kill, and a time to heal . . .
A time to weep, and a time to laugh;
A time to mourn, and a time to dance . . .
A time to keep, and a time to cast away . . .

Change rules our lives and hearts. Some moments will be pleasant, open, and sweet; others will be dark, painful, and difficult. One will inevitably follow another. Each will arise and each will fade away. Peace becomes war—and war, peace; love turns to hate, and softens again into love.

Yet, for all we may know of the inevitability of change, we still resist it.

Change frightens us. We watch people growing old and dying around us every day, and still we try to believe it will never happen to us. We imagine having lives that will not include sickness, tragedy, or death. We try to make everything good, warm, and nice, and if we do stumble upon a moment of joy, we try to repeat exactly what we did the next day and the next, hoping to keep it forever. All the while, we are terrified that some change will come and take it all away.

For the young child as well, change can often be unpleasant and frightening. One child watches a seemingly calm discussion at dinner evolve into a family fight; another sees Mom turn from being a loving parent into a crying, screaming drunk after a few drinks; one feels their brothers and sisters shut down emotionally, keeping more and more to themselves as they grow older; still another senses their family becoming increasingly unsafe with each outburst of anger, each parental absence, every argument, every withdrawal. Families get close, blow apart, and then repeat the cycle again and again. For these children, all change feels as if it is for the worse.

So we learn to fear any sign of change. It disrupts what little calm or peace we manage to carve out for ourselves. Change always seems to bring trouble, pain, or sorrow. Just when we have got things calm and safe again, another piece of trouble comes wandering in. After a while, change itself—in the heart and mind of the frightened child—begins to feel like the enemy.

The Habit of Attachment

There is a certain type of monkey trap used in Asia. First, a coconut is hollowed out and attached by a rope to a tree. Then, a small hole is made at the bottom of the coconut and some sweet food is placed inside. The hole in the bottom is just big enough for the monkey to slide his open hand into the coconut, but not big enough for a closed fist to pass through. The monkey smells the sweets, reaches in with his hand to grab it, and then, with the food clenched tightly in his fist, he is unable to withdraw it. The clenched fist cannot pass through the opening. When the hunters come, the monkey becomes frantic, but it cannot get away. There is nothing keeping the monkey captive except the force of his own attachment. All he has to do is open his hand, let go, and he is free. Even so, it is a rare monkey that manages to escape.

The habit of attachment ignores the reality of the present moment, while stubbornly holding onto what it has already decided. With stunning persistence, we hold to what we already "know." For the monkey, his thought process is predictable and inflexible: (1) Food is good. (2) If I hold onto this, I will get food. (3) The more I hold onto this food, the better my chances of keeping it.

Once this set of truths is planted in his mind, the monkey is unable to accept any new information. The sight of the hunters may make him frantic because they contradict what he has already decided is true, but the information that the hunters are coming brings distress, not freedom. As long as he holds onto what he already "knows," any new information that contradicts his habit simply produces discomfort. If only he were able to let go of his old truths, he could use this new information—"the hunters are coming"—as an opportunity to change his thinking and quickly set himself free.

Our habits of seeing, while designed to keep us from danger, eventually become so inaccurate and flawed that they begin to bring more suffering than safety. Yet we continue to disregard any new information about ourselves and the world, preferring instead to repeat the same old strategies with renewed vehemence. The fault, we think, is not with the strategy, the fault is with our execution. So we keep on trying, doing it faster or harder or longer, hoping it will all work again, just like it used to, if we can just keep trying, just keep holding on.

In Alcoholics Anonymous, they define "insanity" as the tendency to repeat the same behavior over and over, each time expecting a different result. For an alcoholic, this means drinking more and more as things get worse and worse, each time expecting the next drink to bring relief. For our monkey, it means holding on tighter and tighter, when only letting go will bring him freedom. For many of us, it means manufacturing the same childhood situations again and again, hoping that if we do it one more time, our parents will finally bless us, the family will finally respond with unconditional love, and the world will finally come to its senses and give us what we wanted. If we repeat the same behavior often enough, sooner or later it will turn out differently. This, in short, is the habit of attachment.

The Habit of Waiting

Some of us, however, after years of watching our relationships fail, our jobs become unsatisfying, or our dreams die unfulfilled, do begin to suspect that our view of ourselves and the world might be due for a change. Perhaps (we begin to think) it is not the *world* that is doing all this to me, but it is the way I am *seeing* the world that is bringing me so much suffering. But even as this thought arises, we inevitably encounter a profound fear of change. One part of us wishes to be free, yet another part is frightened, passionately convinced that our habits of seeing and behaving should not be tampered with. Even though we feel limited and confined by our old habits of thinking and feeling, at least we know we can handle it the way it is. The pain we already know is somehow acceptable and familiar; we know how bad it can get, and we know we can survive the worst. Any hurt we are having now definitely feels safer than what we might risk if things began to change.

Stuck between these contradictory feelings—wanting to change, yet at the same time afraid of change—many of us discover that one way out of this dilemma is simply to wait. We prepare ourselves for change, but then we set forth a host of unspoken conditions for our healing. We cannot change until things are right, until we feel safe enough, until we have enough therapy, until the right person comes along to help us, until the precise combination of circumstances arises to set us free.

Once a psychotherapist friend made a list of all the things his patients seemed to be waiting for. The list began:

Instead of making a move to change and grow and love, I am waiting for . . .

1. Santa Claus (a miracle)
2. Rigor mortis (a catastrophe)
3. Others to change
4. Knowing who I am
5. Clearer understanding
6. All the rules
7. A push or a kick
8. Perfect conditions
9. Consensus
10. Certainty
11. An invitation
12. My turn

The list goes on to include: getting it all together, hitting bottom, time almost to run out, the right reason, permission, and being old enough.

Our familiarity with our life story can become so habitual that even when we decide to change, we feel seduced by a lingering resignation that we are powerless to move or grow. And so we wait. In our waiting, we lose hope, we settle into despair, and our dreams of joy and fulfillment are left to wither away. The longer we wait to become fully alive, the more something vital within us slowly dies.

Becoming Awake

Habits are thoughts and behaviors born in the past to protect us from the future. The habitual mind is set in motion by the pain of days gone by; it sets itself up as a bulwark against change, against danger, against surprise. Preoccupied with the prospect of further harm, it designs strategies and formulas that strain to protect us from the unpredictable sorrows of the future.

Yet there inevitably comes a moment in our lives when being swept along is not enough, when our habitual, safe, and familiar behaviors no longer feed our deep hunger for vitality, creativity, enthusiasm, and growth. When this moment comes, we are challenged to empty ourselves of our preconceptions about how our life will be and cultivate a beginner's mind, a mind that can see not only the tangled stories of the past and the nameless perils of the future but can also courageously appreciate the unexplored gifts of the present moment.

To the habitual mind, the present moment is useful only insofar as it gives us valuable clues about the past or the future. It uses current information either to validate our theory about the past or to recalibrate our strategies for protecting us in the future. Today, if we do something well, the mind quickly uses that as information to support that we made the right choices in the past, or supposes it to mean we will continue to do well in the future. Rarely do we savor this moment, this instant, merely for what it is. We move quickly through the present moment like a train passing through the railway station, glancing out the window only to confirm that we are traveling in the correct direction.

How will we wake up? Some of us try to get free by fixing the past, others by trying to arrange the future. But freedom will never be granted by the past, and liberation in the future will always be elusive. Real freedom comes when we become awake in the present, when we mindfully become alive in this very instant, right here, right now.

Soon after his enlightenment, the Buddha passed a man on the road who was struck by the Buddha's extraordinary radiance and the peacefulness of his presence. The man stopped and asked, "My friend, what are you? Are you a celestial being or a god?" The Buddha replied, "No I am not." "Are you then a magician or a wizard, or some kind of very special man?" Each time the Buddha replied, "No, I am not." "Well, my friend, what then are you?" The Buddha replied, "I am awake."

For the Buddha, to become awake is to become mindful of each moment, each thought, each step we take along the path. As we train our minds to pay closer attention to all the details of our lives—not simply the details that remind us of our old, tired habits—we begin to discover that every person and every situation we encounter may hold some teaching, some guidance, and may become a doorway to our awakening.

Cultivating Mindfulness

> "I see nobody on the road," said Alice.
> "I only wish I had such eyes," the King remarked in a fretful tone. "To be able to see Nobody! And at that distance too!"
>
> —Lewis Carroll, *Through the Looking Glass*

When we carry in our minds the old categories of what is possible, we effectively limit what we are able to feel, hear, sense, and know. On the other hand, when we cultivate a mindful awareness of everything that is before us, we may learn to see what we have never seen before.

Distracted by the old stories of our childhood, preoccupied with fears of the future, how many moments during the day are we fully present and alive? How often do we really pay attention to the food we eat, tasting each morsel as we place it in our mouths, noting the texture and flavor of each and every bite? How often do we feel the touch of the clothes we put on our bodies, noting the color and texture and feeling the warmth and comfort they bring? How often do we notice the earth, the temperature of the air, the hardness or softness of the ground, the subtle passing of the seasons, the gradual changes in the light, and the lengthening or shortening of the days?

Rather than explore the sensations of the moment, the habitual mind prefers to compare all new data to old information already collected. Suppose, for example, we find ourselves in the midst of a group of strangers, and we begin to notice a knot in our stomach. The habitual mind will quickly explain that knot in terms of some experience in childhood: "I never felt safe in my family, so I still don't feel safe with anyone"; or, "Since my parents never loved me, I always had low self-esteem, so I get nervous in groups." In each case the mind automatically shifts our attention away from a strong sensation in the present and begins a mental review of our old childhood stories. We are no longer present, no longer alive with this current feeling—we have escaped into the mind, into the past, where nothing can change, where we will always and forever repeat the same old story.

A practice of mindfulness, however, invites us to remain present and to explore all the sensations of our bodies and hearts, even the knots in our stomach, not as an indication of the past or as a harbinger of things to come, but as current, useful, valuable information about ourselves. If we stay attentive to the sensation of the knot, for example, what do we notice? Does the knot have a sense of pressure or temperature? What is its texture? What is its shape? Place your hand over the knot—does it change? If it had a voice, what would it say to you? What would it teach you about what you are needing in this moment? As you explore the sensations in your stomach, do you begin to notice other feelings in your body? What are they?

If we allow ourselves to remain present and attentive to our own hearts and bodies, feeling our feelings, staying with our discomforts, and exploring our sensations, then we may become more fully alive, fresh and awake in this instant. Of course, we may always feel some painful residue from the wounds of childhood, wounds we may experience as a knot in the stomach, a tightness in the shoulders, or a pain in the forehead. These are the scars of being human. But we need not use these scars to return us to the past or warn us about the future. Instead, we may use these feelings to teach us about who we are in this moment. We may simply pay attention to what is arising within us, noting, "Ah, here is some tightness," or "Here is a knot, this is how it feels, this is what I imagine it looks like, this is what it is telling me about myself in this moment." When we use our feelings, not as evidence of the past but as information about the present, we learn to meet and accept ourselves with compassionate curiosity.

A good place to begin mindfulness practice is during those times when you notice yourself preoccupied about something in the past or the future. If you find yourself lost in thought about some childhood wound or some worry about how things will go in the future, stop yourself for a few moments and try the following mindfulness exercise to reorient yourself back into the present moment.

As soon as you notice yourself worried or preoccupied, stop whatever you are doing. As we have seen in earlier chapters, we may begin our mindfulness practice with the breath. First, become aware of the breath, noting the sensations in the throat, lungs, and abdomen. How does the breath feel? Close your eyes if it helps you to concentrate. Follow the path of the breath as it moves gently in and out of your body, noticing where it flows easily, and also where it gets caught. Without changing the tempo of your breathing, note if your breaths are long or short, fast or slow, shallow or deep. The point is not to change—only to observe and to be mindful of each breath.

Then, after a moment, allow your mindfulness to extend to the sensations of the body. Be aware of any places where there are particularly strong feelings of pain or pleasure, tension or relaxation. As you come upon these sensations, you may silently note to yourself, "tension, tension" or "pain, pain." Again, the point is not to change how you feel, just to explore the feeling itself. What kind of pressure, texture, or color arises with the feeling? Is it sharp or dull, large or small, solid or fluid? Stay with each sensation until you feel you have fully comprehended the nature of that feeling in your body. Over time, watch as it changes of its own accord, and then move on and explore the next sensation that arises.

Continuing your mindfulness practice, simply allow your awareness to notice any emotions you may be experiencing. Be aware of any states of mind, like fear, joy, sadness, love, or anger. Without trying to change, simply identify the emotion and silently note to yourself "fear, fear" or "sadness, sadness." Again, the point is not to try to feel anything different, but rather to accurately and fully explore whatever feelings may arise within you. At the end of this exercise, open your eyes and pay attention to how you feel now.

As an extension of this exercise, you may expand the mindfulness practice as you continue on with whatever work you were doing. As you continue to read, or wash the dishes, or clean the house, or sit in a meeting, or make tea, mindfully watch yourself perform each detail. Do not let a single act, a single movement, go by without being mindful of it, how it feels, what it looks like, how it is finished. Do not hurry to get the job over with. Savor each step of the way as you lift the pot, place the pen on paper, or take out the garbage. This way, you begin to invite a mindfulness in your daily life, one that will, over time, become a far more interesting source of information about you and your life than all the old childhood stories.

For many of us, learning to pay closer attention to our lives might require no small amount of discipline. But we should not be afraid of discipline; the word *discipline* comes from *disciple,* which essentially means "to follow what you love." Thus, the discipline of mindfulness invites us to cultivate a deep love and affection for paying attention to the daily, precious moments of our lives, allowing us to receive and experience each new moment in a fresh way. In mindfulness, we truly begin to learn about love, for we learn to appreciate the full range of our experience with unconditional acceptance. We learn to welcome the quality of the breath, the texture of the earth as it rises to meet our footsteps, the taste of the air, the sounds of the city, the touch of another's hand, and the feelings in our body. We see with a devout vitality the wonder of all things great and small. Like a soft rain, our attention falls on all things equally, with a compassionate acceptance of exactly who we are and what we feel. The whole universe of our experience is no longer about our childhood; rather, it is being born anew in every instant, with every breath, if we simply open our eyes and hearts to receive it.

When we see with eyes hardened by habit, we tend to see our childhood playing itself out over and over again in the present moment. Yet if we are truly attentive, where is our father in this moment? Where is our mother? In this breath, in this step, in this bite of food, where is our childhood? We see the hurt, the loss, the abuse only in our memory, not in this moment. When we touch all we feel and all we are with mindful, loving attention in the present moment, we are able to be set free from the demons of our remembered smallness, free to grow and change, and to blossom in ways we never dreamed possible.

Mindfulness and Liberation

If the eye is clear, said Jesus, our body will be full of light. When our attention is receptive and accepting, everything we see may become an object of meditation, a source of teaching. Even the most difficult and painful feelings and emotions, as we experience their arising in the present, can become teachers and companions for us. According to Kabir, the fifteenth-century Indian poet, "When the eyes and ears are open, even the leaves on the trees teach like pages from the scriptures."

Where shall we place our attention? As we move through the days of our lives, how shall we keep our eye clear, our hearts open, and our spirits alive and awake in the present moment? If we find ourselves thinking all day about whether or not we are loved, or how we can protect ourselves from danger, or how we can impress others with our skills and achievements, then we are condemned to languish in a prison of our own making. Where we look and how we see gives birth to the kind of life we will live. If we see only danger, we live in fear; if we seek what is gentle and true, we will find ourselves on a path of serenity and peace. All we are, said the Buddha, is a result of what we see and think.

Jesus said that beauty, truth, and the spirit of God may be found in every thing and every moment. "Split a piece of wood, and I am there. Lift up the stone, and you will find me there." Everything that is, preaches the word of God; everything teaches the Dharma. Every person we meet, every relationship, every leaf, every pebble, every flower, every tree is teaching us about what is possible for us in this very instant. Every instant we may discover what we missed in childhood—for every moment contains some teaching about love, balance, healing, and truth.

Mindfulness allows our childhood to recede into the background of our experience, inviting the present moment to fill our hearts with clarity and fullness. When we are caught in our habitual mind, all creation seems to conspire to validate the teachings of our childhood. But as we practice mindful, compassionate awareness of each moment of our lives, then, as Thomas Merton observed, "All creation teaches us some way of prayer."

Mindful awareness is a practice that may bring us a lifetime of healing and freedom. Thich Nhat Hanh speaks of the importance of mindfulness as a daily practice:

> While washing the dishes, you might be thinking about the tea afterwards, and so try to get them out of the way as quickly as possible in order to sit and drink tea. But that means you are incapable of living during the time you are washing the dishes. When you are washing the dishes, washing the dishes must be the most important thing in your life. Just as when you're drinking tea, drinking tea must be the most important thing in your life. When you're using the toilet, let using the toilet be the most important thing in your life.
>
> And so on. Chopping wood is a meditation. Carrying water is a meditation. Be mindful twenty-four hours a day, not just during the one hour you may allot for formal meditation or reading scripture and reciting prayers. Each act must be carried out in mindfulness. Each act is a rite, a ceremony. Raising your cup of tea to your mouth is a rite.
>
> Does the word *rite* seem too solemn? I use that word in order to jolt you into the realization of the life-and-death matter of awareness . . .

EXERCISE
Naming Our Emotional Habits

There are a few core beliefs we carry within us to explain the world and our place in it. Along with those beliefs, there are a few particular emotions that become most familiar and most trustworthy, the ones we feel most often when we are in distress. We will use this exercise to clearly identify our habitual emotional states.

The next time you feel a particularly strong emotional response to a person or event, stop yourself for a moment. Perhaps you had an argument with someone you care about, something happened that frightened you, or someone said or did something that hurt you deeply. Notice the feelings that arise within you.

Now, as you experience the power of that feeling, imagine that in that very instant I approach you and ask you to complete the following sentence: "You see, it's just as I have always known, _____." What response immediately comes to mind? Without censoring your response, what phrase leaps in to fill the blank?

Almost everyone has a sentence or two that instantly explains why things go badly, that succinctly describes our destiny. It may be "you see, it's just as I've always known, I will always be alone." Or it may be "there will never be enough for me." Perhaps the feeling is "I can't trust anyone to really care about me," "I will always have to work harder than everyone else," or "I will never be allowed to be happy." In any case, if you listen closely, there will almost always be a sentence that will instantly present itself to explain why this powerful feeling of sadness, hurt, anger, or rejection has come to you at this time. That sentence defines the essential nature of your emotional habit.

Each sentence naturally carries with it a corresponding feeling. If we believe we will always be alone, then when we feel isolated or misunderstood, we are probably in our habitual emotional state. If we are convinced there will never be enough for us, then when we feel cheated, overworked, or jealous of others' success, we are firmly planted in our habits. Each of us has one particular set of emotions that comes up more often than others. As we explore these habitual states of mind and heart and listen for the sentence that describes our emotional philosophy, we can learn much about where we get caught, where we get stuck in the past. Then we may slowly develop the capability to let these habits naturally fall away, and become mindfully aware of our feelings in the present moment.

Take time to experiment with the wording of your particular sentence until it feels precise and accurate. Then, for a few days, each time you feel badly about something that happens to you, silently repeat the sentence to yourself: "You see, it's just as I've always known, I'll never be happy . . . etc." How does it feel when you speak the sentence so explicitly? What emotions arise within you? Repeat the sentence a few times, each time using a different tone of voice—saying it once with a sad voice, then an angry one, then a playful one.

These are the sentences that are your unconscious companions. By making them explicit and bringing them into your conscious awareness, they become less potent, less able to influence your emotional state of mind. If you can learn to be playful with these voices, you may slowly disempower

*their ability to keep you stuck in the same old states, and you become more
quickly free to shift to a new and different state of mind and heart.*

*An interesting companion exercise is to take a camera and, for an hour or
two, take a walk in the neighborhood where you live. Without loading the
camera with film, use it to take pictures of whatever captures your eye.*

*What sort of things do you find yourself noticing? What people, subjects,
or relationships draw your attention? Focus and snap as many "pictures"
as you like, since there is no film and no pressure to take a "good"
photograph. The object is simply to notice what you notice. After a while,
what patterns of perception seem evident to you? What things appear most
frequently through the lens? Which things seem important, which things
move your heart? At the end of an hour or two, reflect on the way your eyes
led you through the experience. Be aware of the things, people, and events
that seem to hold the most meaning for you. This exercise may help you
become aware of the feelings and emotions that are most familiar, most
habitual, and most powerful in the story of your life.*

Meditation
EXPANDING MINDFULNESS PRACTICE

*Find a comfortable sitting position in your place of refuge. This time you
will sit for thirty minutes, using techniques to expand the mindfulness
practice we have explored in earlier chapters.*

*Close your eyes and allow your awareness to rest in the breath. Gradu-
ally become aware of the sensation of breathing as the air moves in and out
of your body. Observe the qualities of the breath, noting the speed, depth,
and texture of each inhale and exhale. You may silently note "rising . . .
falling" as a way to focus your concentration on the breath.*

*Then, as you become more relaxed and centered in your body, allow
yourself to notice any physical sensations that may be arising. Be aware of
any pain or tension, any pressure or relaxation in the body. Gently bring
your awareness to that area of the body, investigating the quality of the
sensation itself. What does the pain or pressure feel like? Is it sharp or dull,
does it throb or tingle, is it hot or cold? Watch the shape and substance of
the feeling, making a silent note of its predominant character: "pressure,
pressure"; "aching, aching"; or "tensing, tensing." Watch the sensation
until it naturally begins to recede. Then gently bring the awareness back to
the breath.*

Now begin to observe any reactions the mind may have to the various bodily sensations. For example, when you are noting painful sensations, you may also feel aversion, impatience, or fear. Make a note of these mind states, observing their qualities until the next mind or body state arises. Sometimes you may experience pleasant sensations in the body, and there is a corresponding mind state of happiness or attachment. Make a note of these also.

As various thoughts arise, you may similarly note, "thinking, thinking," and, without following the thought, let it go and gently return to the breath. Be aware of any plans, worries, memories, or fantasies that are occurring as you sit quietly. What seem to be the predominant themes? Again, silently note each thought as it goes by, noting "planning, planning," "wandering, wandering," or simply "thinking, thinking." The object is not to follow the thoughts themselves, but rather simply to note that a thought has arisen. Then, after making a mental note of its presence, allow the thought to fade away. You can always think about it later on. For now, simply let it go, and gently return to the breath.

Lastly, you may scan your inner emotional landscape. What feelings do you notice that are present within you? Do you feel relaxed, impatient, or angry? Do you feel sad, tired, or peaceful? Without trying to change them, note which feelings seem the strongest. Choose one feeling and investigate it more thoroughly. If you are feeling sad, for example, what are the sensations that arise with sadness? Perhaps there is a warmth in the stomach or a tightness in the throat? Maybe there is an empty feeling or tension in some part of the body. Take as much time as you need to explore the feeling that has arisen, and stay with that feeling until it passes.

Even though we expect our feelings to stay for a long time, you may notice that most feelings actually pass in a moment or two, giving way to a different emotion. A moment of pride may dissolve into a moment of anger; a sense of sadness may dissolve into a moment of self-pity; a voice of judgment may give way to a voice of courage. If you watch your emotions for any length of time, you may see yourself experience a dozen different feeling states in rapid succession. Each voice pleads its case until it automatically melts into the next. The more you remain present and mindful of the emotions within your body and heart, the more you may see how fluid your feelings actually are. At the end of thirty minutes, you may open your eyes.

It is the nature of feelings to change from moment to moment. If we feel sad, angry, or rejected for long periods of time, we are probably holding onto that feeling out of habit. As we practice mindful investigation of the sensations around our feelings, we may become more present and alive in *this moment, allowing our feelings to change and evolve naturally. We may watch them arise and fall away without attachment, without holding onto them out of fear and habit.*

EXERCISE*
Developing Daily Wakefulness

This exercise lasts one month. At the beginning of each week, choose a simple regular activity of your life that you usually do unconsciously, on automatic pilot. Resolve to make that particular activity a reminder, a place to wake up your mindfulness.

For example, you might choose making tea, shaving, bathing, or perhaps the simple act of getting into the car. Resolve to pause for a couple of seconds before each time you begin the activity. Then do it with a gentle and full attention, as if it were the heart of a meditation retreat for you.

As you go through the week, try to bring a careful mindfulness to that act each time it arises in your life. Even the simplest acts can be powerful reminders and bring a sense of presence and grace. If you choose the opening of doors throughout the day, you can open each door as if Jesus or the Buddha were to pass through with you. If you choose the act of making tea or coffee, you can do it as if it were a gracious Japanese tea ceremony.

At the end of the week, add another activity, until by the end of the month you have included four new areas of your life into daily mindfulness. Then, if you wish, continue this exercise for a second and third month, bringing the power of attention into more and more of each day.

* Special thanks to Jack Kornfield and Joseph Goldstein for this exercise.

CHAPTER ELEVEN

Isolation and Intimacy

Our experience as separate individuals stands in perpetual tension with our experience as members of a larger community. Where does our individuality end and our involvement with others begin? When do we keep our hearts to ourselves, and when do we seek out the hearts of our families, friends, and neighbors? When do we stand alone, and when do we seek the company of those we love?

For children raised in troubled families, these questions often seem painful and confusing. For many of us, the experience of being a separate individual has frequently been accompanied by a tremendous sense of fear and isolation. Our sense of individuality has been colored by memories of feeling unspeakably alone, misunderstood, unheard, and invisible. In our families, we kept the aches in our hearts and spirits to ourselves; hurtful episodes were left unspoken, and we guarded our wounds and fears in secret silence. When there was pain, no one spoke of it; when there was sorrow, no one gave it a name. And so we learned to shrink into ourselves, separate and apart from everyone else.

We learned to use our separateness as protection—a shield against pain, a private fortress against fear and intimacy. Yet, while we may have initially felt that our isolation kept us safe, over time our separateness actually intensified our unspoken hurt, sadness, and shame. Our tendency to isolate ourselves gave birth to a terrible loneliness, a profound feeling of being set apart from the rest of our family, from the rest of humanity. Eventually we came to fear that we might never feel close to anyone but ourselves.

Alice's father was an alcoholic. For Alice's whole life, her mother had refused to speak to her about her father's drinking, even after Alice had moved away. As a child, Alice learned to watch the drinking and the fights in secret, while her mother maintained that there was nothing wrong. Alice quickly learned that she could not speak the truth about what she saw and felt, and developed a habit of staying in her room, reading and keeping to herself.

Rachel, who grew up in a "normal" household, was fifteen years old when she developed a crush on an older exchange student who was staying in their home. After some time the older boy took Rachel to bed, and she became pregnant. The family, filled with shame and embarrassment, sent Rachel far away to an unwed mothers' home. There, without any family or friends, she gave birth all alone, just before Christmas, to a child she gave up for adoption. Rachel, now a grown woman, says she feels terribly alone much of the time, even when she is in the company of others. She feels she must do everything by herself, and that no one can be trusted to help her. She long ago decided it was safer to remain alone. Over time, her feelings, dreams, and yearnings became buried in the frightened isolation of her heart.

As we perfected our ability to withdraw, we found it increasingly difficult to form alliances or partnerships that felt safe or trustworthy. When I ask people, "Who were your allies in childhood?" more often than not I am met with a blank stare, a look of confusion and disbelief. "What do you mean?" they reply. "There was never anyone I could really trust." Perhaps there was an occasional aunt or grandparent who took them in, someone who listened, someone who felt safe. But often the most powerful memories are of being alone, ignored, and set apart, painfully separate from the rest of the world.

As children, when we are deeply hurt, we sometimes seek safety by creating a subspecies of one, neatly dividing the world in two equal parts: (1) me, and (2) everyone else. No one else can name or share the pain I feel, so it must be mine alone. My life, my hurt, and my fear must belong only to me. When I was hurt, no one saw; when I was in need, no one came; when I was sad, there was no one to comfort me. I am afraid I am in this alone. There is no one like me, there will be no one for me. I will learn to survive by myself.

The experience of childhood pain can accelerate our psychological tendency to isolate ourselves from others within our human family. Erik Erikson has described how human beings often "pseudospeciate," that is, we create subgroupings within our own species, groups that we then decide are somehow different, inferior, or dangerous. It is precisely this psychological process that can enable a human being who is a "Nazi" to emotionally justify sending human beings who are "Jews" to the ovens. It gives "Spaniards" psychological permission to wipe out "Incas" and "Aztecs"; it permits "whites" to mentally justify enslaving "blacks."

Similarly, when our fears and hurts cause us to withdraw from the rest of our family, we begin to see ourselves as one kind of person and the rest of the world as another. When we see ourselves as "I" and everyone else as "other," then we can objectify other human beings to such a degree that they no longer seem to have the qualities of being human. They are simply "other"—or, even worse, "dangerous" or "enemy." If we can completely establish our separateness from them, we make it easier to find the permission we need to be totally separate, to feel disconnected from their actions, their feelings, their lives, and their humanity. They are not like me, they are not my family. I have no relationship with them.

As we close ourselves inward, we create a sphere of safety that becomes smaller and smaller until it has room enough only for ourselves, removed from anything or anyone who could ever love us, from anyone who would touch, caress, or heal us. Isolated in our secret hurts and sorrows, there is no room for anyone to help us, no room for healing. "In separateness," said the Buddha, "lies the world's great misery."

Our Sense of "I" and "We"

We spend much of our childhood and adult lives trying to discover who "I" am, who "you" are, and to solve the puzzle of how "you" and "I" might become "we." If we begin our lives with such painful confusion about how to safely belong in loving community with others, how can we successfully understand an experience of "we"?

Perhaps we may start by exploring our sense of "I." Much Western psychological literature speaks of the need to develop an identity, an "I," that is separate and distinct from our mother, our father, our siblings, and our peers. This critical process of "individuation" is considered to be of paramount importance in healthy psychological development, so that we may evolve a strong sense of self and an ability to perform as individuals in society. However, some of us respond to childhood suffering by *overin-dividuating* in an unhealthy way, choosing to isolate ourselves entirely as a way of protecting us from danger.

But even if we do successfully individuate and learn to establish clear ego boundaries and precise limits on our personal identity, constructing a strong and well-defended ego can never be the end of our story. When we overemphasize the need for a powerful sense of "self"—when we learn to "set limits," "ask for what we want," and make sure we "take care of ourselves"—we subtly perpetuate our isolation by pitting "our" needs against "theirs." So even if we finally muster up enough courage to extract "our" share from "them," "they" still feel like the enemy. Even though we "get" what we "want," we still end up feeling isolated, separate, and set apart from true community with those who would be our lovers, our allies, and the family of our spirit.

The greater evolution of our sense of "I" is still incomplete because, in fact, our "I" never really stands alone; we are inextricably interdependent with everyone else who shares our friendship, our family lineage, and our planet. Our sense of "I" comes to full flower in a healthy, loving community of "we." Unfortunately, children touched by family sorrow become excruciatingly sensitive to the tension between "I" and "we." Our contacts with others reveal a certain uneasiness, and even those close to us can begin to feel like the enemy. Whom can I trust to be there for me? Who can really hear my pain? Can anyone understand my heart? How far can I let you in, how safe will I be? Might it not be better to remain alone, separate and protected?

Separateness and Interdependence

After a lifetime of withdrawal and isolation, many of us develop a deep ambivalence about being seen or known by others. Using our invisibility as a shield against pain, we become comfortable in our anonymity and unsure about how close or intimate we really want to be, even with those closest to us. Even as we feel handicapped by our separateness, at the same time we ache to be made whole with our friends, our family, and with God. We experience a deep, profound knowing that we do not belong in exile. We sense the possibility of a rich connection with others—yet we feel confused about where we belong, and mistrust that we will ever be welcome. For those of us who habitually withdraw in order to feel safe, our ability to feel part of a larger whole is clumsy and impaired. Reluctantly, and with great fear, we gradually make our home in isolation.

Even though we wrap ourselves in separateness out of fear and habit, the truth is that we are still connected, intimately bound to one another. It becomes extremely difficult to maintain the illusion of our separateness when we observe how intricately we are all woven together. "I am part and parcel of the whole," said Gandhi, "and I cannot find God apart from the rest of humanity." Thich Nhat Hanh beautifully describes the subtle interplay of factors that connect us all, using as an example the making of a piece of paper:

If you are a poet, you will see clearly that there is a cloud floating in this sheet of paper. Without a cloud there will be no water; without water, the trees cannot grow; and without trees, you cannot make paper. So the cloud is in here. The existence of this page is dependent on the existence of a cloud. Paper and cloud are so close.

Let us think of other things, like sunshine. Sunshine is very important because the forest cannot grow without sunshine, and we humans cannot grow without sunshine. So the logger needs sunshine in order to cut the tree, and the tree needs sunshine in order to be a tree. Therefore you can see sunshine in this sheet of paper.

And if you look more deeply, with the eyes of a bodhisattva, with the eyes of those who are awake, you see not only the cloud and the sunshine in it, but that everything is here: The wheat that became the bread for the logger to eat, the logger's father—everything is in this sheet of paper.

Like the piece of paper, we, too, carry within us everything and everyone who taught us, held us, nourished, and loved us as we have grown: The food we eat, the people who grew and harvested it, the plants and animals that gave their lives for our well-being; the people who manufactured the materials and built our house for us; the clothing we wear and the people who wove the fabric and sewed the garments for us. Every moment, with every step, we live in intimate communion with all the beings and elements that work to bring us life, food, music, shelter, transportation, and clothing. In short, we are never alone. We are awash in a sea of intimacy and interdependence with all beings.

Several years ago, when I was in the seminary, my refrigerator stopped working. It continued to hold my food rather well but kept it warm instead of cold. When I called a repair shop, they said it would cost fifty dollars just to send someone to look at it. Since I was an impoverished graduate student without a great deal of disposable income, I courageously resolved to fix the refrigerator myself.

First I went back to the used furniture man who had sold the refrigerator to me. He said it sounded like it needed a particular electrical part that would cost only a few dollars, and told me where to buy it. I then went to the electrical supply store, and the man who sold me the part explained how to put it in the refrigerator. Excited and rather pleased with myself, I went home with my precious part, and managed to install it in about an hour. The refrigerator worked.

I couldn't have been more proud. I had fixed my broken refrigerator all by myself. The epitome of American ingenuity and know-how, I was a picture of self-reliance. I could take care of myself.

Later that day, as I began to reflect on my achievement, the question arose in my mind—who fixed the refrigerator? Was it really me, or was it the man who told me which part to buy, and where I could put it? Or was it the people who made the part in some faraway factory? Maybe it was whoever gave me the money so I could buy the part, or perhaps it was the man who sold it to me and told me how to install it? Who fixed the refrigerator?

In fact, it is almost inevitable that we all end up fixing the refrigerator. We are so delicately woven into the fabric of all beings, so intricately involved in the common dance of life, that only tremendous fear and resistance can keep us apart. We depend upon one another for food, for care, for love, for life itself. While it may sometimes feel like it is hard for us to belong, in fact the opposite is often true: It requires an enormous amount of energy to remain separate.

In Africa, the Bantu people say, "A person is a person through other persons." Our psychological experience may convince us that we are isolated and separate from others, and the lingering memories of unspoken fears may cause us to shrink from intimacy. Yet in spite of all our fear and trembling, we are still, in every moment, sharing our very breath with all creation. Our membership in the family of the earth is so strong, our belonging so deep, that our mental and emotional separations cannot truly keep us apart. "When we pick out anything by itself," said John Muir, "we find it hitched to everything else in the universe."

As a child, Joanne had always felt misunderstood and alone; her parents had rarely had time to listen to her fears or her worries, nor did they support her talents or her gifts. She learned to feel that the world was simply a large collection of people who would forever misinterpret her, and decided she would forever remain alone. She joined one of our therapy groups, but after only a few weeks she said she was noticing she felt different from everyone else, and wasn't sure she belonged in the group. She mentioned that she might prefer to see me individually. Even though I suggested she might work on these feelings of isolation with the group, the feelings of separateness were powerful, and were driving her to quit. "I just don't belong here," she said. "My needs are just different from everyone else's."

"Joanne," I said, "you are certainly welcome to leave, and you are just as welcome to stay. You must follow your own heart." We decided to meet privately a few times. There, we spoke at great length about her habitual need to be special and different from everyone else. All her life she had felt misunderstood, unheard, and unseen by those around her. She spoke of how painful it was to be separate, yet how equally frightening it was to let go of the familiar safety of her barriers and boundaries. I could sense her deep confusion and sadness. I felt how desperately she wanted to feel welcome in the company of others, yet she simultaneously felt a powerful pull to withdraw, to run away. After a few weeks, I asked her to try to express these feelings to the group, just to see what would happen. If she still felt uncomfortable, she could leave knowing she had done her best. She agreed that she would try.

The following week, Joanne spoke to the group about how she felt so different from everybody else, that her problems and her ways of working on herself were just not going to fit in the group, and that she wanted to leave. Several members of the group reflected that they had noticed her coming late to several meetings, and her poor excuses for missing a few others. They wondered if she might not be afraid of belonging to the group. Others told her that when she *was* present, Joanne was always compassionate and insightful—it just seemed like she couldn't ever decide if she wanted to stay. They suggested perhaps this was a pattern for her life, since she had changed partners, careers, and living situations many times in her life. Others spoke of the care and affection they had for her, and of the disappointment they would feel if she left.

Joanne seemed a little surprised by the honesty and care offered to her by the other members of the group. Perhaps she expected them to be annoyed, or pull away, or in some way reject her. Instead, they seemed to be more open and truthful—they even seemed to be moving closer. Sensing her confusion, I sat next to her and gently met her eyes with mine. "I know that you feel yourself apart from us, and that brings you much sorrow. But Joanne, wherever did you get the idea that everyone here is not your sister and brother? How could you believe that we are not *already* your family?"

As the truth of the question settled in her heart, some of the barriers of years of fearful isolation began to melt, and Joanne wept. She cried long and deep, feeling the pain of the separateness that she had carried for a lifetime. As she allowed her heart to grieve the ache of her isolation, she also began to allow herself to feel the possibility that perhaps she could stay in one place long enough to be seen, to be known, and to be heard; perhaps someday she could belong here, with us, in this moment. Maybe there could be a place for her after all.

Our separateness is a painful fiction, a psychological device we use to feel protected, a mere illusion of the mind. For if we look honestly at our childhood, was there truly anyone in our family without sorrow? Once pain was injected into the family bloodstream, was anyone truly immune from suffering? Even though we may have felt alone in our hurt, we were subtly connected by our sorrow, bound together as we each in our own way shared the tender sufferings of our common family.

The habit of our emotional seclusion only serves to bring additional violence to ourselves, denying ourselves the gift of sharing the sorrows and joys of being human with all who live. The word *person* is a compilation of *per* (through) and *sonare* (sounding). Each person is simply a vessel through which the spirit of life gently passes, a spirit that weaves us all into a fabric of the human family. It is impossible to think we could really go away—where could we go? We are never really cut off from the body to which we belong.

Some cultural traditions honor this interdependence with particular wisdom and grace. Chief Seattle, a native American writing in 1854, said, "This we know . . . all things are connected, like blood which connects one family. Whatever befalls the earth befalls the children of the earth. Man did not weave the web of life—he is merely a strand in it. Whatever he does to the web, he does to himself."

Healing Our Isolation: A Mutuality of the Heart

Most of us, however isolated, have a deep yearning for true intimacy, for an experience of community with others, for the kinds of safe and loving relationships we never had. Yet the inertia of our isolation has become so habitual, so painfully familiar, that many of us only dream of such communion. Even so, there are times when we unexpectedly experience a moment of mutual love and care so sweet and powerful that it takes our breath away. Some of us may have this experience while making love, when the fragile boundaries of "I" and "you" dissolve, and we feel ourselves participating in physical and spiritual union with another. Others may feel it in a moment of tenderness with an old friend; some of us feel it with our children, when we open our hearts so wide that it feels we are carrying these little beings in our very soul.

Still others discover a rewarding intimacy in providing care for someone in need. I have most recently witnessed this compassionate mutuality among people living with AIDS. Unfortunately, when AIDS first became public, some used the infectious HIV virus as an opportunity to reassert their separateness from their brothers and sisters. They began to speak the language of pseudospeciation, frantically labeling who "had" HIV and who did not. But over time, as many of us have sat with friends who were dying from the effects of AIDS, holding their hands and listening to their fears, joys, and sorrows, we are more likely to feel our common humanity than our separateness. We feel a deep kinship of spirit as we share the experiences of life and death, health and disease, fear and love.

How do we cultivate such intimacy? What practices are available to allow us to gently outgrow our isolation? First we must recognize that we are most often propelled into isolation by fear, sadness, or hurt. When, in the company of others, we become sad, afraid, or hurt, our survival impulse is to hide out, to disappear, and to make ourselves small, protected, and alone. Our assumption is that if we withdraw from everyone else, we can make the painful, uncomfortable feelings go away.

Ironically, as we have seen, our withdrawal into isolation can actually serve to increase our suffering. When we separate out of fear, our fears may multiply, our sadness congeals, and our wounds continue to germinate in the fertile greenhouse of our seclusion. Consequently, the first step in healing our isolation requires us to reverse our natural tendencies to hide our fear and camouflage our grief. Rather than hide, our challenge is to speak what is true, to share the tender contents of our hearts, to describe for others the emotional geography of our deepest concerns. By locking away our most terrible feelings, we keep them alive and strong; by attending to them, mindfully exploring and acknowledging them, by speaking them aloud in the company of others, we allow them to recede, to fade, and to gradually take up less space in our body and soul. Only then are we able to open ourselves to intimate communion with others.

During one of my therapy groups, I began to notice that some of the members had started to withdraw, speaking infrequently and becoming less involved. We had all been together for a few months, and already several people had spoken of how the group had been a tool in their healing. Still, a few of the members had gradually become more quiet over the last weeks, and I soon noticed that each of the quiet members was female. So I asked the three women who were present that evening to form a small circle in the middle of the group, and to have a group of their own. I asked them to spend an hour sharing among themselves how it felt to be a little girl growing up in their family, and what it felt like to be a woman now. I asked all the men, in the outside circle, simply to listen in silence.

Although they were slightly tentative at first, soon each woman was speaking passionately about the fears and hurts they had experienced as children. They spoke of the afflictions, the abuses, the violations, and betrayals that polluted their childhoods. As women, they were able to speak of the promises broken, the gentle moments of love, and the terrible disappointments they experienced with their mothers. They also spoke of how painful it was to never feel real intimacy with their fathers, their husbands, or their lovers. Each in turn found herself weeping about how difficult it had been to be a little girl, and over the unspoken grief, fear, and anger they had carried as grown women, alone and unheard, for so long. At the end of the evening, all spoke of how comforting it had been to be in the company of other women who could listen, understand, and care. Several of the men were in tears.

What had happened? Clearly, I had done nothing more than ask these women to gather for a few moments, to speak what was true in their hearts, and to share the fear and sadness they had carried in secret. Gently the isolation melted away as each felt the company of the other and they shared the excruciating pain of being isolated, hurt, and alone. In that moment they activated in one another a sense of mutual care, respect, and trust. After that evening, the intimacy among the members of the group grew very quickly. Not surprisingly, the men asked if they could do the same exercise. When it was their turn to gather in the inner circle, many of the same emotions emerged, as these men had also learned to isolate themselves at an early age.

Whatever we feel, however deeply we feel it, most of us learn to camouflage our true emotions. We show the world only what we imagine will be acceptable and keep the rest secret and hidden. Thus, no one really sees us, no one ever knows who we are. Even if people love us, they love us for who we pretend to be—so we never really feel loved at all. But when we name our feelings truthfully—first to ourselves, then to others—when we speak about the sorrow, the terror, and the grief, we invite a rush of sympathetic vibration from those who are suddenly free to enter into our lives, to become allies, to love and touch and share our deepest hearts. The truth sets us free to enter fully into a relationship with another, opening the door to a mutuality of love and support. Whether we are with a spouse, a close friend, a support group, a therapist, or on a spiritual retreat, we take our first step out of isolation when we speak to others about what is most deeply true in our hearts.

Healing Our Isolation: A Mutuality of the Spirit

There is a rich, extensive lineage of spiritual teachers and saints who maintain that the membrane that divides "me" from "you" is not quite so solid as we may think. They explain that the passionate distinctions we draw between who "I" am and who "you" are are simply a matter of perception, the clumsy device of a frightened mind. In other words, rather than feeling myself as separate from you, it may be more accurate to recognize that, as the Mayan saying goes, "I am your other self." When the Quakers gather together, they speak of honoring "that of God which is in

every person"; in the Hindu tradition, the greeting *Namaste* may be translated as "I see and honor the divine within you, as you see and honor the
divine within me."

For children accustomed to emotional isolation, this may seem a difficult
practice at first. Yet as we learn to feel confident enough to see and name
what is most deeply true about ourselves, we often find we become more
skillful in naming what is true and beautiful in others. Over time, as we
cultivate an ability to see ourselves with mercy and kindness, as we
become more sensitive to where there is fear, hurt, tenderness, or love
within ourselves, we begin to recognize those same feelings in others. We
learn to see all beings as children of the same God, children who share our
sorrows and joys, our lineage, and our spirit. As we name more accurately
the outline of our own spirit, we begin to look for that same spirit in those
we meet. Slowly we may begin to feel less alone and more part of a family
of children, all of whom hurt, all of whom ache for love.

We have all experienced this compassionate sense of mutuality from
time to time. Either on a walk with a stranger, at a gathering, or even during
an unexpected conversation over a cup of coffee, people who may have
seemed closed, hard, unfeeling, or dangerous suddenly reveal something
about themselves that makes them seem soft, vulnerable, and open. In an
instant our heart shifts and we feel a sense of acceptance, even compassion,
where only a moment before we had felt aversion and dislike. In that
instant, we recognize something deeply human, a part of ourselves in the
other. We experience one another in a new way, not as "me" and "other,"
but somehow as children of the same spirit. Mother Teresa said her practice
is to seek out that spirit in the most difficult leper, the troublesome beggar,
the most demanding vagrant. In doing this, she says she is attending to
Jesus "in all his distressing disguises."

Rumi said:

What I tell about "me" I tell about you
The walls between us long ago burned down
This voice seizing me is your voice
Burning to speak to us of us.

Jesus taught that whatever one does to any other being—when they feed or
clothe someone, when they help or hurt someone, when they anger or heal
someone—they are doing it to God. Every being, however awkward or
unappealing, harbors a spark of the divine light within him. When we are
able to discern the same spirit in ourselves and others, we become more
pliable, and our experience of "we" naturally begins to expand, nourished

by increasing tolerance, patience, safety, and love. If everyone I meet is a mirror of my own spirit, how can I possibly cut you out of my heart without bringing us both much pain and anguish?

Joseph Campbell told a story of two policemen who were driving up a road in Hawaii when they saw, on a bridge, on the other side of the guard rail, a young man preparing to jump. The police car stopped, and the policeman on the right jumped out to grab the man. But he caught him just as the man jumped. As he himself was being pulled over, the second policeman arrived and pulled the two of them back in time. Campbell continued:

> Do you realize what had suddenly happened to that policeman who had given himself to death with that unknown youth? Everything else in his life had dropped off—his duty to his family, his duty to his job, his duty to his own life—all of his wishes and hopes for his lifetime had just disappeared. He was about to die.
>
> Later, a newspaper reporter asked him, "Why didn't you let go? You would have been killed." And his reported answer was, "I couldn't let go. If I had let that young man go, I couldn't have lived another day of my life."

"Why?" asked Campbell. Why should any human being suddenly defy the law of self-preservation, supposedly the first law of nature? Perhaps, he argues, it is because there are deeper laws at work within us. There is a deep mutuality that resonates within us, an inner knowing that we share the same life, the same breath, the same spirit, and the suffering of any single being somehow diminishes us all. "Our true reality," said Campbell, "is in our identity and unity with all life."

On Not Taking Childhood Personally

Some of us, weary of the pain of continually isolating ourselves, have sought relief through individual psychotherapy. Yet while these encounters may give us new information about ourselves and bring us welcome healing and relief from our loneliness, one of the subtle dangers of individual psychotherapy is that it perpetuates the illusion that we are, in fact, so uniquely alone in our sorrow that we require intensive individual attention in order to be understood at all. We may literally spend years in individual therapy, never having to let go of the illusion of our separateness from our sisters and brothers.

Katie was a young woman who had seen me privately for several months.

She had hoped to heal some of the pain of her childhood sexual abuse and to discover some way of feeling less closed down, less tight, less alone. We explored how her body armored itself in response to intimacy, the fear and hurt lodged deep within her. After a while, I suggested she may want to join one of my therapy groups, where she would have the opportunity to explore new ways of being close with others in the safe setting of a group.

Katie committed herself wholeheartedly to the group, using it as a laboratory to speak about herself and her feelings in the company of others. She shared her tender feelings, her fear, her hurt, even her anger. She spoke of feeling isolated and stuck, and she told us about the numbness she used to protect herself from danger. She allowed others in the group to confront her, to question her thoughts and feelings, and to invite her to go deeper within herself. Over time, she learned to feel much more a part of everyone else's life, and became a valued member of the group.

Yet Katie still felt isolated because of her childhood abuse. She felt broken in some unique and terrible way, and was convinced the secret to her healing lay somewhere deep inside. She could not rest until she had uncovered all the violations, hurts, and mistakes that had happened to her as a little girl. Because she was abused, there was something terribly wrong with her, something that needed to be fixed. And until she could find out exactly what was broken and how to make it all better, she would never be able to let anyone in to help her, to comfort her, to love her. Her perseverance and determination to heal herself, while admirable, also served to keep her closed, tight, and inaccessible. Regardless of how much she shared with others, she still felt isolated in her own feelings. After all her good work, she still felt frustrated and disappointed with herself.

It became clear to me that Katie had personalized the abuse to such a degree that she felt her childhood pain was something that happened not just *to* her but *because* of her. She was convinced that if she could only find out the truth of what had happened *to* her, she would finally be able to learn what she needed to know *about* her. Her whole life had become a problem to be solved, and until she solved it, she couldn't let anyone else in.

When we isolate ourselves, we perpetuate the illusion that our pain somehow *belongs* to us, that because it came to us personally it is somehow ours alone, unlike anyone else's. We begin to think that if we were a different kind of person, if we were better, stronger, or smarter, the pain would not have come. So we end up examining our childhood pain in the hope of discovering some deep psychological defect, some toxic catalyst that may be lurking still in our psyche. Who knows when it could manufacture that same kind of pain again? As long as we are unsure of what, in us, caused so much suffering to happen, as long as we are still trying to solve the puzzle of our childhood, we keep everyone else at bay. Only when we have located the answer, only when we have cleared away any questions, do we feel safe enough to come out of our isolation and invite another into our heart.

I said to Katie, "It seems to me that you still look at yourself as a problem to be solved. You seem to think the abuse that happened to you has something to do with you personally, as if it were somehow *about* you. But your abuse didn't have anything to do with you at all. Pain comes to children in all kinds of ways: Some children are born Jewish in Germany in the 1930s; others are born black in South Africa; others are born during a civil war, or a drought or famine. You just happened to be born into a family of people who were sexually confused, and you were terribly hurt by their unskillfulness. It was never about you; you had nothing to do with it. In fact, the fact that you were abused has nothing to do with you at all. It was simply one image that arose in the emotional collage of your life. This week, as you think of yourself, your childhood, and your hurt, you might want to experiment with not taking the story of your life so personally. Imagine that what happened to you was simply something that happened to a child of God. Not for any particular reason other than it happened, and it was very sad, and it hurt deeply. Perhaps this perspective might begin to free you from feeling so tainted with the brush of your childhood story."

I didn't know quite how Katie would respond; many of us have become powerfully attached to the unique peculiarities of our suffering. But I felt she was genuinely ready to let go of this endless, exhaustive investigation that had only served to leave her feeling disappointed, inadequate, and alone. When she came in the next week, she looked much softer. "I feel so much lighter, like a big weight was lifted from me," she said. "What you said felt so true, it just allowed me to let go a little, to not take what happened to me so personally. When I let myself think that I was just born in a family of sexually clumsy people—and it could have just as easily been Germany or South Africa—somehow, I can stop feeling so responsible for figuring it all out. It doesn't change what happened, or even take the hurt away. It just makes me feel less alone. I just got a piece of the pain that everybody gets, and it wasn't my fault, and I don't have to fix it. It just wasn't about me at all."

In Community with the Larger Family

Stephen Levine reminds us that when we move from seeing our particular suffering as "our" pain and begin to experience it simply as "the" pain—the pain of all creation, of all beings—then we move on from being separate and alone, and our suffering becomes a doorway into community with the family of the earth. The pain we have felt is intimately connected with the pain felt by a woman giving birth; by the families torn apart by civil war; by the children dying of cancer, and by the fathers and mothers who hold them as they die; and by all those who suffer hunger, war, or oppression. Every one of us is given some quantity of suffering; some are given more than others, some more violently, some more subtly. But the suffering we feel has never been ours alone; it is simply a fragment of the suffering given us all as children of flesh and spirit. The *form* of the suffering may change from person to person, but the *fact* of our suffering is something we inevitably hold in common with all sentient beings.

Have you ever, when you were alone, entered a temple, church, or synagogue when it was empty and quiet? In those moments, if you allow yourself to listen, you may sometimes hear the echo of thousands of prayers that have been prayed in that place by a thousand hearts in pain. You may feel the tears, the cries, the petitions that have been spoken by parents, children, friends, or lovers who ached for some kind of healing, gift, miracle, or blessing for someone who was suffering. In that place, we may feel our own prayers and petitions mingle with all those who have gone before and all who will come after.

The saints of the world emphatically insist that each one of us is an invaluable member of the family of creation. The Christians teach that everyone is a shining cell in the body of Christ. The Buddhists teach that everyone has deep within them a Buddha nature, and that they may take refuge in being part of the *sangha*, a member of the family of all sentient beings who seek to be healed. Gandhi said that we are so inextricably bound together in a common family that everything we do and say has an effect on the entire fabric of humanity. As a reminder of this delicate interdependence, he suggested that whenever we had to make a significant decision in our lives, we first imagine the poorest person in the world sitting right in front of us. The point is not to induce guilt but rather to remind us that we are intimately related to all our sisters and brothers, and that any decision we make regarding ourselves must take into account the effect we will have on the family to which we undeniably belong.

Desmond Tutu said there was once a woman in California who wrote him to say she awoke every morning at two o'clock to pray for peace and healing for the people of South Africa. Now, in the face of all the political, military, and economic conflicts in his homeland, Bishop Tutu could have easily dismissed her efforts as being too little, too late. But what he said was, "How do I know that this is not the woman who will save us all? Every prayer, every word of hope is a blessing for us, an invaluable part of our work for peace. So I wrote her back, and said 'Keep praying! We are all part of the body of peace. Every one of us is necessary.' "

Each of us is necessary. When we isolate and withdraw from humanity, we not only deny ourselves the love, comfort, and nurture available from our friends, family, and neighbors, we also deny others access to our gifts, our wisdom, our heart, and our spirit. Our global family aches for the gifts of each one of us as we seek political and ecological healing among the peoples and species of the earth. All creation awaits our gifts.

Thomas Merton speaks of a moment in his own life when he experienced a mutuality of spirit with the community of all people:

Then it was as if I suddenly saw the secret beauty of their hearts . . . the person that each one is in God's eyes. If only they could see themselves as they really are. If only we could see each other that way all the time, there would be no more war, no more hatred, no more cruelty, no more greed . . .

I suppose the big problem would be that we would all fall down and worship each other . . .

EXERCISE
Speaking the Truth

One of the most powerful healing practices is speaking the truth. We often use silence, dishonesty, and confusion of language to keep ourselves hidden and separate from the rest of humanity. We either confuse ourselves so we can no longer hear what is really true, or we become too frightened to speak what is true for fear of being vulnerable and exposed. Learning to speak the truth with clarity and courage is a potent doorway to intimate community and relationships with others.

Choose one person with whom you wish to do this exercise. It should be someone you feel comfortable with, such as a close friend, lover, or spouse. Ask them to sit with you for ten minutes and just listen in silence to what you have to say.

Use this time to speak honestly, clearly, and intentionally about what is in your heart. Mindfully consider your choice of words, allowing your speech to become slower and more accurate. You may share some secret you have kept hidden, something about yourself, or how you feel about them. If there are feelings of fear or discomfort you have never spoken about, use this time to tell them the truth of how you feel. What concerns or experiences have you never told them? What would you like them to know about you? Tell them as much as feels comfortable and true. The object is not to expose yourself beyond what feels safe but rather to name honestly and precisely the nature of your innermost feelings.

What do you notice as you speak? Observe any impulse to censor or alter your feelings. Watch how isolated or intimate you feel, noting which feelings tend to make you want to pull back and which seem to invite a closeness with your companion. Observe what happens as you move closer and closer to the truth. Watch any fears or uncertainties that arise, and note how they affect your speech. With each word, try to speak as accurately as you are able about those things that are deeply true about yourself.

At the end of ten minutes, ask your friend to summarize what he has heard. Ask if he has any questions. Notice your responses to being questioned and responded to in relation to your most private feelings, and observe your ability to respond openly. Notice if you begin to feel confused about what is true, or if you tend to present yourself in a different light depending on the question.

After five or ten minutes of dialogue, you may stop. How do you feel now? Are you more open, close, and intimate or more isolated? Have you spoken the real truth? Which parts were most difficult? Which produced the greatest sense of relief?

You may use the practice of speaking what is true with other friends, in groups, even in business meetings or social gatherings. In each situation, try to ascertain if what you are saying is clear and true. Notice when you are trying to be obscure or manipulative, and when you are speaking what is honestly in your mind and heart. The point is not to use honesty as a device to be cruel or hurtful but rather to reveal a more accurate representation of ourselves in community with others. As we become more comfortable speaking the truth, we are able to move out of isolation.

Meditation
TOUCHING THE PAIN OF OTHERS

We are never alone in our suffering. The pain of being human is shared by all who live. In this meditation, we use our own pain to make contact with the simultaneous suffering of all other beings.

Find a comfortable sitting position in your place of refuge. Gently close your eyes and allow your attention to rest on the breath. Slowly become aware of the sensations of breathing, noting "rising, falling" with each inhale and exhale. Take a few moments with this practice to center yourself in your body.

After a while bring your attention to your heart, noticing any sensations in the area of the chest. Going deeper, become aware of any places within where there is sadness, grief, or loss. Allow the images to arise one after another, feeling the depth of your sadness. Acknowledge to yourself that all your friends, your children, and your family will die some day; feel the place that knows that you, too, will die one day, and perhaps leave so much undone. Become aware of all the things left unspoken, all the love you didn't get or give, all the hurts and disappointments that have touched your life. As feelings arise, let them come. Be soft and feel them as fully as you can. Feel the depth of the sorrows that have come, that will come, that will be a part of your life until you die.

Take a few cleansing breaths into your heart area. As you exhale, begin to let go of the holding and the tightness around the pain. Allow the pain to soften and to loosen its grip on your heart.

Now, shifting your perspective, gently allow the image of someone close to you to arise, someone you care for deeply. Allow yourself to become aware of her pain, the places in her life where she has felt sadness, hurt, or loss. Be aware of the deep sorrows this person has experienced over the course of her life. Take all the time you need to feel her pain, her sadness, her hurt; be aware of any anguish or grief she may have been given. Try to feel it in your own heart, in your own body.

How do your feelings change in relation to this person? What do you notice about your own pain, your own sorrow? What words arise within you, what do you feel you wish to offer this person? Silently imagine yourself giving this person some comfort, some care, some loving kindness. Be aware of the intimacy made possible when you share deep sorrow with another.

After a while, allow images of others who are in pain to arise. Begin with people close to you who are suffering illness, loss, or physical or emotional discomfort. Become aware of the nature of their pain, the sadness and grief they feel deep within. Feel how their pain is a mirror of the sorrows you carry within yourself. Feel how the pain connects you; feel also how touching this pain together, with mindful attention, opens a door to mutual love and intimacy.

Next, allow images of others to arise: men, women, and children suffering the horrors of war; mothers losing their children to violence and illness; mothers and fathers dying of hunger, trying to keep their children from starving; old men and women in hospitals and nursing homes, uncomfortable and alone; men and women sleeping in the cold, homeless. Allow each image to arise for a moment, one by one, feeling the depth of their suffering and sorrow, becoming aware of the kinship between the pain you feel in your life and the pain felt by all other beings. Allow the pain to open and soften the heart with compassion, allowing a sympathetic vibration to exist between your heart and the hearts of all who suffer.

Observe how birth, suffering, illness, and death touch each one of us who lives on the earth. This is the pain we all share, in which we all partake, the pain of being human that touches our common bodies, hearts, and minds. You may say to yourself as each image arises, "I am your other self."

Embrace each image with forgiveness, mercy, and love, touching the pain with your heart, touching all the beings who suffer with your heart. This is the inheritance of the family of creation. This is your family.

Feel the depth of connection to all beings as you allow the pain to be a doorway into community with your greater family. Feel the truth of your belonging. Gradually return to the awareness of your breath as it naturally flows in and out of your body; feel your body as a tiny cell in the larger body we all share. When you are ready, you may gently open your eyes.

Afterward, you may wish to make a collage celebrating the family of all beings. Using pictures from magazines, family photos, or your own drawings, gather a pile of images that speak to the multitude of joys and sorrows experienced by all living beings. Select from your collection of pictures those images that most accurately describe the common pulse we all share as children of the earth. Arrange them to make a collage of the larger community to which you belong. You may also use the collage to explore and identify your place in the human family.

CHAPTER TWELVE

Obligation and Loving Kindness

When we come to the moment of our death, it is likely that a few simple questions will arise in our hearts: Did I love well? Was I generous and kind? Did I allow myself to be loved? How did I share that love with others?

Few people facing the end of their lives worry that they didn't spend enough time at work; not many wonder if they made enough money, or went to enough meetings. Instead, as they prepare themselves for death, they become focused on the deep love they have for their family, their children, and their friends. What could be more important? To hold those we love, to give our love freely, to be open and generous with our care— these are the measures of our life, the priceless rewards of our time on earth.

Perhaps our most painful childhood legacy is that we have few, if any, clear memories of exchanging unconditional, trustworthy care and affection with someone close to us. Many of our families were confused about love; love was neither given nor received with ease, and we were cautious and unsure about how to care for one another. Around tender feelings we were clumsy and awkward. Even when love was intended, it could often be misinterpreted or mistrusted.

To many of us, the idea of "unconditional" love seems abstract, foreign, somehow utopian. Much of the care in our families involved an intricate maze of contracts and conditions: If I do this or that for you, then you will behave in a caring way toward me—or (at the very least) you will not hurt me. Our experience of care was fraught with covert, reciprocal contracts designed to minimize the harm we would bring to one another. In this way, gestures of affection were actually strategic maneuvers calculated to fulfill our obligations to those around us. Caring acts were primarily defensive: If we didn't hold up our part of the caring bargain, we could be rejected, hurt, or abandoned. So we learned to be attentive, to listen to everyone else's problems, to try to be helpful when others were in pain. We cultivated an ability to construct the correct phrase, create the proper atmosphere, and generate sufficient support so that anyone in pain would feel better after they had been with us. We used the language of care to buy safety, belonging, and peace, and this was a language we mastered to perfection.

We learned to use care and kindness as a weapon for our defense, manufacturing sympathetic words and caring behaviors for whomever came our way. But this was not true love or generosity; this was a desperate response to a fearful obligation. Even as we perfect our ability to care for others in order to secure a reciprocal kindness from them, our own hearts are often closed, empty, and removed. By all outward appearances, we may seem to be freely giving care to those in need—a beautiful thing to do, and a lovely practice—but in reality, when we care for others as a defense, with no hope of drinking from the fountain of loving kindness ourselves, we set up an imbalanced, resentful, and dishonest situation in which we quickly burn out. Ultimately these seemingly endless demands for care simply drive us deeper into isolation and despair.

When Bill was a child, his mother seemed in constant need of care and attention, and she often came to Bill for advice. Even though he was small, it felt to Bill that his mother wanted *him* to take care of *her*, and not the other way around. Since Bill naturally wanted her love, he would always try to help her; maybe if he gave her enough love and attention, she would eventually be strong enough to take care of him. But after repeatedly giving her advice on her life, her friends, her marriage, and her family, Bill felt drained and empty. He eventually decided that his mother would never be able to care for him. Further, he concluded that he would never be loved without first paying a great price. So he gradually stopped looking to his mother for love and affection. Over time, he stopped going to anyone. He had come to see care as a necessary evil: something relentlessly required by the world around him, but something he despaired of ever receiving himself.

We feel obliged to provide care for others in order to earn our place, to placate those around us, to be accepted, and to protect ourselves from harm. Over time, we begin to see care as a substance, something that we "have" that we are required to "give" in order to satisfy the endless demands of a desperate world—and so that we may finally "get" some care ourselves. Like dipping into some secret stash, we have to determine when to give whatever care we have, who needs it most, how to distribute it so that everyone feels satisfied, and how to figure out how much is left at the bottom of the barrel. Then, when we are "empty," we have to find some way to "get" some more. This forces us to "take care" of ourselves until we are full again, then we resurrect the cycle of "giving" care all over again.

Yet true love, by definition, is unconditional and abundant. It is not gained by contractual arrangements with those around us. When we say, "I will love you if you will love me back," we are still bargaining in fear. And out of that fear, we place endless demands on those we love: "I will love you as long as you don't change, as long as you stay the way you are, as long as you behave the way I want." When these contracts become confused with true love, they actually separate us from one another, as we become objects of one another's desperation.

When we love, are we really doing anything at all? In fact, we are likely to feel most loved when we simply hold one another. A simple, loving touch, a small gesture of care, a single word of kindness help remind us of a place deep within where we know we are already loved, that we are cared for by God, by the spirit, by the earth itself. A single moment of care can remind us that we are safe and whole. When we touch that place in ourselves, it is a very powerful moment indeed. Our practice is to continually remind one another of this place, to remember with a gentle heart the tremendous care available to each one of us in every step we take.

Even in the most painful situations, we may still experience tremendous love and care. When we encounter someone who is suffering the heartbreak of a divorce or the loss of a family member, when we sit with a friend who is struggling with cancer or AIDS, when we speak with people who were terribly hurt as children—even in the midst of our most poignant losses, we may still feel a loving connection as members of a common family. Here, there is no contract, no obligation; no one "has" the care, no one is giving, no one is taking. As we share the pain of being human, we also share the love that is part of our lives together.

Care and Dishonesty

Regardless of how loving we are, it is impossible to expect that we will have genuine feelings of care for everyone all the time. There will inevitably be moments when we become weary, hurt, or afraid, when we feel vulnerable and in need of care ourselves, and experience a scarcity of loving kindness in our hearts. In these moments, if we continue to feel obliged to manufacture care for others, we quickly learn to equate care with dishonesty. If we were truly honest and said "No, I don't have time for you today," or "I am not feeling well," or "I'm sorry, I am finding your behavior difficult and I don't enjoy spending time with you," then we might appear cruel and insensitive. If we spoke what was true, we may hurt someone's feelings, and they would be angry. They would probably reject us, dislike us, even abandon us, and so we decide that the most expeditious thing we can do is to lie, to shade the truth, to manufacture a façade of care that conceals our true feelings. We become adept at manufacturing a caring and supportive attitude even when we may be feeling no such thing. We learn to justify our emotional dishonesty in the name of kindness.

When Betty was young, her mother would get drunk late at night. She would then wake Betty up and make her sit and talk and keep her company while she drank. Betty, half asleep, would try her best to look interested and attentive so her mother wouldn't get mad or yell at her. But all the while, as she endured one drunken monologue after another, all Betty ever wanted was to be left alone so she could go back to sleep.

To this day, Betty is known as a person who will sit and listen to anyone's problems, and people always leave feeling better. But Betty confided to me that she often has no real love for them—in fact, she feels angry and resentful that they take so much of her time. "I can't believe I let all these jerks just use me up. I keep hoping if I listen to them long enough, they will finally just go away and leave me alone."

Terri and Jay were seen by everyone in their circle as an ideal couple. She was an artist, he was a musician, and they were both successful and admired for their work. However, after some time Terri realized that even though they shared many interests, she was not really in love with Jay. She enjoyed his company and liked him as a good friend, but she did not feel the deep, passionate love of a wife for her husband. For many years she never spoke to any of her friends about her ambivalent feelings; she feared they would be disappointed if they knew how she really felt. More important, she was afraid that if she said anything about her true feelings, the marriage would instantly come to an end. So Terri decided that keeping the truth to herself was necessary to preserve her marriage. It seemed the kindest thing to do for everyone concerned.

In our families, few people dared to be honest about their thoughts and feelings. No one wanted to be the one to say that our mother was emotionally disturbed, that our father seemed incredibly angry, that our parents were unkind to us, or that we weren't happy. If we said what was true, people would likely become even more angry and upset. So we equated not telling the truth with being kind, with not causing pain, and with preserving the peace. After a while, we convinced ourselves that dishonesty—while necessary for our survival—was the most expedient form of kindness.

But denying the truth actually served to prolong our family suffering. Indeed, it would have been infinitely kinder if someone in our family had had the courage to clearly name our sorrows, our fears, and our hurts. By not telling the truth about ourselves, we intensified our secret suffering and we made any exchange of authentic love impossible. How could we feel loved when we pretended to be someone else? It is not that we were maliciously dishonest, it was just that hiding the truth had become such a fearful habit, we simply knew of no other way to be kind; kindness and honesty had become seemingly incompatible.

But, as we have seen, telling the truth is often the seed that gives birth to love. When we are able to honestly name our fear, our sadness, and confusion—and when we can meet ourselves, just as we are, with acceptance and compassion—then we cultivate the possibility of an authentic loving kindness toward ourselves. Self-acceptance is impossible if we cannot speak truthfully about ourselves. Without the truth, we may learn to accept who we appear to be, but what we are accepting is a lie. Mindfully naming where we are stuck, frightened, or caught opens the door to genuine self-acceptance and loving kindness toward ourselves and others. Jack Kornfield, a gentle teacher of Buddhist meditation, says that the essence of spiritual practice is self-acceptance:

> . . . It is the ground out of which any other freedom or understanding can come. Our practice is to begin to listen to where we are closed to ourselves, to our bodies, our feelings, our hearts . . . and out of this can come a very deep opening, and forgiveness, and healing of the heart.

Suffering and Love

In Vietnam there is a traditional folk tale that describes the difference between heaven and hell. In hell, everyone is given an abundance of food, and then given chopsticks that are a yard long. Each person has all the food they need, but because the chopsticks are too long, the food never reaches their mouths.

In heaven, the image is exactly the same: Everyone is given an abundance of food, and their chopsticks are also a yard long. But in heaven, the people use their chopsticks to feed one another.

A single act of compassion can instantly transform hell into heaven. The word *compassion* comes from the Latin *pati*, which means "to suffer." *Com-pati* means "to suffer with," to feel the pain of another as it reflects our own. Compassion, then, is not something we give to another; rather, it is something we share through a mutual recognition of our common suffering.

When we share the hell of our hearts in the company of others, we open something deep within us, something warm and alive, a rich sensation of being part of one another. Through the practice of compassion we may love and be loved without holding, without keeping score.

There is a story from the time of the Buddha; Kisa Gotami, a young woman, married a man who loved her very much. In time, she gave birth to a son. She and her husband were exquisitely joyful and together lived quite happily. Sadly, two years after their son was born, the child became ill and died very quickly. Kisa Gotami was devastated; her heart was broken. She was so stricken with grief that she refused to admit that her son had died. She carried his small corpse around, asking everyone she met for medicine to make her boy well again.

Kisa Gotami went to the Buddha and asked him if he could please cure her son. The Buddha looked at Kisa Gotami with deep love. He said, "Yes, I will help you; but first I need a handful of mustard seed." When the mother in her joy promised to collect the seed immediately, the Buddha added, "But the mustard seed must be taken from a house in which no one has lost a child, husband, wife, parent, or friend. Each seed must come from a house that has not known death."

Kisa Gotami went from house to house asking for the mustard seed, and always the response was the same: "Yes, we will gladly give you some mustard seed. But alas, the living are few and the dead are many." Each had lost a father or mother, husband or wife, son or daughter. She visited one home after another, and every home told the same story. By the time she got to the end of the village, her eyes were opened, and she saw the universality of sorrow. Everyone had experienced some great loss, each had felt tremendous grief. Kisa Gotami realized she was not alone in her suffering; her sorrow had given birth to a compassion for the larger human family. Thus, Kisa Gotami was finally able to grieve the death of her son and bury him, and she returned to the Buddha to thank him and receive his teachings.

Many of us have had moments when—sitting at the bedside of someone close to death, surrounded by friends, family, and our community of loved ones—the presence of shared loss has opened everyone's heart. The sadness, hurt, and grief slowly melted our separateness and we were able to feel tremendous love for the person who was dying, and an abiding compassion for one another. We could each feel how the other was in pain, and simply by holding hands, sitting quietly, even just making tea or preparing a meal together, we were exquisitely conscious of our whole community caring for itself. In a family gathered together by sorrow or death, we felt a tremendous abundance of love available to us all. "Love," said Teilhard de Chardin, "is capable of uniting living beings in such a way as to complete and fulfill them, for it alone takes them and joins them by what is deepest in themselves."

The Practice of Loving Kindness

There was once a young rabbi who lived in a small mountain village. He was a clever young man who believed himself to be very wise, and he had a great desire to be recognized for his tremendous gifts. But to his disappointment, the people of the village had never honored or respected him to his satisfaction. This had left him feeling bitter and resentful.

One day an old rabbi, famous for his wisdom, came to the village. The clever young rabbi saw this as a great opportunity; the old master was going to speak before a gathering of the villagers the following morning, and the young rabbi decided to devise a test for him. At the right moment, in the middle of the gathering, the young man would approach the elder rabbi holding a tiny bird in his hand. Then he would ask him the following question: "Rabbi, I have a bird in my hand. Can you please tell me, is the bird alive, or is it dead?" If the rabbi answered, "The bird is alive," the young man could easily crush the small creature and hold it out for all to see, proving that the old rabbi was wrong. On the other hand, if he replied, "The bird is dead," the young rabbi would simply let the bird fly away into the sky, clearly demonstrating his superior cleverness and wisdom.

The next day, when the rabbi sat before the assembled villagers, the young man stood up and challenged him with his question. "Rabbi, we all know that you are clever and wise; but please, sir, if you will, can you tell me if the bird I hold in my hand is alive or dead?"

The rabbi was silent for a moment; everyone awaited his response. Then, with eyes of infinite compassion, he looked at the young man and gently replied, "It is up to you, my friend. It is up to you."

At this point in our lives, we hold the key to our healing in our own hands. The wounds of childhood are long past, and we have thoroughly investigated the lingering scars that color our emotional landscape. We have learned to speak the truth about our sorrows and hurts, and to describe the inner geography of our hearts with clarity and precision. We have also begun to discover that, as children of a larger family, we have available to us a wealth of healing practices bequeathed to us from the spiritual traditions of the world.

Beginning in this moment, starting with this very breath, our healing is up to us. As the rich mixture of sorrow and wisdom that saturates our life becomes more evident, as we mindfully explore the tremendous depth of who we really are, our challenge is to integrate these healing practices into our daily lives. Each emotional wound we have identified, every exercise, meditation, and practice of mindfulness ultimately serves to engender an acknowledgment and trust in a deep spirit of strength, wisdom, and wholeness we carry within ourselves.

The fundamental thread that runs through the fabric of these teachings is the practice of loving kindness. Each childhood wound and every spiritual teaching has been presented to help us cultivate a particular aspect of mercy and compassion toward ourselves. At each juncture we have been confronted with a choice: Do we meet ourselves and our wounds with judgment or with mercy? Do we touch our childhood memories with anger, or soften them with love and forgiveness? Do we recall our violations with shame, or embrace them with genuine acceptance; do we react with fear and isolation, or with faith and courage? Do we add to the violence within ourselves, or do we cultivate unconditional love and kindness for all we have been and all we have become?

Every day we live, each moment, offers a fresh opportunity to be more gently loving with ourselves and others. We begin by learning to belong in the sanctuary of our own breath, to feel more at home in our own bodies, more confident in our rightful place as a member of the human family. This enables us to accept wholeheartedly ourselves and others just as we are, thereby planting the seeds of a genuine, secure experience of belonging.

Second, as we make a forgiving peace with the childhood we were given, we become more able to respond compassionately to those who, intentionally or unintentionally, brought us harm. As we loosen our habitual attachment to the old childhood stories, we begin to cultivate a mindful appreciation of our current gifts and capacities. We are free to be more creative and spontaneous in our generosity with ourselves and others.

In the same way, as we soften the tyranny of our judging mind, and as we let go of an exaggerated sense of our importance, we begin to experience a quality of mercy and inner peace. Through self-acceptance, mercy, and humility, we are set free to care for ourselves and others with less resentment, less anger, and less fear. As we slowly recognize that there may be enough love available for us all, we come to feel that our kindness and affection may be given freely without judgment or fear of depletion.

Finally, our healing is deepened through a mindful cultivation of simplicity, stillness, and nonattachment. These practices enable us to listen more precisely to the voices of our heart and spirit. We learn to name what is most deeply true within ourselves and to embrace what we have been given with gratefulness. As we become quiet and still, we gain access to an abundance of inner resources that give us permission to be kind and generous with ourselves and others.

Every spiritual practice is an act of love. Each act of mindfulness, of meditation, and of compassion helps soften our fearful holding to the past and allows us to speak more clearly and precisely from the heart. Each time we mindfully attend to the present moment, we make space for great healing. Each time we hold the pain with love and mercy, we create one less moment of fear, one less act of judgment, one less instance of bringing harm to ourselves or others. With every gesture of mercy and compassion, we refuse to add to the mountain of suffering we all share. Each moment that we meet ourselves with loving kindness, we perform a revolutionary act. Over time, the potent impact of a thousand loving moments inexorably combines to profoundly alter the basic emotional assumptions that have governed our lives.

Compassion for Ourselves and for the World

For many of us, an authentic love for others has been virtually impossible when we have had so little love for ourselves. Wherever there is judgment, fear, or holding within ourselves, we inevitably encounter a resistance to be free and open with our love for others. If we judge ourselves, we will judge the world; if we are angry and impatient with ourselves, we will be angry and impatient with our friends and family. Peace and healing in the world must begin within ourselves. As Ramana Maharshi, the Indian sage, once said: "As we are, so is the world."

The Dalai Lama is the exiled spiritual and political leader of Tibet who was granted the Nobel Peace Prize for his nonviolent work on behalf of the oppressed Tibetan people. Speaking of the unending quest for world peace, the Dalai Lama said:

> The question of real, lasting world peace concerns human beings, so basic human feelings are also at its roots. Through inner peace, genuine world peace can be achieved. In this the importance of individual responsibility is quite clear; an atmosphere of peace must first be created within ourselves, then gradually expanded to include our families, our communities, and ultimately the whole planet.

In the Judeo-Christian scriptures, sages and prophets had predicted for centuries that a great savior would come who would be the King of Kings, the Lord of Lords. But when Jesus the Savior came, he arrived as a tiny, helpless infant born to poor refugee parents. Everyone had assumed that God would save them, love them, and take care of them. But when Jesus arrived, they unexpectedly found themselves providing nourishment and care for a tiny, divine infant.

We practice truly loving ourselves by learning first to imagine that the God-child is alive and present in the manger of our own heart, within our own body and spirit. Next, we must accept that part of our spiritual practice is to care for that divine child that lives most tangibly within us. If we are gentle, kind, and loving with ourselves, we may begin to see ourselves as God sees us, as a child of light, a child in whom the spirit of God has made its home. As a young child, we may have been hurt badly, our families may have brought us great suffering, and our hearts may have been broken. The practice of loving kindness insists that we meet this wounded child of God with tenderness and mercy; as God's child, we deserve all the love in the world.

How do we learn to love and honor the God within us? How do we hold the divine spirit that lives within all beings with mercy and loving kindness?

A troubled woman came to the Indian saint Ramakrishna, saying, "Oh, Master, I do not find that I love God." He asked, "Is there nothing, then, that you love?" To this she answered, "My little nephew." He replied, "There is your love and service to God, in your love and service to that child."

We do not find God apart from ourselves, apart from our sisters and brothers. The face of every being that lives is a reflection of the divine, every one of us carries a spark of the spirit of God. When we love anyone, we are loving God. When we care for anyone, we are caring for God. Jesus said that whatever you do for anyone who suffers, you do for Him. When we open our hearts, our homes, or our hands in service to anyone in need, we are making a place for God. Every act of loving kindness toward ourselves or others is an act of love for God.

This kind of love needs no religion, no theology, no church; a simple act of kindness is a precious sacrament and a moment of love is an epiphany. No more is required of us than this: that we love ourselves and one another with gentleness and mercy, for we each carry within us the tender heart of God.

Many people with AIDS have spoken to me of a certain quality of loving attention that they now bring to themselves and others as a result of their illness. "I always had a hard time loving myself," said Angela, a friend with AIDS. "But since I have been sick I've been looking at my life and learning to be kinder and more loving toward myself. It feels good. I am so thankful."

Growing up with a scarcity of love and care in our families, many of us are reluctant to be too generous or loving with ourselves. To be kind to ourselves seems self-centered and selfish. But love for ourselves and love for others are not mutually exclusive. A compassionate heart makes no distinction: You are a child of God, as I am a child of God, and we both need loving care. True love does not sacrifice others for our own needs— nor does it sacrifice ours for others. Loving kindness does not require that we decide who will be deprived; there is enough care available for everyone. As Jesus said, "Go and learn the meaning of this: I desire mercy, not sacrifice."

The practice of loving kindness must find its root deep within us. The story is told that Mohandas Gandhi once settled in a village and at once began serving the needs of the villagers who lived there. A friend inquired if Gandhi's objectives in serving the poor were purely humanitarian. Gandhi replied, "Not at all. I am here to serve no one else but myself, to find my own self-realization through the service of these village folk."

As Gandhi wisely points out, even as we serve others we are working on ourselves; every act, every word, every gesture of genuine compassion naturally nourishes our own hearts as well. It is not a question of who is healed first. When we attend to ourselves with compassion and mercy, more healing is made available for others. And when we serve others with an open and generous heart, great healing comes to us.

As we investigate the sorrows of childhood and their lingering effects on our minds and hearts, we gradually come to realize that we ultimately share our suffering with all the children of the earth. All beings who are born are given a portion of that pain, and all beings stand in need of deep healing, love, and care. Consequently, our healing is not just for us; the more we feel our place in the human family, the more we undertake our own healing as part of our love for all beings who suffer. As we extend our circle of kindness and compassion to include all living things, the more we engender the possibility of true, lasting peace within ourselves and for all humanity. As Thomas Merton observed, "The whole idea of compassion is based on a keen awareness of the interdependence of all these living beings, which are all part of one another and all involved with one another."

As we heal the wounds of the past, we carry less pain into the world, less confusion and anger, and we bring more clarity and peace. Here, our work is not simply for personal gain; it becomes our gift, our offering to the human family, to the earth, and to the divine spirit within us all. Albert

Schweitzer, after a lifetime of compassionate service, noted a profound correlation between our own happiness and the happiness of others. "One thing I know," he said, "the only ones among you who will be really happy are those who have sought and found how to serve."

The Buddha said, "If you knew what I know about the power of giving, you would not let a single meal pass without sharing it in some way." Most of us are naturally compassionate, but for some of us, the wounds of childhood have suffocated our natural generosity toward ourselves and others. We often feel sad and troubled because we are unsure how to love, how to be helpful to ourselves and others, how to be most useful to the family of the earth. Our task is not to learn how to be loving; the love within us is already full and alive. Our practice is to melt the fear and armor that imprisons our hearts. Then our impulses to love and our inclinations to be generous and kind blossom easily and surely within us.

These are the fruits of our practice: to become kind and loving with ourselves and others. The painful legacy of our family sorrow turned us fearfully inward, isolating our deepest gifts from ourselves and one another. These practices gently reveal the wealth of courage, wisdom, and loving kindness that has been imprisoned, in exile, hidden away deep within our bodies and hearts for most of our lives.

Mindfulness and Loving Kindness

In Sanskrit, the words for *mind* and *heart* share the same root. So when we use the practice of mindfulness to heal the remaining wounds of childhood, it might be more accurate to say we are cultivating *heart*fulness, a courageous discipline of attending to ourselves with an open heart. The practices of heartfulness and mindfulness are potent methods that enable us to gently extricate ourselves from the seductive morass of our childhood memories. Mindful loving kindness may be our most powerful healing tool—and it may only be found in the present moment. All healing is available to us just as we are—not when we are old enough, or more evolved, or free from the difficulties of being human. Healing comes when we are able to meet ourselves and others, just as we are, with unconditional appreciation, gratefulness, and compassion.

Love is not something we can extract from the past. When we look to the past for the love we never received, we remain forever entangled in regretful preoccupations with our childhood disappointments. On the other hand, love is equally impossible in the future. Regardless of how much we plan, scheme, and strategize about how we will arrange to be loved, how often do we feel truly cared for while dreaming of the future? Our dreams of future love are more likely to cause worry and anxiety as we perform our desperate orchestrations, and in spite of our best efforts, we are often left feeling dissatisfied and disappointed.

Our only hope for loving kindness is today, in this moment, this instant; there is no other soil in which love can grow. If the heart is to open, it can only happen in this very breath. What are you waiting for? How can you be kinder or more loving to yourself in this moment? Where will you place your care? What in your body or heart is in need of special attention? Which person or situation in your life would benefit from a moment of loving kindness?

Acts of love are often uncomplicated, small gestures that require little effort: a touch on the shoulder, a word of appreciation, a cup of cocoa, a warm bath, or a note of thanks. It could be so simple, so easy to be more loving in this instant. Loving kindness is the most powerful enzyme of healing and is always available to us in this very moment. How much longer can we afford to wait? And, more important, how can we begin?

Perhaps we may begin with ourselves. You could take just a few moments each day to cultivate a simple practice of loving kindness. It requires such little time. You may even start this moment: Take a minute to arrange yourself in a comfortable position, and slowly let your attention come to rest in your breath. Then, sitting still, slowly begin to recite this prayer of loving kindness:

May I be happy.
May I be peaceful.
May I be free from suffering.
May I be healed . . .

What happens as you repeat this prayer over and over, quietly within the heart? Do you notice any resistance or hesitation to be gentle and loving with yourself? What thoughts or worries impede your loving in this moment? Observe any tension that arises in the body, any struggle in the mind or heart. As you repeat the prayer, also be aware of softening, of letting go. Observe any sensations of warmth or love that arise within you. How do you feel?

This prayer of loving kindness is called *metta*, and in Buddhism is considered the heart of spiritual practice. The Buddha taught that all beings require loving kindness, and in this moment, you may begin with yourself. You can recite this prayer of loving kindness to yourself every morning you awake, before you get out of bed. Undertake this loving kindness practice for thirty days, choosing phrases most meaningful to you. (You may wish to add, "May I be filled with compassion," "May I be soft and open," "May I be loving." Use words that feel nourishing and true.) As each day goes by, observe how merciful and accepting you are and how much compassion you have available for yourself.

At the end of the month, you may expand your *metta* practice to include others, beginning with your family, then your friends, your community, expanding outward to include all beings, even the earth itself. Practicing this loving kindness meditation every day, you may find it easier to care for yourself and others. You may become less inclined to procrastinate before you perform an act of kindness. As it becomes more natural, you will learn, in the words of the Lotus Sutra, to "look at all beings with the eyes of compassion."

"If you have love," wrote Thomas Merton, "you will do all things well." As we reclaim our inner strength, wisdom, and resilience, we take our place of belonging as children of the earth. Through all the practices we have explored—as we cultivate mercy, simplicity, humility, nonattachment, lovingkindness, and all the rest—we begin, each day, in small simple steps, to create a world in which there is more kindness, peace, and love for our children—and for all the children of the earth for generations to come.

The Dalai Lama explains that the core of all healing, the heart of all spiritual teaching, may be found in the practice of loving kindness:

My true religion is kindness. If you practice kindness as you live, no matter if you are learned or not learned, whether you believe in the next life or not, whether you believe in God or Buddha or some other religion, in day-to-day life you have to be a kind person. With this motivation, it doesn't matter whether you are a practitioner or a lawyer or politician, administrator, worker, or engineer. Whatever your profession or field, you carry your work as a professional. In the meantime, deep down, you are a kind person. This is something useful in daily life.

We shall not cease from exploration
And the end of all our exploring
Will be to arrive where we started
And know the place for the first time.
Through the unknown, remembered gate
When the last of earth left to discover
Is that which was the beginning;
At the source of the longest river
The voice of the hidden waterfall
And the children in the apple-tree

Not known, because not looked for
But heard, half-heard, in the stillness
Between two waves of the sea.
Quick now, here, now, always—
A condition of complete simplicity
(Costing not less than everything)
And all shall be well and
All manner of thing shall be well
When the tongues of flame are in-folded
Into the crowned knot of fire
And the fire and the rose are one.

—T. S. Eliot, *The Four Quartets*

For information about tapes, workshops, and retreats, please write:

Wayne Muller
P.O. Box 6627
Santa Fe, NM
87502-6627

Part of the proceeds from this book will help support Bread for the Journey, Inc., a nonprofit organization that assists individuals and communities who suffer poverty, hunger, or life-threatening illness.

REFERENCES

Frontispiece

Henry David Thoreau, "Where I Lived, and What I Lived For," *Thoreau's Vision*, ed. Charles R. Anderson (Englewood, NJ: Prentice-Hall, 1973), 167.

Chapter One: Pain and Forgiveness

Daniel Goleman, *Vital Lies and Simple Truths* (New York: Touchstone, 1985), 30.

Stephen Levine, *Healing into Life and Death* (New York: Anchor/Doubleday, 1987), 103.

Pir Vilayat Khan, *Introducing Spirituality in Counseling and Therapy* (New York: Omega Press, 1982).

The Bhagavad Gita (Berkeley: Nilgiri Press, 1985).

Ette Hillesum, *An Interrupted Life: The Diaries of Ette Hillesum* (New York: Pantheon, 1983).

Chapter Two: Fear and Faith

Dr. Herbert Benson, *The Relaxation Response* (New York: Morrow, 1975).

Mohandas Gandhi, *The Message of Jesus Christ* (Bombay: Bharatiya Vidya, 1971).

Jelaluddin Rumi, *Open Secret*, tr. John Moyne and Coleman Barks (Vermont: Threshold Books, 1984).

Chapter Three: Performance and Belonging

Nate Shaw, *All God's Dangers: The Life of Nate Shaw*, ed. Theodore Rosengarten (New York: Knopf, 1974).

Jelaluddin Rumi, cited in Joseph Goldstein and Jack Kornfield, *Seeking the Heart of Wisdom*, (Boston: Shambhala, 1987).

Kabir, *The Kabir Book*, ed. Robert Bly, (Boston: Beacon Press, 1977), 33.

Chapter Four: Scarcity and Abundance

Brother David Steindl-Rast, *Gratefulness, the Heart of Prayer* (New York: Paulist Press, 1984).

Wendell Berry, *The Country of Marriage* (New York: Harvest/Harcourt Brace Jovanovich, 1973), 19.

Thich Nhat Hanh, *Being Peace* (Berkeley: Parralax Press, 1987), 7.

Martin Buber, *Tales of the Hasidim*, trans. Olga Marx, (New York: Schocken Books, 1948).

Mohandas Gandhi, cited in *Peacemaking: Day by Day*, (Erie: Pax Christi USA, 1989), 50.

Chapter Five: Judgment and Mercy

Thomas Merton, *A Thomas Merton Reader*, ed. Thomas P. McDonnell, (New York: Harcourt Brace and World, 1962).

Rainer Maria Rilke, *Letters to a Young Poet*, trans. M. D. Herter Norton, (New York: W. W. Norton, 1954), 46–47.

Mohandas Gandhi, *From Yeravda Mandir* (Ahmedabad, India: Navajivan, 1932).

Mohandas Gandhi, *An Autobiography* (Boston: Beacon Press, 1957).

Eknath Easwaran, *Meditation* (Berkeley: Nigiri Press, 1978).

Mohandas Gandhi, *Non-Violence in Peace and War* (Ahmedabad: Navajivan, 1948).

Chapter Six: Grandiosity and Humility

Shunryu Suzuki, *Zen Mind, Beginner's Mind* (New York: Weatherhill, 1983).

Walker Percy, *Lost in the Cosmos* (New York: Washington Square Press, 1984).

Yushi Nomora, *Desert Wisdom* (New York: Image/Doubleday, 1984).

Thomas Merton, *The Way of Chuang Tzu* (New York: New Directions, 1965).

Kurt Vonnegut, *Cat's Cradle* (New York: Dell, 1970).

Joseph Campbell with Bill Moyers, *The Power of Myth* (New York: Doubleday, 1988).

Jelaluddin Rumi, *Open Secret*.

Richard Katz, *Boiling Energy* (Cambridge: Harvard University Press, 1982).

Mohandas Gandhi, cited in *Peacemaking: Day by Day*, 8.

Chapter Seven: Drama and Simplicity

Terry Tempest Williams, *Pieces of White Shell* (New York: Scribner's, 1984).

Walpola Rahula, *What the Buddha Taught* (London: Gordon-Fraser, 1982).

William Blake, *The Poetical Works of William Blake*, ed. John Sampson (Oxford: 1913).

Sujata, *Beginning to See* (Berkeley: Celestial Arts, 1987).

Ralph Waldo Emerson, *The Portable Emerson* (New York: Penguin Books, 1987).

Thich Nhat Hanh, *A Guide to Walking Meditation* (Berkeley: Parralax Press, 1985).

Chapter Eight: Busyness and Stillness

Pablo Neruda, "Keeping Quiet," in *Extravagaria*, trans. Alastair Reid (New York: Farrar, Straus, Giroux, 1972).

Thomas Merton, cited in *Peacemaking: Day by Day*, 140.

Brother David Steindl-Rast, *Gratefulness, the Heart of Prayer*.

Thomas Merton, "In Silence," *The Collected Poems of Thomas Merton* (New York: New Directions, 1977), 280.

Chuang Tzu, *Inner Chapters*, trans. Gia-fu Feng and Jane English (New York: Knopf, 1974).

Matthew Fox, *Meditations with Meister Eckhart*, (Santa Fe: Bear and Company 1983).

Henri Nouwen, *The Way of the Heart* (New York: Seabury Press, 1981), 52, 53.

Joseph Goldstein and Jack Kornfield, *Seeking the Heart of Wisdom*.

Paul Reps, *Zen Flesh, Zen Bones* (New York: Anchor/Doubleday, 1961), 62.

Mother Teresa, cited in Malcolm Muggeridge, *Something Beautiful for God* (New York: Image/Harper and Row, 1977).

Nanao Sakaki, *Break the Mirror* (San Francisco: North Point Press, 1987).

Chapter Nine: Disappointment and Nonattachment

Erik Erikson, *Childhood and Society* (New York: Norton, 1963).

Brother David Steindl-Rast, *Gratefulness, the Heart of Prayer*.

William Blake, *The Poetical Works of William Blake*.
Mother Teresa, *Something Beautiful for God*.
Sasaki Roshi, *Buddha Is the Center of Gravity* (Lama Foundation, 1974).
Eido Tai Shamano, cited in David Steindl-Rast, "A Deep Bow: Gratitude as the Root of a Common Religious Language" Mt. Savior Monastery.

Chapter Ten: Habit and Mindfulness

Thich Nhat Hanh, *Being Peace*.
James Tate, "Four Prose Poems," *Zero: A Journal of Contemporary Buddhist Life and Thought*, vol. 3 (Los Angeles: Zero Press, 1979).
Joseph Goldstein and Jack Kornfield, *Seeking the Heart of Wisdom*.
Lewis Carroll, *The Annotated Alice: Alice in Wonderland and Through the Looking Glass* (New York: Potter, 1960).
Thomas Merton, cited in *Peacemaking: Day by Day*, 78.
Thich Nhat Hanh, *The Miracle of Mindfulness* (Boston: Beacon Press, 1987).

Chapter Eleven: Isolation and Intimacy

Thich Nhat Hanh, *Being Peace*.
Mohandas Gandhi, cited in *Peacemaking: Day by Day*, 14.
Linnie Marsh Wolfe, *John Muir: Son of the Wilderness* (Madison: University of Wisconsin Press, 1978).
Jelaluddin Rumi, *Speaking Flame*, tr. Andrew Harvey (Ithaca: Meeramma, 1989).
Joseph Campbell, *The Power of Myth*.
Thomas Merton, cited in *Peacemaking: Day by Day*, 7.

Chapter Twelve: Obligation and Loving Kindness

Pierre Teilhard de Chardin, *Building the Earth* (Wilkes-Barre: Dimension Books, 1965).
Tenzin Gyatso, the Dalai Lama of Tibet, *Ocean of Wisdom* (Santa Fe: Clear Light Publishers, 1989).
Jag Paresh Chander, *Teachings of Mahatma Gandhi* (The India Book Works, 1945), 375.
Thomas Merton, "Marxism and Monastic Perspectives" in John Moffit, ed., *A New Chapter for Monasticism* (Notre Dame, 1970), 80.
T. S. Eliot, "The Four Quartets," *Complete Poems and Plays* (New York: Harcourt Brace, 1952).

RECOMMENDED READING

Buddhism

Robert Aiken. *The Mind of Clover*. San Francisco: North Point Press, 1984.

Joseph Goldstein. *The Experience of Insight*. Boulder: Shambhala, 1983.

Jack Kornfield and Paul Breiter. *A Still Forest Pool*. Wheaton: Theosophical Publishing House, 1987.

Thich Nhat Hanh. *Old Path White Clouds*. Berkeley: Parallax Press, 1991.

Christianity

Brother Lawrence. *The Practice of the Presence of God*, trans. John J. Delaney. Garden City: Image/Doubleday, 1977.

Stephen Clissold. *The Wisdom of St. Francis and his Companions*. New York: New Directions, 1978.

M. Basil Pennington. *Centering Prayer*. Garden City: Image/Doubleday, 1982.

Matthew Fox. *Original Blessing*. Santa Fe: Bear and Company, 1983.

Poetry

Stephen Mitchell. *The Selected Poetry of Rainer Maria Rilke*. New York: Vintage/Random House, 1984.

Stephen Mitchell. *The Poetry of the Enlightened Heart*. New York: Harper and Row, 1989.

Spirituality, Healing, and Service

Ram Dass and Paul Gorman. *How Can I Help?* New York: Knopf, 1985.

Erik Erikson. *Gandhi's Truth*. New York: Norton, 1969.

Dominique Lapierre. *City of Joy*. New York: Warner Books, 1986.

Stephen Levine. *Meetings at the Edge*. New York: Anchor/Doubleday, 1984.

Stephen Levine. *Who Dies*? New York: Anchor/Doubleday, 1982.

Thomas Merton. *The Asian Journal*. New York: New Directions, 1975.

INDEX

197